W9-BYR-288

Craft Academy

Craft Academy

PHOTOGRAPHY BY

TIM IMRIE AND PETER WILLIAMS

HERMES
HOUSE

First published in 1998 by Hermes House

Hermes House is an imprint of
Anness Publishing Limited
88-89 Blackfriars Road
London SE1 8HA

© Anness Publishing Limited 1998

Published in the USA by Hermes House
Anness Publishing Inc., 27 West 20th Street,
New York, NY 10011; (800) 354-9657

All rights reserved. No part of this publication
may be reproduced, stored in a retrieval system,
or transmitted in any way or by any means, elec-
tronic, mechanical, photocopying, recording or
otherwise without the prior written permission of
the copyright holder.

A CIP catalogue record for this book is available
from the British Library.

ISBN 1 84038 043 8

Publisher: Joanna Lorenz
Series Editors: Clare Nicholson, Lindsay Porter
                and Judith Simons
Photographers: Tim Imrie and Peter Williams
Designer: Peter Butler
Stylist: Georgina Rhodes
Illustrator: Lucinda Ganderton

Printed and bound in China

10 9 8 7 6 5 4 3 2 1

American-English terminology is used in this book.
The conversion list below may be helpful to some readers:
CARDBOARD — CARD
FIBERBOARD — HARDBOARD
MATTE LATEX — MATT EMULSION
METHYLATED ALCOHOL — METHYLATED SPIRIT
STEEL WOOL — WIRE WOOL
TIN CLIPPERS — TIN SNIPS
TURPENTINE — WHITE SPIRIT
WET AND DRY PAPER — WET AND DRY SANDPAPER
WHITE GLUE — PVA GLUE

PUBLISHER'S NOTE
Working with craft materials is great fun and can fill
many rewarding hours. For safety, protective gloves
should be worn when cutting wire or tin, and a mask
and goggles should be worn when soldering or cutting
MDF. The publishers cannot accept responsibility for
any injury incurred in the making of the projects.

CONTENTS

INTRODUCTION

THE ARRIVAL OF CHEAP AND HIGHLY WORKABLE MODERN MATERIALS HAS MEANT THAT OUR DEPENDENCY ON TRADITIONAL CRAFTS HAS DIMINISHED ON A GRAND SCALE OVER THE LAST CENTURY. WHILE THIS TREND LOOKS SET TO CONTINUE, THERE HAS BEEN, IN RECENT YEARS, A REVIVAL OF INTEREST IN FOLK ART, AND GALLERIES AND MUSEUMS ARE NOW TURNING THEIR ATTENTION TO OLDER CRAFT FORMS, PRESENTING EXHIBITIONS OF CONTEMPORARY ARTISTS WHO ARE KEEN TO REDISCOVER THE BEAUTY OF THESE FORGOTTEN SKILLS. WIRE, MOSAIC, TIN, PLASTER AND POLYMER CLAY ARE VERSATILE AND REWARDING MATERIALS. THIS BOOK WILL ENABLE YOU TO MAKE YOUR OWN CREATIONS BY FOLLOWING THE STEP-BY-STEP INSTRUCTIONS FOR EACH PROJECT. A COMPREHENSIVE TECHNIQUES SECTION TAKES YOU THROUGH THE ESSENTIALS FOR EACH CRAFT, AND A GALLERY OF STUNNING CONTEMPORARY PIECES AIMS TO INSPIRE YOU TO DEVELOP YOUR OWN WORK ONCE THE BASIC SKILLS HAVE BEEN MASTERED.

WIREWORK
MARY MAGUIRE

THE CRAFT OF WIREWORK HAS BEEN SADLY NEGLECTED IN RECENT YEARS BUT IS NOW MAKING A COMEBACK, AND WIRE CREATIONS CAN BE SEEN IN FASHIONABLE STORES, MAGAZINES AND GALLERIES. WIRE IS AN AMAZINGLY VERSATILE MATERIAL REQUIRING FEW TOOLS TO MANIPULATE IT, BESIDES YOUR HANDS. THIS SECTION WILL ENABLE YOU TO MAKE YOUR OWN WIREWORK CREATIONS BY FOLLOWING THE STEP-BY-STEP INSTRUCTIONS FOR EACH PROJECT. THE BASIC TECHNIQUES SECTION EXPLAINS THE DIFFERENT WAYS OF MANIPULATING AND SHAPING WIRE USED IN THE PROJECTS. THE GALLERY SHOWS A RANGE OF WIRE STRUCTURES MADE BY ARTISTS, AND AIMS TO INSPIRE YOU TO DEVELOP WORKS OF YOUR OWN DESIGN.

Left: These whisks and baskets are typical examples of the wirework items being produced in Britain and France at the turn of the twentieth century. With the renewed interest in wirework, there are many reproductions of such kitchen implements available today.

HISTORY OF WIRE

WIREWORK IS AN ANCIENT ART FORM, PROBABLY FIRST PRACTICED BY THE EGYPTIANS AROUND 3000 BC. EARLY EXAMPLES HAVE BEEN DISCOVERED IN THE BURIAL CHAMBERS OF IMPORTANT PEOPLE THROUGHOUT THE ANCIENT WORLD. IN 2600 BC, WIRE WAS USED IN GOLD AND SILVER RIBBONS FOR ENTWINING IN THE HAIR OF COURTLY LADIES IN THE SUMERIAN CITY OF UR. THE ART OF WIREWORK SPREAD IN VARIOUS FORMS FROM BABYLON TO BAGHDAD, DAMASCUS AND CONSTANTINOPLE BEFORE FINALLY REACHING EUROPE.

Wire was originally made by chiseling thin strips from a sheet of metal. The strips were either twisted and then rolled between two flat surfaces to smooth them, or spirally wound around a mandrel.

Today wire is made by drawing rods of metal through conically shaped holes in a drawplate. The metal drawplate was first used in Persia in the sixth century BC but did not reach Europe until the tenth century AD when wire first started being made on a commercial scale. The iron-wire trade was mainly for chain mail, but wool carders, girdles, chains, fish hooks, and needles were also made. Up until this time gold and silver wires were made almost exclusively for jewelry but during the Middle Ages embroidery became their principal use. In England, the two trades were governed by different bodies, the Broiders' Company and the Girdler and Pinmakers' Company. It was not until the late seventeenth century that they became distinctive guilds, known as the Worshipful Company of Gold and Silver Wireworkers' and the Worshipful Company of Tin Plates alias Wireworkers.

By the mid-sixteenth century, there were at least 6000 wire drawers in London alone, and it was around this time that the first mechanical drawing machines were used in England. The water-driven drawplate system used in these machines was invented by Rudolf of Nuremberg in the fourteenth century, but was not introduced to England until 1564. Gold and silver wirework flourished

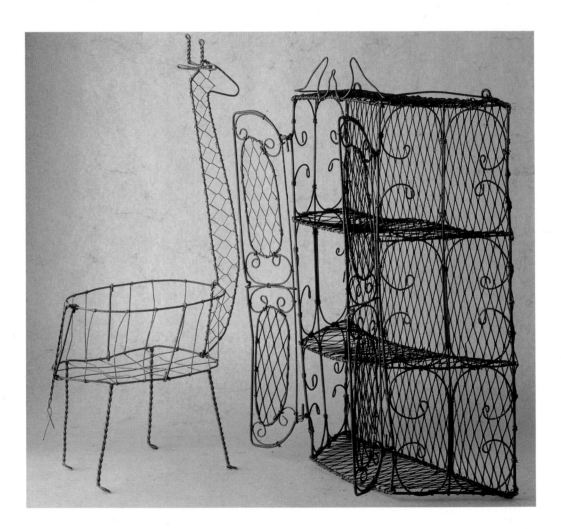

until the time of the French Revolution, when fashions changed and the industry went into decline.

Because of the corrodible nature of iron, very few examples of the broad range of objects once made from iron wire have survived to this day, save the items mentioned above and a few toys and

Above: These two pieces of wirework were made in Mexico. The enchanting giraffe design doubles as a basket. The wire cupboard stands 2 ft high.

Left: This motorcycle and Volkswagen car were made in Zimbabwe.

Below: These horses were made by apprentice wireworkers in Zimbabwe. They are made from recycled flip flops.

Bottom: The levers and cables on this vehicle are fully operational.

traps. By the early nineteenth century, tinning and black-japanning had become popular ways of protecting the wireworker's craft. Not only did these treatments prevent rusting, they also helped cement items made from unsoldered wire.

America imported its wire from England and Germany until 1812, when the war with England meant that supplies were cut off. From this point, the Americans started building their own factories for producing wire. By the mid-nineteenth century, the steam engine enabled wire, woven wire and wire fencing to be mass produced. The industry flourished, reaching its peak in Europe and America at the turn of the century, when an impressive range of products was available from wire whisks and baskets to wire gazebos. The craft of wireworking was applied to every possible household device until the advent of plastic gradually led to its demise.

Wirework is still alive and well in many countries around the world, as shown by the examples from Africa and Mexico. In Europe, with the renewed interest in folk art, the craft is enjoying a renaissance.

GALLERY

IN THE 1920S, THE AMERICAN ARTIST ALEXANDER CALDER BROUGHT WIRE INTO PROMINENCE IN THE WORLD OF FINE ART WITH HIS WIRE SCULPTURES AND DRAWINGS OF PEOPLE AND ANIMALS, WHICH ARE AS FRESH AND ALIVE TODAY AS THEY WERE THEN. TODAY THERE ARE MANY ARTISTS WORKING IN WIRE. THE GALLERY ILLUSTRATES A BROAD CROSS-SECTION OF CONTEMPORARY WIREWORK USES AND TECHNIQUES.

Above: CANDLE HOLDERS
The lantern, candle holder and candlestick have all been made from small-gauge chicken wire. The base of the candle holder has been crafted from wire-mesh spoons which are available from oriental shops. Chicken wire makes beautifully light candle holders which are safe to use indoors as well as outside.
CLARE NICHOLSON

Right: VENUS
This standing sculpture, which measures 7 x 3½ in, was knitted in colored enameled fuse wire around a copper wire frame. Objects such as electrical components and glass beads add to the rich texture of the piece.
JAN TRUMAN

Left: NOAH'S ARK
This wire sculpture, which is approximately 11 ft long, is made from chased, rolled and etched copper and binding wire, then cast silver and bronze have been added. Several parts of the sculpture are made from recycled materials such as rusty beer cans.
CATHY PILKINGTON

Right: CROCHETED GLOVES
These elegant gloves are made of flat panels crocheted in 0.008 in silver wire which have been seamed together with gussets in the same way that leather gloves are made. French knots have been embroidered along the main gauntlet, and hammered silver discs sewn on between the knots. The bobbles were made from a double thickness of crocheting. The gloves have been oxidized to give them their dark patina.
SUSAN CROSS

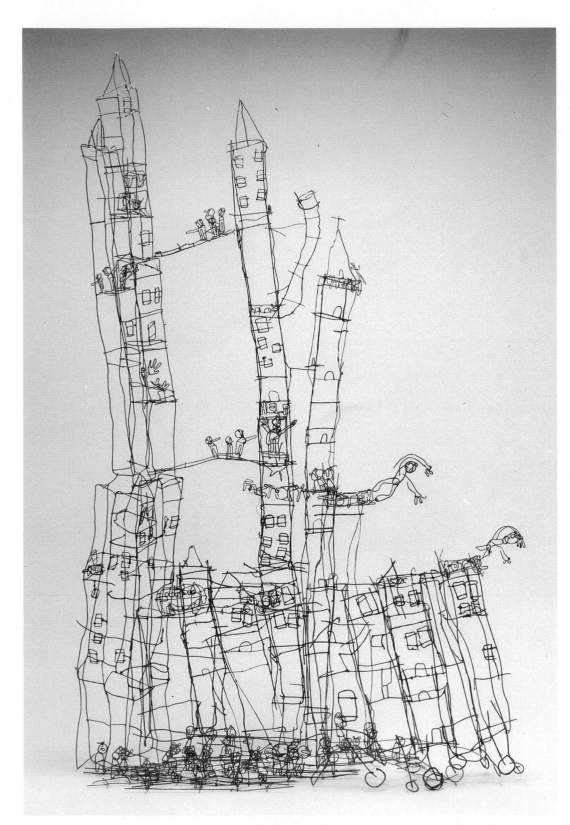

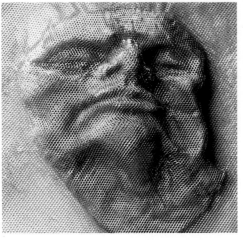

Above: TORTURED HEAD
The head was first drawn from life, then a piece of Lucite was placed over the drawing and a relief model built up around it in clay. A plaster mold was made of the clay model as a negative image, from which a second mold was made as a positive image. Aluminum mesh was compressed between the two molds to take the form of the head, and finally layers of aluminum were applied. It is 12 x 12 in in size.
JANE MACADAM-FREUD

Opposite: WIRE-MESH GEESE
These sculpted life-size animals are caught in mid-action while exploring a kitchen. The malleability of wire lends itself well to sections such as the necks, which are stretched curiously into nooks and crannies. The geese are made from recycled rabbit netting which has been reclaimed from old pheasant-rearing pens.
RUPERT TILLS

Left: METROPOLIS
Inspired by a trip to Las Vegas, Metropolis is Paul's response to the alienation of urban life. Constructed from 1 yd lengths of silver wire soldered together, the structure is approximately 3 x 2 ft. It has been painted in places.
PAUL DAVIS

Right: FRUIT FUNNEL
Hans makes predominantly functional food-related constructions; this beautifully undulating funnel is designed to gauge fruit according to its size. The starkness of its form and color contrasts with the bright colors of the vegetables. The funnel was made from spot-welded mild steel wire which was then heat-blackened.
HANS STOFER

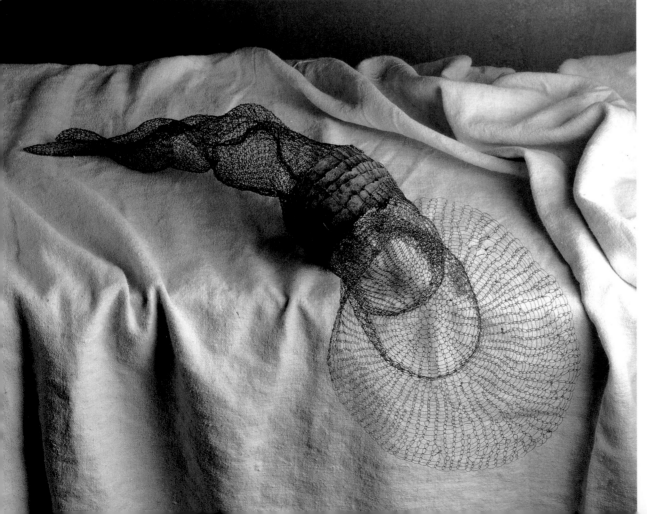

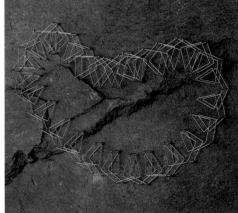

Left: DISCARDED SKIN
This wire sculpture, measuring 26 in in length, is made from a section of etched and colored steel strips which are held together with woven soft wire. Amanda Bright works exclusively in steel with soft wire and is inspired by the material properties of steel.
AMANDA BRIGHT

Above: NECK PIECE
This neck piece was made from articulated lengths of stainless-steel wire. Its success lies in the simplicity of line and the beautiful movement within the piece when handled or worn.
ESTER WARD

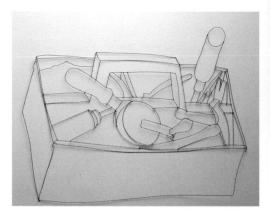

Above: TOOL BOX
Tony Eve uses wire as everybody else uses a pencil. He creates a simple wire outline to "draw" objects, from tool boxes to bicycles. These structures have a charming wit and simplicity.
TONY EVE

Right: HAT AND SHOES
These pieces have been woven out of enameled copper wire. The hat was inspired by ancient Greek helmets. The ornamentation on the shoes is attached through the laces.
ADELE TIPLER

Left: TREASURE BASKET
Drawing on her textile background and basket-making skills, Hillary has created a wirework basket approximately 6 x 8 in in size. A grid was drawn on a wooden former and thumbtacks were hammered in at the intersections. The structural wires were anchored to make them manageable, then short lengths of assorted wire were woven around the main struts and through metal and rubber washers and grommets. The ends of the wires were then looped around and wrapped.
HILLARY BURNS

MATERIALS

W IRE IS MADE BY DRAWING RODS OF METAL THROUGH CONICALLY SHAPED HOLES IN A DRAWPLATE. ROUND WIRE IS THE MOST COMMON BUT SQUARE, HEXAGONAL AND HALF-ROUND WIRES ARE ALSO AVAILABLE. AS WELL AS MEASURING WIRE IN MILLIMETERS OR INCHES, GAUGES ARE ALSO USED, IN WHICH THE MEASUREMENTS RANGE FROM 0 TO AROUND 50. THE SMALLER THE NUMBER, THE THICKER THE WIRE. DIFFERENT COUNTRIES HAVE DIFFERENT GAUGES. HOWEVER, THE MEASUREMENTS FOR WIRE IN THE PROJECTS ARE GIVEN IN INCHES.

Enameled copper wire is primarily used in the electronics industry but is ideal for wirework because of the wide range of colors. Available from some craft and electrical stores but, for the full range of colors and gauges, by mail order from suppliers. It also comes on industrial-sized spools for the real enthusiast.

Wire coat hangers are cheap and widely available. They come in different finishes.

Tinned copper wire is shiny and does not tarnish, so it is particularly suitable

KEY
1, 2, 4, 5, 7, 11, 14, 15 Enameled copper wire
3 Coat hanger
6, 8, 9, 20, 23 Tinned copper wire
10, 26 Aluminum wire
12 Twisty wire tape
19, 21 Garden wire
16, 18, 24, 28 Copper wire
17, 25, 27 Straining wire
13, 22 Galvanized wire

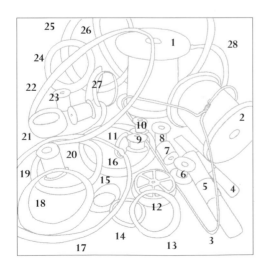

for kitchenware. Available by mail order from suppliers in a broad range of gauges.

Aluminum wire is a dull blue-gray color. Of all the wires listed, it is the easiest to work with because it is so soft and easy to bend. Available by mail order from suppliers.

Garden wire is easy to manipulate and kind to the hands as it is plastic-coated. It comes in various shades of green and in different thicknesses. It is perfect for crafting bathroom or kitchen accessories because it is waterproof, long-lasting and colorful. Available from hardware stores and gardening stores.

Copper wire has an attractive, warm color and can be bought in different tempers (hardnesses). Soft copper wire is easy to work with and has been used for the projects in the book. Available in a broad range of gauges from some hardware stores and craft stores, or by mail order from suppliers.

Straining wire is made up of thin strands of galvanized wire that have been twisted together, which give this wire a nice texture and make it very strong. As the wire is hard, caution needs to be taken when working with it. Available from hardware stores.

Galvanized wire is zinc-coated steel wire. The zinc coating prevents rusting, making this wire ideal for outdoor use. Galvanized wire is a hard wire, so it does not bend as easily as some of the other wire, and, because it is springy, caution needs to be taken when working with it. Available in approximately five gauges from hardware stores.

Chicken wire is made from galvanized steel wire. Usually used for fencing and animal pens, it comes with different-sized holes and in various widths. For the purposes of the projects in the book, we have used the smallest gauge. Chicken wire is a versatile craft material as it is

easy to manipulate and inexpensive. Available from hardware stores.

Silver-plated copper wire comes in small coils in many different gauges, and is particularly suited to jewelry making and small, fine wirework. Available from jewelry craft stores.

Twisty wire tape is a thin, flat tape with a hidden wire core. It comes in various shades of green for gardening purposes and in blue and white for household usage. Strips of multicolored freezer-bag ties can also be bought. This material is not usually associated with crafts but it is a pleasing wire to work with and can be used by children if they are supervised. Available from gardening stores and supermarkets.

Above: Pipe cleaners and paper clips are less obvious wirework materials, but, being inexpensive and coming in a variety of colors, shapes, and sizes, they are great fun to work with. There are also many ways to decorate wire structures, such as coloring wire with car-spray paint as in the Seashore Mobile project, or using beads to embellish wire frames such as the Lantern project.

EQUIPMENT

ONLY THE MOST BASIC KINDS OF WIRE CUTTERS AND PLIERS ARE NEEDED TO MAKE THE PROJECTS IN THE BOOK. FOR SOME OF THE PROJECTS, YOU COULD GET AWAY WITH USING JUST ORDINARY GENERAL-PURPOSE PLIERS, ALTHOUGH THE MORE SPECIALIZED PLIERS MAKE SOME MODELING JOBS MUCH EASIER. ROUND-NOSED PLIERS, WHICH ARE AVAILABLE FROM CRAFT SHOPS, ARE A WORTHWHILE INVESTMENT.

General-purpose pliers are the pliers that you are most likely to own already. They often have serrated jaws to give a strong grip. This can be a disadvantage in wirework as the serrations leave marks. Place a piece of leather between the pliers and the wire to prevent any marking.

Round-nosed pliers (also known as round-nosed jewelry pliers) are a good investment as they can be used for many different crafts as well as for repairing broken jewelry. With these pliers, wire can be bent into tiny circles (see the Angel project). If you are planning to make many of the projects in the book it is worth investing too in half-round pliers (also known as half-round jewelry pliers). These are useful for bending wire into broad curves (see the Seashore Mobile project). Both types are available from craft shops.

Wire cutters are extremely useful, even though the cutters on ordinary general-purpose pliers will do for most projects. Don't buy the smallest cutters available, as good leverage with long handles is needed when cutting galvanized wire.

Parallel or channel-type pliers are useful because the jaws open and close parallel to each other, unlike ordinary pliers. Even when the jaws are smooth, they still grip well, as they hold along their full length rather than at just one point. For this reason they are suitable for straightening bent wire and for bending angles.

Needle-nosed pliers are useful for reaching into difficult places and are the best kind of pliers for working with chicken wire.

Hand drills are useful for twisting soft wires, together (see Basic Techniques and the Fused Flowers project).

Wooden coat hangers can be used for twisting galvanized wire together (see Basic Techniques and the Spice Rack project). Always make sure that the handle is securely attached and will not unscrew.

Permanent marker pens are essential for marking measurements on wire, as felt-tips will just rub off.

Rolling pins and wooden spoons are two of many household items useful for making coils in wire (see Basic Techniques and the Hook Rack project). Keep your eye out for cylinders and pipes in varying sizes, which also might be useful for making coils.

Gardening gloves will protect your hands when working with chicken wire and other scratchy wire, such as straining wire. Wearing goggles is also advisable when manipulating long lengths of wire, especially if the wire is under tension, as a loose end could whip up accidentally in your face. It is best to take precautions.

Ruler Many of the projects require accurate use of measurements, and careful use of a ruler will ensure a good result.

Scissors are always an essential piece of equipment when working on craft projects. Sharp scissors will cut through thin wire, but this is not advisable because it will blunt the blades. Always use wire cutters for this purpose.

Hammer A hammer is useful for flattening the ends of cut lengths of wire (see the Toasting Fork project).

Block of wood When shaping wire (see the Toilet-tissue Holder project) it is sometimes useful to use a gib, which can be made with a screw and a piece of wood.

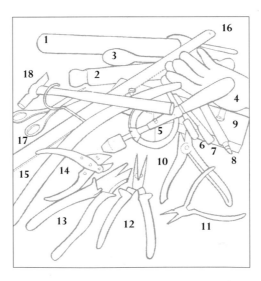

KEY
1, 2 Rolling pins
3 Wooden spoon
4 Gardening gloves
5 Hand drill
6, 7, 8 Permanent marker pens
9 Piece of wood
10 Wire cutters
11 Round-nosed pliers
12 Needle-nosed pliers
13 General-purpose pliers
14 Parallel (or channel-type) pliers
15 Wooden coat-hanger
16 Ruler
17 Scissors
18 Hammer

BASIC TECHNIQUES

WIRE IS A WONDERFULLY VERSATILE MATERIAL. IT CAN BE BRAIDED, CORDED, COILED, WRAPPED, TWISTED, WOVEN, CROCHETED, SPRUNG, SPIRALED, FILIGREED AND FASHIONED INTO INNUMERABLE DIFFERENT SHAPES. OF THE MANY TECHNIQUES COMMONLY USED IN WIREWORK, INSTRUCTIONS ARE GIVEN HERE FOR THOSE USED TO MAKE THE PROJECTS IN THE BOOK. LOOK THROUGH THIS SECTION BEFORE STARTING ANY OF THE PROJECTS.

TWISTING WIRE

Twisting is a simple and effective way of joining two or more wires to add to their strength and texture.

Soft wires such as copper are the easiest to twist, and using a hand drill speeds up the process. Harder wires such as galvanized wire require more effort and caution must be taken. Letting go of the wires prematurely may cause them to spin out of control, which can be dangerous. If using a coat hanger to twist the wires, choose the wooden type with a wire hook that revolves, ensuring that the handle is securely attached and will not unscrew.

Twisting Hard Wire

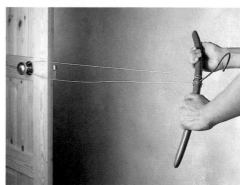

1 Cut a piece of wire at least three times as long as the required twisted length, depending on the degree of twist you want in the wire. Double the length of wire and loop it around a door handle or other secure point. Wrap the loose ends very firmly three times around the hanger on either side of the handle. Make sure that you hold the wire horizontally, otherwise you may get an uneven twist.

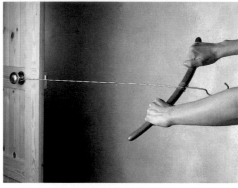

2 Brace yourself backward to keep the wire taut and begin twisting the coat hanger around. Do not relax your grip as this may cause an uneven texture.

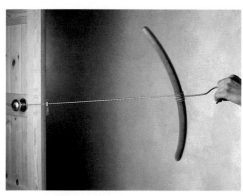

3 Twist the wire to the degree required, taking care not to overtwist as the wire may snap. To release the tension in the wire, hold the hanger firmly in one hand and grip its handle in the other. Quickly release your hold on the hanger, which will spin around a bit.

4 Remove the wire from the door handle and cut off the ends.

Twisting Soft Wire

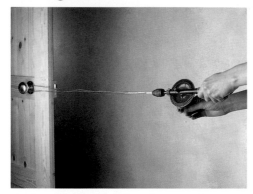

1 Double the lengths of wire to be twisted. Two lengths have been used here. Loop the wires around a door handle and wrap the other ends with masking tape before securing them into the hand-drill chuck.

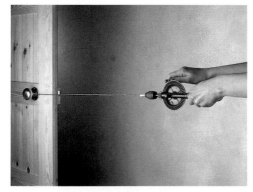

2 Keeping the wire taut, rotate the drill to twist the wire to the degree required. With soft wires there is no need to release the tension in the wire before removing from the drill bit and trimming.

WRAPPING WIRE

When wrapping wire, ideally the core wire should be thicker and harder than the wrapping wire, although two wires of the same thickness can be used as long as the wrapping wire is soft enough for the job. Copper wire is the most suitable. When cutting the core wire, remember to allow an excess length of at least 2½ in to form the winding loop. The long lengths of soft wire used in wrapping can be unmanageable, so coil the wire first, as described in Method B.

Method A

1 Using round-nosed pliers, make a loop at the end of the core wire. Attach the wrapping wire to this loop.

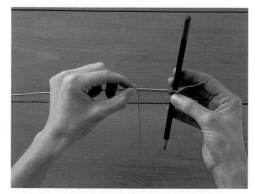

2 Insert a pencil or other suitable object into the loop and use it as a winder. While winding, hold your thumb and index finger right up against the coil to ensure that the wire is closely wrapped.

Method B

1 Using round-nosed pliers, make a loop at the end of the core wire and bend the wire into a spiral along half its length. Form a loop at the other end of the core wire and secure the wrapping wire to the loop. Insert a pencil into the loop and use it as a winder.

2 Wrap a quarter of the wire, remove the pencil and coil the wire that has just been wrapped. This section can now be used as the winder. Change the position of your hand so that it supports the core wire from beneath, with the wrapping wire running between your fingers and thumb.

Tips for Wrapping Wire

When using wire from a skein, keep it on the floor with your foot holding it in place. This will enable you to achieve the necessary tension for wrapping the wire.

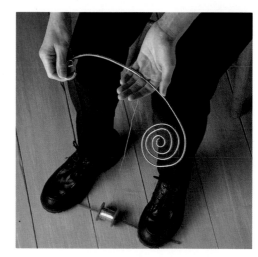

When using wire from a spool, insert a long stick through it and hold it in place with your feet. This allows the spool to unwind quite freely while keeping the wire taut.

COILS

Coils are probably the most commonly used decorative device in wirework. They also have a practical use as they neaten and make safe what would otherwise be sharp ends, while adding grace and style.

Closed Coils

1 Using round-nosed pliers, make a small loop at the end of the wire.

2 Hold the loop firmly with parallel (channel-type) pliers. Use them to bend the wire around until you have a coil of the size required. Keep adjusting the position of the pliers as you work.

Open Coils

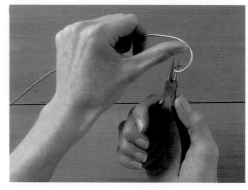

1 Using round-nosed pliers, make a small loop at the end of the wire. Holding the loop in the pliers, place your thumb against the wire and draw the wire across it to form a curve.

2 Use your eye to judge the space left between the rings of the coil.

3 Finally, carefully flatten the coil with parallel (channel-type) pliers.

Flattened Extended Coils

The flattened extended coil is a common structural and decorative device used in wirework. It is a quick and easy way to make the side walls of a container, for instance, and has been used to make the decorative trim at the front of the Spice Rack and the bracket at the back of the Hook Rack.

1 Wrap the wire several times around a broomstick or other cylindrical object to make a coil. If using galvanized wire, you will need to brace your thumb firmly against it.

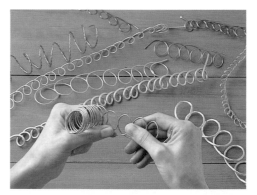

2 After removing the coil from the broomstick, splay out the loops one by one, holding them firmly between your fingers and thumbs.

3 Keep splaying out the loops until the whole coil has been flattened. The loops will now look more oval than round. You can stretch the coil further to open the loops if you wish.

WEAVING
Many basketwork and textile techniques can be applied to wirework, as illustrated in the gallery section by the woven hat and shoes and the crocheted jewelry. Knitting and lacemaking techniques can also be employed. Fine enameled copper wire is especially suitable for weaving as it is soft and pliable and comes in a wide range of colors. Of the techniques described here, methods B and C will give a more closely woven and tidier finish than method A. Method A is the simplest.

Method A

The quickest and easiest way to weave is to wind the wire in and out of the struts to create an open texture.

Method B

Weave around the struts by passing the wire over each strut and looping it around the wire to create a smooth, closely woven surface. Use this technique to weave the Fused Flowers, the Candle Sconce, the Woven Chair and the Woven Bottle.

Method C

Follow Method B but reverse the weave, this time passing the wire under each strut before looping it around the wire to create ridges in the weave. This technique will give the same result as method B except that the rib will be on the outside, not the inside.

CHICKEN WIRE TECHNIQUES
Chicken wire is a fantastic medium as it is cheap, attractive and readily available. Its malleability and lightness make it suitable for creating large structures, and as such it is commonly used by sculptors. For ease of explanation, the instructions refer to struts (the horizontal, twisted wires in the hexagons) and strands (the single wires). When working with chicken wire, it is advisable to wear gloves. Finish off any project made of chicken wire by tucking away all the sharp ends.

BINDING CHICKEN WIRE
Method A

Place a length of wire along the edge of the chicken wire. Loop a thinner binding wire around the length of wire and the chicken wire to bind them together. Use this technique to bind the chicken wire in the Picture Frame, to bind the sides and bottom of the Utility Rack, and to bind the rim of the Lantern and its lid.

Method B

When binding diagonally, it is convenient to bind along the diagonal strands of the chicken wire. If a more acute diagonal is needed, as for the top of the Utility Rack, allow a ¾ in excess length of chicken wire. Bind evenly around the length of wire, taking in each strand or strut of chicken wire as you come to it. Trim and wrap any ends around the length of wire using round-nosed pliers.

TRANSFORMING THE HOLE SHAPES

The hexagonal shape of the holes gives chicken wire plenty of molding potential, which can be increased still further by breaking the rigidity of the horizontal struts.

Heart Shapes

Hold the center of each strut in turn with round-nosed pliers and twist up the wire to each side to create a cleft in the center. When this process is repeated a pattern of heart shapes will emerge.

Brick Wall

Insert general-purpose pliers into the holes in the chicken wire so that the sides of the pliers are up against the struts. Pull the handles gently apart to transform each hexagon into a rectangle. Work carefully to keep the mesh from buckling.

Fishing Net

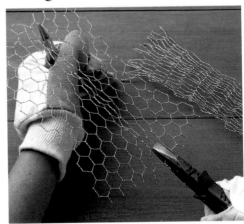

Hold the chicken wire securely with small pliers and pull it with general-purpose pliers to elongate the holes and create a fishing-net effect. You could hook the chicken wire over nails hammered into a piece of wood if you were stretching a larger area.

JOINING CHICKEN WIRE

1 Cut the chicken wire at the point just before the wire strands twist into struts so that one edge is a row of projecting double strands and the other edge is a row of projecting twisted struts.

2 Place the piece of chicken wire with the projecting struts on top of the other piece so that they overlap slightly and the rows of struts lie on top of each other. Using round-nosed pliers, wrap each projecting strand around the corresponding strand on the uppermost piece of chicken wire.

3 Twist the overlapping struts together using round-nosed pliers.

SHAPING CHICKEN WIRE

Depending on the type of shape and the rigidity of structure required, chicken wire can be shaped with the struts running either horizontally or vertically. Generally, for a stronger, fatter shape, work with the struts running horizontally and, for a longer, more elegant shape, work with the struts running vertically. Although any number of shapes can be made, the ones described here can be used for making the Lantern project.

Shaping with the Struts Running Vertically

1 Using general-purpose pliers, squeeze the struts together to form the neck, pulling all the time to elongate the wires.

2 To make the bulge, stretch the holes by inserting general-purpose pliers as described for the brick wall, but only stretch a little for a more elegant shape.

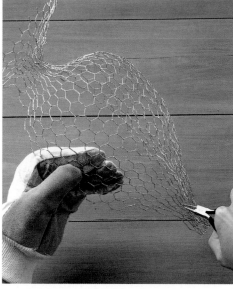

3 Using round-nosed pliers, squeeze the struts together to make the bottom tip, pulling to elongate the wires.

Shaping with the Struts Running Horizontally

1 Transform all the hexagons to heart shapes. To contract the wire that will become the neck, squash together the cleft in each heart shape with round-nosed pliers and mold with your thumbs.

2 To make the bulge in the body of the structure, mold with your fingers from inside, pressing outward. Using round-nosed pliers, grip and then pull the wires outwards.

3 To make the bottom tip, squash together the clefts as for the neck, contracting them more tightly to form a tight core.

TOILET-TISSUE HOLDER

TRANSFORM ONE SIMPLE, FUNCTIONAL OBJECT INTO ANOTHER WITH THIS CHARMING TOILET-TISSUE HOLDER MADE FROM A WIRE COAT HANGER. THE LESS EXPERIENCED WIREWORKER IS ADVISED TO START WITH THIS PROJECT. HEARTS ARE A TRADITIONAL MOTIF IN FOLK-ART DESIGNS, AND TRANSFORM FUNCTIONAL OBJECTS INTO WARM, PERSONAL ONES. ADAPT THE BASIC DESIGN TO MAKE OTHER BATHROOM ACCESSORIES, SUCH AS TOOTHBRUSH, GLASS OR SOAP-DISH HOLDERS. IF YOU PREFER, YOU COULD USE GALVANIZED OR PLASTIC-COATED GARDENING WIRE INSTEAD OF A WIRE COAT HANGER.

1 Cut the hook and twisted wire from the coat hanger. Straighten the wire using parallel (or channel-type) pliers.

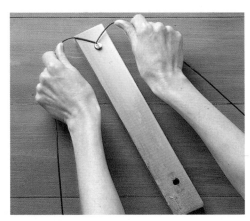

2 Drill a hole in a piece of wood and wind in a screw. Wrap the wire around the screw halfway along its length. Tighten the screw so that it holds the wire securely in place as you mold the curves of the heart shape.

3 Allow 2½ in between the eye and the bottom of the heart shape. Twist the wires together twice at the bottom of the heart. Bend out the remaining wires at right angles.

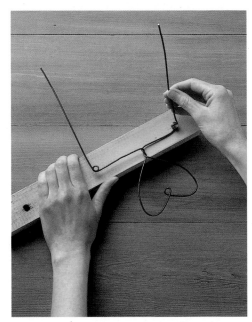

4 Unscrew the heart and replace the screw in the wood. Measure 2½ in from the bottom of the heart along each wire. Wrap each wire once around the screw at this point and then bend up the end at a right angle.

5 Using permanent marker pen, mark each remaining length of wire at intervals of 3 in, 1¼ in, 1¼ in, ¾ in, and ¾ in. The measurements may have to vary slightly depending on how much wire is left. Bend the wire into right angles at the marked points, so the ends that will hold the toilet roll point inwards. Finally, to decorate, loosely wrap a length of 0.031 in galvanized wire around the whole structure.

MATERIALS AND EQUIPMENT YOU WILL NEED

WIRE COAT HANGER • WIRE CUTTERS • PARALLEL (OR CHANNEL-TYPE) PLIERS • PIECE OF WOOD • DRILL • SCREW • RULER •
PERMANENT MARKER PEN • GENERAL-PURPOSE PLIERS • GALVANIZED WIRE, 0.031 IN THICK

POCKET CLIPS

ADORN YOUR POCKETS WITH THESE HIGHLY ORIGINAL AND DECORATIVE CLIPS THAT WILL ADD A TOUCH OF FLAIR TO THE MOST ORDINARY OF JACKETS. DESIGN YOUR OWN CLIPS FOR THE TOP POCKET OR LAPEL OF A MAN'S JACKET OR A TEENAGER'S SCHOOL BLAZER. YOU COULD COPY AN EXISTING EMBLEM OR LOGO OR EVEN SCULPT A NAME OR WORD. A SMALLER DESIGN MADE IN FINE WIRE WOULD MAKE AN ATTRACTIVE TIE CLIP. GALVANIZED WIRE HAS BEEN USED HERE WHICH COULD BE SPRAYED WITH METALLIC CAR PAINT. FOR A MORE SOPHISTICATED LOOK USE GOLD- OR SILVER-PLATED WIRE.

1 Cut 40 in of 0.047 in galvanized wire. Make a coil at one end. Bend out the wire to make an S-shape, referring to diagram 1. Square off the loop below the coil with half-round pliers.

2 Bend in the wire to form one side of a neck, then make a large loop in the wire. Make a mirror-image loop and coil on the other side of the large loop, and cut off any excess wire.

3 Fold the structure in half at the neck and bend the top of the large loop at both sides to make shoulders. Nip in the bottom of the large loop to make a scallop shape. The large loop should measure approximately 4½ in from top to bottom.

DIAGRAM 1

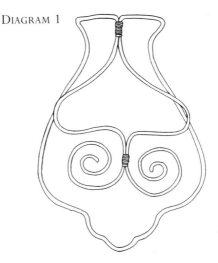

4 Using the 0.025 in wire, bind the coils together. Bind the neck for ½ in.

MATERIALS AND EQUIPMENT YOU WILL NEED
GALVANIZED WIRE, 0.047 IN AND 0.025 IN THICK • RULER • WIRE CUTTERS • ROUND-NOSED PLIERS •
HALF-ROUND PLIERS

PICTURE FRAME

THIS LIGHT AND AIRY PICTURE FRAME IS MADE FROM THICK ALUMINUM WIRE, WHICH IS SOFT AND BENDS EASILY TO FORM THE FILIGREE FRAME SURROUND. THE PASTEL RIBBON AND OLD-FASHIONED PICTURE CREATE A VICTORIAN EFFECT. IT IS VERY EASY TO CHANGE THE RIBBON AND PICTURE TO FIT IN WITH ANY SETTING AS THE FRAME CONTAINS NO GLASS. SUBTLY COLORED PICTURES AND BLACK-AND-WHITE PHOTOGRAPHS ARE ESPECIALLY EFFECTIVE. CHOOSE A RIBBON THAT IS THIN ENOUGH TO THREAD EASILY THROUGH THE WIRE MESH AND THAT MATCHES OR CONTRASTS WITH THE PICTURE.

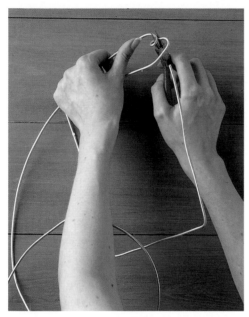

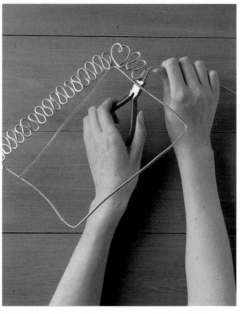

1 Using round-nosed pliers, carefully bend the 0.128 in aluminum wire into a rectangle measuring 6 x 8 in. At the fourth corner, form a heart shape. Do not cut off the wire.

2 Bend the wire into a series of filigree loops to fit along each side of the frame. Form a heart at each corner.

3 Leave ½ in of excess wire spare at the last corner and cut off. ▶

MATERIALS AND EQUIPMENT YOU WILL NEED

ROUND-NOSED PLIERS • SOFT ALUMINUM WIRE, 0.128 IN AND 0.039 IN THICK • RULER • WIRE CUTTERS • SMALL-GAUGE CHICKEN WIRE • GLOVES (OPTIONAL) • GALVANIZED WIRE, 0.065 IN THICK • PERMANENT MARKER PEN • RIBBON

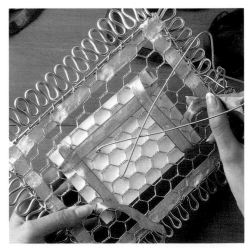

4 Cut a piece of the small-gauge chicken wire 6 x 16 in and fold it in half. Bend the filigree out of the way and use 0.039 in aluminum wire to bind the chicken wire to the inner rectangle (see Basic Techniques).

5 Bend the filigree back into place and bind on to the inner rectangle.

6 To make the support for the frame, cut a 19 in length of galvanized wire. Using a permanent marker pen, mark the wire at intervals of 7 in, 2½ in, 2½ in, and 7 in. Bend the wire into a crossed-triangle shape, making a loop in the center and a loop at each end. Cut two short pieces of wire and make a loop at each end. Link the two pieces together and close the loop firmly.

7 Thread a piece of ribbon around the edges of the chicken wire, looping it around the frame at each corner so that it lies flat.

8 Attach the support to the frame by opening the loops slightly and then closing them around the chicken wire about two-thirds of the way up from the bottom. Attach one end of the two short linked pieces to the loop in the bottom of the support, and the other end to the base of the frame. This piece prevents the support from collapsing and allows the frame to be folded flat.

9 Position your picture on the frame and secure it by threading a ribbon through the wire from the back, and looping it around the corners, as shown.

UTILITY RACK

The shelf at the bottom of this useful and simply designed rack is wide enough to hold four food cans. Stripped of their labels, the cans make attractive storage containers that complement the design of the rack. Alternatively, the shelf will hold three small plant pots.

Hang the rack in the house, studio, garage or shed. Screwed to the wall at each looped point, it will be quite secure and capable of holding a considerable weight. The basket hanging from the bottom is made from a small Chinese sieve.

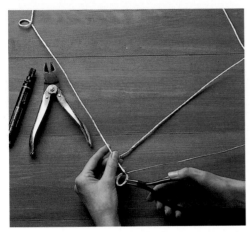

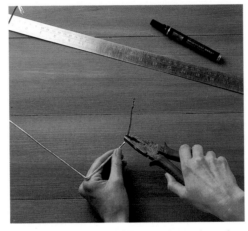

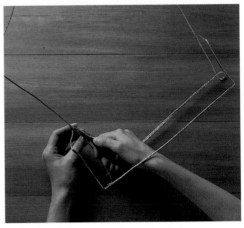

1 To make the frame, cut a 79 in length of straining wire. Twist the ends tightly to stop them from unraveling and, with permanent marker pen, mark the wire at intervals of 11½ in, 2 in, 13 in, 2 in, 10 in, 2 in, 10 in, 2 in, 13 in, 2 in, and 11½ in. Using round-nosed pliers, make a loop with each 2 in section, making sure that the pen marks match up and that all the loops face outward (see diagram 1).

3 To make the shelf, cut a 29 in length of straining wire and mark it at intervals of 1 in, 3½ in, 4 in, 12 in, 4 in, 3½ in, and 1 in. Using general-purpose pliers, bend the wire at right angles at the marked points (see diagram 2).

4 Mark each side of the frame 4 in from the bottom. Twist the 1 in ends of the shelf wire tightly around the frame at these points.

▶

2 Using the 0.025 in galvanized wire, bind the two 11½ in sections together to make the bottom of the frame.

DIAGRAM 1

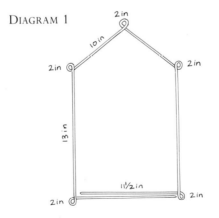

DIAGRAM 2

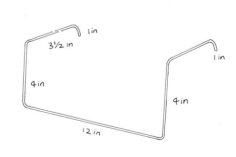

MATERIALS AND EQUIPMENT YOU WILL NEED
STRAINING WIRE • RULER • WIRE CUTTERS • PERMANENT MARKER PEN • ROUND-NOSED PLIERS • GALVANIZED WIRE, 0.025 IN AND 0.065 IN THICK • GENERAL-PURPOSE PLIERS • TACKING WIRE • GLOVES • SMALL-GAUGE CHICKEN WIRE

DIAGRAM 4

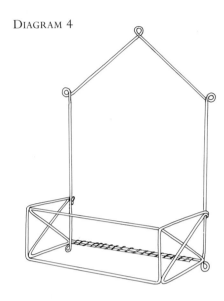

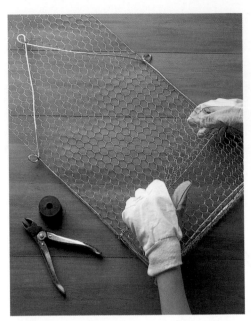

5 To make the rim and sides of the shelf, cut a 41 in length of 0.065 in galvanized wire and mark it at intervals of 1 in, 5 in, 3½ in, 5 in, 12 in, 5 in, 3½ in, 5 in, and 1 in. Using round-nosed pliers, make a loop with the 1 in section at each end of the wire. Bend the wire at the 5 in and 3½ in points at each end at 45° angles to form the side crosses of the shelf. Bend the 12 in section in the middle at right angles to form the top rim (see diagram 3).

DIAGRAM 3

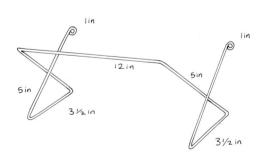

6 Tack the loops at the ends of the rim wire to the 4 in markings on the sides of the main frame. Tack each corner of the side crosses to the frame (see diagram 4).

7 Wearing gloves for protection, lay the frame on to the flat piece of chicken wire and cut around the frame. Allow 12 in at the bottom for wrapping around the shelf, so that there is a double thickness of chicken wire at the front of the shelf where it tucks inside. Using 0.025 in galvanized wire, bind the edges of the chicken wire to the frame (see Basic Techniques). Wrap any rough edges at the top around the frame before binding. Bind the shelf firmly to the frame as you bind on the chicken wire, and remove the tacking wire.

HIPPY HAPPY NECKLACE

WIRE COMES IN MANY FORMS AND APPEARS HERE IN DISGUISE AS PIPE CLEANERS. THE RANGE OF PIPE CLEANERS USED IN THIS PROJECT IS AVAILABLE AT EDUCATIONAL TOY SHOPS. THE NECKLACES ARE GREAT FUN TO CREATE AND ARE THE PERFECT PROJECT TO MAKE WITH CHILDREN. MAKE MATCHING ACCESSORIES USING CLIP-ON EARRING BACKS AND HEADBAND BASES. GLUE A SMALL PIPE-CLEANER FLOWER ON TO EACH EARRING BACK AND LARGER ONES ON TO THE HEADBAND BASES. TO MAKE A BRACELET, ATTACH FLOWERS TO A LARGE FURRY PIPE CLEANER IN THE SAME WAY AS FOR THE NECKLACE.

1 Using round-nosed pliers, make small flowers from plain pipe cleaners. Make the centers of the flowers by straightening striped paper clips and coiling them into spirals (see Basic Techniques). Then bend a furry pipe cleaner with your fingers to make a five-petaled flower. Twist the ends together. Coil a plain pipe cleaner and striped paper clip into spirals to make the center of the large flower.

2 To attach the centers, cut a length of twisty wire tape and tie a knot in it. Thread it through the flower so the knot is at the front and there is a long end behind.

4 Form a loop at each end of the pipe cleaner and attach twisty wire tape to each loop. Form two paper clips into cones. Trim them, then slide them on to the ends.

3 Bend a thick, bumpy pipe cleaner into a semicircle. Bind the small flowers to the pipe cleaner with the twisty tape, tucking in the ends behind the flowers. Bind the large flower to a paper clip and clip on to the pipe cleaner.

5 Bend the ends of straightened clips into coils. Join the double spirals together to make two chains. Make a hook-and-eye catch from paper clips. Attach the chains to the ends of the pipe cleaner, then attach the hook-and-eye catch.

MATERIALS AND EQUIPMENT YOU WILL NEED
ROUND-NOSED PLIERS • PLAIN, FURRY, AND THICK, BUMPY PIPE CLEANERS • STRIPED AND COLORED PAPER CLIPS • TWISTY WIRE TAPE • WIRE CUTTERS

GREETING CARDS

A HOMEMADE CARD MAKES A PERSONAL GIFT THAT WILL BE CHERISHED. OFFER THIS CHERUB CARD TO THAT SPECIAL SOMEONE ON VALENTINE'S DAY. APPLY YOUR CREATIVITY TO MAKE WIRE CARDS FOR BIRTHDAYS, CHRISTMAS, AND HALLOWE'EN DAY USING APPROPRIATE MOTIFS. METALLIC SPRAY PAINTS CAN BE BOUGHT FROM CAR ACCESSORY SHOPS AND ADD A COLORFUL LUSTER TO THE WIRE, AS CAN BE SEEN IN THE SEASHORE MOBILE PROJECT. IF YOU ARE DELIVERING YOUR CARD BY HAND, WHY NOT WRITE THE RECIPIENT'S NAME IN WIRE AND ATTACH IT TO THE ENVELOPE?

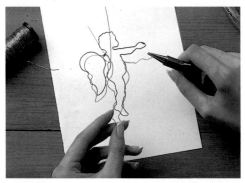

2 To make the cherubs, use round-nosed pliers to bend the 0.025 in galvanized wire around the template on page 400. Bind the cherub shapes where the wings join the body. Then make two hearts from the 0.047 in wire.

1 Cut an 8½ x 13 in rectangle of red cardboard and a 5¾ x 8¼ in rectangle of pink cardboard. Score a line down the centre of the red cardboard and fold. Draw around the small heart template on page 93 in the center of the red cardboard, 1 in from the bottom. Draw around the large heart template in the center of the pink card, ⅝ in from the bottom. Cut out the hearts and reserve the cut-out hearts. Erase all the pencil marks. Spray the bottom edge of the pink cardboard gold.

3 Use a straight pin to make pairs of holes around the cherubs and one of the hearts, where they will be positioned on the pink cardboard.

4 Thread the nylon through the holes in the cardboard from behind to attach the cherubs and heart. Secure at the back with masking tape. Hang the second heart from the first with cotton thread so that it hangs in the heart-shaped hole. Glue the pink cardboard on to the red cardboard. Glue the pink heart on to the inside of the cardboard so that, when the greetings card is closed, the inner heart is pink.

MATERIALS AND EQUIPMENT YOU WILL NEED

RED AND PINK CARDBOARD • RULER • PENCIL • SCISSORS • UTILITY KNIFE • ERASER • GOLD SPRAY PAINT • ROUND-NOSED PLIERS • GALVANIZED WIRE, 0.025 IN AND 0.047 IN THICK • WIRE CUTTERS • STRAIGHT PIN • THIN NYLON THREAD • MASKING TAPE • RED COTTON THREAD • PAPER GLUE

FUSED FLOWERS

FASHION YOURSELF A BUNCH OF FABULOUS FLOWERS, WOVEN FROM RICHLY COLORED FUSE WIRE. ONCE YOU HAVE MASTERED THE FLOWER DESCRIBED IN THE STEP INSTRUCTIONS, ADAPT THE DESIGN TO MAKE THE TWO VARIATIONS SHOWN IN THE PICTURE. ENAMELED COPPER WIRE COMES IN A VAST ARRAY OF COLORS, SO YOU CAN ADD LEAVES AND TENDRILS BY SPIRALING AND COILING THE ENDS OF LENGTHS OF THICKER AND DARKER ENAMELED COPPER WIRE. DISPLAY THE FLOWERS TO DRAMATIC EFFECT IN A METALLIC VASE OR IN THE WOVEN BOTTLE, WHICH IS MADE USING THE SAME WEAVING TECHNIQUES.

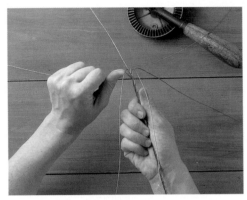

1 Cut six 20 in lengths of 0.039 in enameled copper wire. Twist them together along half the length using a hand drill to form the stem (see Basic Techniques). Bend back the wires loosely.

3 Weave a bulb-shaped stamen, 1 in high and ⅝ in wide.

5 Using a different-colored wire, weave a flower shape 2½ in high.

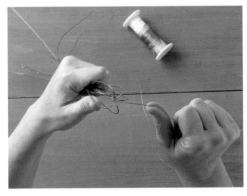

2 Holding the wires in one hand, attach a length of 0.025 in wire to the center. Start weaving around the six wires (see Basic Techniques).

4 Bend each of the wires back up around the woven stamen between your finger and thumb.

6 Using round-nosed pliers, bend each remaining length of wire to form a loose coil. Finally, bind the stem with several lengths of fine enameled copper wire.

MATERIALS AND EQUIPMENT YOU WILL NEED

ENAMELED COPPER WIRE, 0.039 IN THICK AND 0.025 IN THICK IN TWO COLORS • RULER • WIRE CUTTERS •
HAND DRILL • ROUND-NOSED PLIERS

SPOON RACK

THE ELEGANCE OF THIS FRESH GREEN RACK WILL ADD STYLE TO YOUR KITCHEN AND ENSURE THAT YOUR KITCHEN IMPLEMENTS SUCH AS BRUSHES AND SPOONS ARE ALWAYS CLOSE AT HAND. THE SIMPLICITY OF THE DESIGN IS REFLECTED IN THE CHOICE OF MATERIALS. GARDEN WIRE IS INEXPENSIVE AND READILY AVAILABLE, AND IT COMES IN MANY DIFFERENT THICKNESSES AND COLORS.

ALTERNATIVELY, YOU COULD USE GALVANIZED OR TINNED COPPER WIRE. THE CLOVERLEAF, WHICH IS USED FOR THE HOLDERS, IS A RECURRENT MOTIF IN WIREWORK PROJECTS AND CAN BE FORMED AROUND CYLINDRICAL OBJECTS OF DIFFERENT SIZES SUCH AS A WOODEN SPOON, BROOM HANDLE OR A ROLLING PIN (SEE THE BOTTLE CARRIER AND HOOK RACK PROJECTS).

1 Cut three 40 in lengths of thick gardening wire. Wrap one end of each wire three times around a rolling pin. Using round-nosed pliers, make a small loop in the coiled end of each wire large enough to take a screw. Shape the coils to make a spiral in each wire. Bend back the wire from one of the lengths at a right angle to make the central stem.

2 To make the spoon holders, cut three 23 in lengths of wire. Bend each wire at a right angle 5 in from one end.

3 In the next section of wire, make a row of three circles by wrapping the wire one-and-a-half times around a piece of copper piping (or similar tube) for each of the circles.

4 Bend the remaining wire away from the third circle at a right angle. Bend the three circles around to form a clover shape and bind the long end of wire around the 5 in end for 2¾ in. Do not cut off the ends.

5 Arrange the three spiraled wires together with the right-angled one in the center. Measure 12 in from the right angle on the central stem and then mark this point. Cut a 14 in length of wire and make a small loop in one end of it. Leave ¾ in next to the loop, then bind the wire tightly around the spiraled wires, upward from the marked point (see diagram 1).

DIAGRAM 1

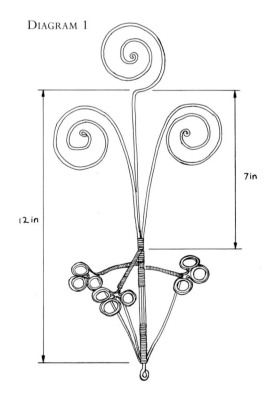

7in

12 in

MATERIALS AND EQUIPMENT YOU WILL NEED

THICK GARDENING WIRE • RULER • WIRE CUTTERS • ROLLING PIN • ROUND-NOSED PLIERS • PIECE OF COPPER PIPING • PERMANENT MARKER PEN

6 Measure 7 in from the right angle of the central stem and, using the excess wire on one of the clover shapes, bind it on to the stem at this point. Bind upward for ¾ in and cut off the wire. Bind on the second clover shape ¾ in below the first in the same way. Attach the third clover shape below the second, binding downward for 1½ in. Make a bend halfway along the stems of the second and third clover shapes to angle them inward slightly.

7 Bend up the three stem wires at the bottom and bind each to the neck of one of the clover shapes. Cut off the ends. Screw the spoon holder to the wall through the loop in each spiral and at the bottom of the stem.

WIRE BASKET

THIS STURDY BASKET IS PARTICULARLY SUITABLE FOR GATHERING VEGETABLES FROM THE GARDEN. THE WIRE MESH ALLOWS THE SOIL TO FALL THROUGH AND, BECAUSE THE WIRE IS GALVANIZED AND RUSTPROOF, THE DIRTY VEGETABLES WITHIN IT CAN BE HOSED DOWN IN THE GARDEN. IN THE PAST, WIRE BASKETS WERE USED FOR COLLECTING CLAMS FROM THE SEASHORE OR FOR CARRYING BREAD HOME FROM THE STORE. FEW DESIGNS ARE PRODUCED TODAY, EXCEPTING KITCHENWARE BASKETS FOR SALADS AND FRYING, MANY OF WHICH ARE COLLAPSIBLE. WEAR GLOVES WHEN WORKING WITH CHICKEN WIRE TO PROTECT YOUR HANDS.

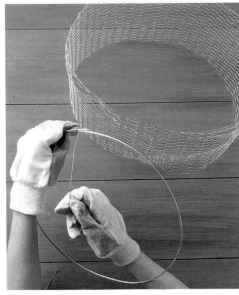

4 Cut two 7 in lengths and two 9 in lengths of 0.065 in galvanized wire. Using round-nosed pliers, attach the wires to the oval to form a grid, binding where the wires cross.

1 To make the cylinder, cut a piece of chicken wire 11 x 35 in. Form it into an oval and join the short edges together (see Basic Techniques). Cut a 37 in length of straining wire and form it into an oval that will fit snugly inside the chicken-wire cylinder. Bind the ends together with 0.025 in galvanized wire.

2 To shape the basket, count up ten holes from the bottom of the cylinder. This section will be the base. Bend all the holes into heart shapes (see Basic Techniques).

3 To make the base support, cut a 27½ in length of straining wire and bind it into an oval.

5 Push the bottom edges of the basket together and bind with 0.025 in galvanized wire to close up the base neatly. ▶

MATERIALS AND EQUIPMENT YOU WILL NEED

SMALL-GAUGE CHICKEN WIRE • WIRE CUTTERS • GLOVES • RULER • STRAINING WIRE • GALVANIZED WIRE 0.065 IN AND 0.025 IN THICK • ROUND-NOSED PLIERS • PERMANENT MARKER PEN • TACKING WIRE • BROOMSTICK

6 Position the base support on the bottom of the basket and bind it on to the chicken wire all the way around.

7 Place the large oval of straining wire inside the basket, 2 in from the top. Fold the chicken wire over it to reinforce the top rim of the basket.

8 Mark a 21½ in length of straining wire but do not cut it. Tack the end to one side of the basket and bend to form the handle. Secure the wire where you have marked it to the other side of the basket. Wrap the next section of straining wire ten times around a broomstick to form ten loops (see Basic Techniques). Bind these loops around the basket to where the handle wire is tacked.

9 Bend the wire over the basket to double the handle. Bend the next section of wire to form a three-petaled decoration, as shown, and bind it to the basket. Loop the handle across again and make another three-petaled decoration on the other side.

10 Bend the wire back over the basket to form a fourth handle loop. Using the broomstick, make ten more loops in the wire and bind around the basket.

11 Using 0.025 in galvanized wire, bind the four handle wires together at the top, tucking the ends inside.

CHANDELIER

CREATE THIS SPLENDID CHANDELIER TO HANG OVER YOUR DINING TABLE. THE ELEGANT STAR-SHAPED FRAME HOLDS LIGHTS MADE BY PLACING A THIN LAYER OF OLIVE OIL AND A FLOATING WICK INSIDE GLASSES HALF-FILLED WITH WATER. TINT THE WATER WITH FOOD COLORING. CHOOSE GLASSES WITH TAPERING SIDES, SO THEY DON'T SLIP THROUGH THE HOLDERS, OR USE BABY-FOOD JARS WITH NECKS WIDE ENOUGH TO TAKE THE WIRE THICKNESS. THE LONG LENGTH OF ALUMINUM WIRE NEEDED FOR THIS PROJECT IS QUITE DIFFICULT TO WORK WITH IN THE EARLY STAGES. WEAR GLOVES TO PREVENT THE WIRE FROM COLORING YOUR HANDS.

1 Using a permanent marker pen and a ruler, mark the 0.128 in aluminum wire at intervals of 21½ in, 2 in, 21½ in, 2 in, 21½ in, 2 in, 21½ in, 2 in, 21½ in, 2 in, and 2 in. Do not cut the wire at this stage. When handling the wire wear a pair of gloves.

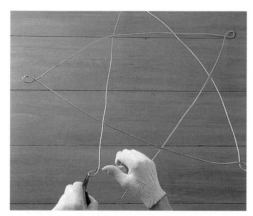

2 Using round-nosed pliers, bend each 2 in section of wire into a loop, leaving the last 2 in straight for joining. Weave the long sections over and under each other to form a star shape. Bind the last 2 in to the beginning of the wire, using 0.039 in aluminum wire. Bind each loop closed.

3 To even up the star shape, divide each 21½ in length of wire into three equal sections of just over 7 in, and mark the points. Match up the marks where the wires cross and bind them together at these points using 0.039 in wire.

4 Enlarge the templates on page 400 to size by photocopying them at 150%. It is essential that all the pieces are enlarged by the same percentage.

5 Cut 13 in lengths of 0.128 in wire. Using round-nosed pliers, carefully bend 15 of these lengths around the nosed double-coil template. ▶

MATERIALS AND EQUIPMENT YOU WILL NEED
GLOVES • SOFT ALUMINUM WIRE, 0.128 IN AND 0.039 IN THICK • RULER • PERMANENT MARKER PEN • ROUND-NOSED PLIERS • WIRE CUTTERS • PHOTOCOPIER AND PAPER • FIVE GLASSES OR JARS AT LEAST 2¼ IN IN DIAMETER • ONE GLASS OR JAR AT LEAST 2½ IN IN DIAMETER • SIX BATH-PLUG CHAINS • METAL RING

6 Using round-nosed pliers, bend the remaining 15 lengths of wire around the templates on page 93 to make five double coils, five arched double coils and five single-looped coils.

8 Using five short lengths of 0.039 in aluminum wire, bind the five double coils on to the central holder.

10 Bind three nosed double coils to each small glass holder: bind one nosed double coil to the coils on the glass holder and the other two to the ring. Position each structure inside the points of the star frame so that the noses of the nosed double coils fit into the corners and the coils of the glass holder face toward the tip. Bind in place (see diagram 1).

7 To make the glass holders, cut five 20 in lengths of 0.128 in wire. Wrap each around one of the 2¼ in glasses or jars. Wrap the wire around twice and overlap the ends. Use the template on page 93 to coil the wire at each end. To make the central glass holder, cut a 24 in length of wire and then wrap it three times around the larger glass or jar to make a plain coil.

9 Bind the double coils together where the sides touch to make the raised central piece. Then bind alternate arched double coils and single-looped coils around the edge.

DIAGRAM 1

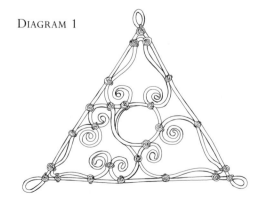

11 Bind the central piece to the star frame at all the points of contact. Attach a bath-plug chain to each of the five points where the wires of the star frame cross. Attach the hooks at the ends of the chains to a metal ring and close up. Attach the sixth bath-plug chain to the top of the metal ring for hanging. Place the glasses or jars in the holders.

GARDEN TRAY

ONE OF THE GREAT THINGS ABOUT WIRE IS THAT IT GIVES STRUCTURE TO OTHERWISE FLIMSY MATERIALS. HERE THE WIRE IS COMPLETELY COVERED WITH RAFFIA TO CREATE A ROMANTICALLY RUSTIC TRAY. A READY-MADE MAT FORMS THE BASE, BUT YOU COULD MAKE YOUR OWN USING 19 IN STICKS OF EQUAL THICKNESS. BIND THEM TOGETHER WITH RAFFIA TO MAKE A MAT APPROXIMATELY 16 IN WIDE. YOU COULD USE ANOTHER TYPE OF MAT AS LONG AS IT IS RIGID ALONG ITS LENGTH. USE THE TRAY FOR GARDENING OR AS AN ATTRACTIVE HOLDER FOR SEVERAL POTTED PLANTS.

1 Cut two 40 in lengths of straining wire. Using a permanent marker pen, mark each wire at intervals of 10 in, 2 in, 16 in, 2 in, and 10 in. Using parallel (or channel-type) pliers, bend each wire at the marked points to create the shapes of two carrying handles. The two 10 in sections double up to form the base. The two 2 in sections make the sides and the 16 in section curves over the top. Hold each handle together at the base with double-sided tape.

2 To make the hearts, cut two 40 in lengths of straining wire and mark at intervals of 15 in, 10 in, and 15 in. Make each 10 in section into a heart shape and cross the wires over at the marked points. Bend up the wire and then secure it with tape. Wrap the heart wires and the handles with tape, then bind them closely with raffia.

4 Position the end of the mat inside one of the handles and bind in place with raffia. Thread the raffia between the sticks of the mat and around the sides and base of the handle. Position the heart wire inside the handle, and bind in place where the coils touch the sides and the heart touches the bottom. Bind the second handle and heart wire to the other end of the mat.

3 Using round-nosed pliers, bend the ends of the heart wires into coils, so that they will fit inside the handles.

5 Make two bundles of twigs and bind tightly to the top of the handles with double-sided tape. Wrap with raffia to cover all the tape.

MATERIALS AND EQUIPMENT YOU WILL NEED

STRAINING WIRE • RULER • WIRE CUTTERS • PERMANENT MARKER PEN • PARALLEL (OR CHANNEL-TYPE) PLIERS • ROUND-NOSED PLIERS • DOUBLE-SIDED TAPE • SCISSORS • RAFFIA • STICK MAT • TWIGS

SEASHORE MOBILE

Amarine theme is ideal for a mobile as the gentle movement suffuses the sea creatures with an "underwater" grace. Here a seahorse, dolphins, starfish, and fish undulate around the central figure of a crab. Wire is an excellent material for mobile-making as it is light and can be fashioned into any imaginable shape. Spray paint the wires different colors to give them a subtle, variegated hue. Design your own mobiles on different themes. Form stars, sun, moon and clouds for a celestial mobile, or pink and red hearts and cherubs for a romantic theme.

1 To make the small supports, cut two 18 in lengths of 0.078 in wire. Bend each wire into an arch, and form a coil at each end using round-nosed pliers. Bend a curve in the wire near each coil using half-round pliers.

2 To make the main supports, cut two 29 in lengths of 0.078 in wire. Bend each wire into an arch, form a coil at each end and bend waves in the wire beside each coil.

3 Cut a 1¼ in length of 0.078 in wire. Using the half-round pliers, bend the wire around to make a ring. Cross the main support wires so that they meet exactly in the center and tape then together, with the ring at the top. Wrap with 0.025 in wire to secure the joint, completely covering the tape.

4 Enlarge the templates on page 401 to size by photocopying them at 180%. It is essential that all the pieces are enlarged by the same percentage.

5 To make the two starfish and the shell, cut three pieces of 0.065 in wire: 8½ in, 13 in, and 20 in long. Using the enlarged templates, form the 8½ in length of wire into a shell, the 13 in length into a small starfish and the 20 in length into a large starfish. Bind the ends together using the thinnest wire.

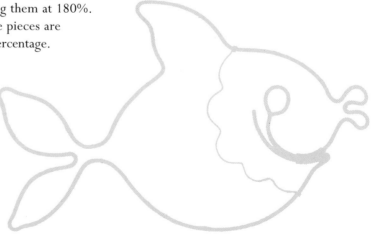

MATERIALS AND EQUIPMENT YOU WILL NEED
GALVANIZED WIRE, 0.078 IN, 0.025 IN, 0.065 IN, AND 0.047 IN THICK • RULER • WIRE CUTTERS •
ROUND-NOSED PLIERS • HALF-ROUND PLIERS • DOUBLE-SIDED TAPE • PHOTOCOPIER AND PAPER • CAR SPRAY PAINTS • NYLON THREAD • SCISSORS

6 Cut a 36 in length of 0.065 in wire and form it into a seaweed shape, using the template as a guide. Bind the ends together using the thinnest wire.

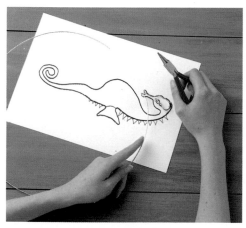

7 Use both the round-nosed and half-round pliers to bend a 36 in length of 0.065 in wire into a seahorse shape.

8 Bind the ends of the wire together at the top of the seahorse's head using the thinnest wire. Use the same wire to make the seahorse's dorsal fin. Loop the wire around the wire of the seahorse's back to make a series of arches. Nip a point in each arch.

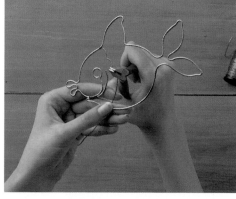

9 To make the fish, cut two pieces of 0.065 in wire, 28 in, and 40 in long. When you have completed the outline of the large fish, add a wavy line of the thinnest wire between the head and body. Bind the point where the head meets the body, then wrap along the bottom of the body. Extend the wire across the body, bind the joint at the top and cut off the excess. Complete the small fish with a wavy line of the thinnest wire between the head and body.

10 To make the dolphin, cut a 42½ in length of 0.065 in wire. Start at the dolphin's eye and, using the template, bend the wire around the outline to the mouth. Bend the wire back to make a curved line inside the body that finishes at the tail.

11 Bind the dolphin at the mouth and tail where the wire meets. ▶

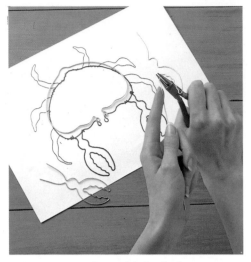

12 Form the crab's body from a 16 in length of 0.065 in wire. Make an eye loop at each end of the wire with round-nosed pliers. Make the front legs of the crab from two 11½ in lengths of 0.047 in wire.

13 Twist the ends of the legs around the wire of the crab's body and squeeze with pliers to secure.

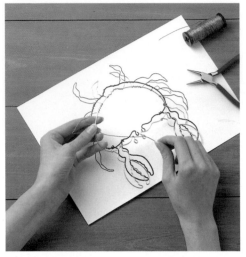

14 Use a continuous length of the thinnest wire to make the back legs, following the template. Wrap the wire around the crab's body between the legs.

15 Spray paint the sea creatures red, yellow, aquamarine, blue and green. Some of the shapes can be sprayed in two colors.

16 To assemble the mobile, attach the sea creatures to the supports with nylon thread. It is important to use the lengths of thread given so that the mobile balances. The crab hangs down 5½ in from the center of the main support. The dolphin hangs 2¾ in and the seaweed 3 in from either end of one of the main supports.

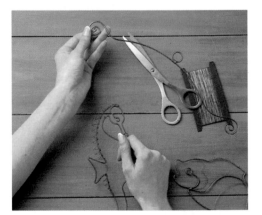

17 Hang the seahorse 4½ in from the end of a small support and the large fish 4¾ in from the other end. Tie this support so that it hangs 5½ in from one end of the second main support. Hang the shell 5 in from the other end. Hang the second small support 3½ in below the shell. Hang the small fish and big starfish 3 in from either end of the small support. Hang the small starfish 3 in below the large one.

CANDLE SCONCE

DESPITE ITS ORNATENESS, THIS MEDIEVAL-LOOKING CANDLE SCONCE IS QUITE EASY TO MAKE. THE BASKET CONTAINER WILL TAKE A NIGHT LIGHT OR THICK CANDLE. BY MAKING THE BASE OF THE BASKET WIDER AND WEAVING THE SIDES DEEPER YOU CAN ADAPT THE SHAPE TO FIT A LARGER CANDLE. USE SILVER-PLATED WIRE TO MAKE A LIGHTER, MORE DELICATE SCONCE TO SUIT A MORE CLASSICAL INTERIOR. ALWAYS SECURE THE CANDLE WITH CANDLE FIXES. CHECK THE DISTANCE BETWEEN THE CANDLE FLAME AND THE WALL AND DO NOT ATTACH THE SCONCE TO A WALL THAT HAS WALLPAPER OR FLAMMABLE PAINT.

3 Bend up the wires at the edge of the circle and weave the side of the candle basket to a depth of about 1 in.

1 Cut 15 in lengths of 0.065 in wire. Bundle them together so that they are even at the top and bottom, and grip them with the general-purpose pliers 6¼ in from one end. Hold the pliers closed with masking tape so that they act as a vice. Using the 0.031 in wire, bind around the bundle of wires for ¾ in from the pliers. Do not cut off the wire. Release the pliers.

2 Using round-nosed pliers, bend a downward-curving loop at the end of each wire in the bundle. Bend down the wires at right angles at the top of the bound section so that they spread out in a circle. Using the length of 0.031 in wire that is still attached to the bundle, weave around the wires to make a base with a diameter measuring 2¾ in (see Basic Techniques).

4 Using parallel (or channel-type) pliers, coil down the wires to the edge of the candle basket.

MATERIALS AND EQUIPMENT YOU WILL NEED

COPPER WIRE, 0.065 IN AND 0.031 IN THICK • RULER • WIRE CUTTERS • GENERAL-PURPOSE PLIERS • MASKING TAPE • ROUND-NOSED PLIERS • PARALLEL (OR CHANNEL-TYPE) PLIERS

5 Using parallel (or channel-type) pliers, make two columns of coils with the wires left underneath the candle basket. Make nine coils in each column, ensuring that the second column is a mirror image of the first. Cut off the end of each wire, increasing the amount you cut off by ½ in each time, so that the coils decrease in size. Using round-nosed pliers, form waves in the three remaining wires. Cut off the ends of the outer wires, so that the central one is the longest.

6 Decide which is the back of the sconce. Using the parallel (or channel-type) pliers, unwind the two coils at the back a little, cross them over each other and twist them flat. Attach the sconce to the wall through the holes in the center of these two coils. Bend back the wavy wires so that they support the sconce at the bottom, holding it away from the wall. Check the distance between the candle flame and the wall.

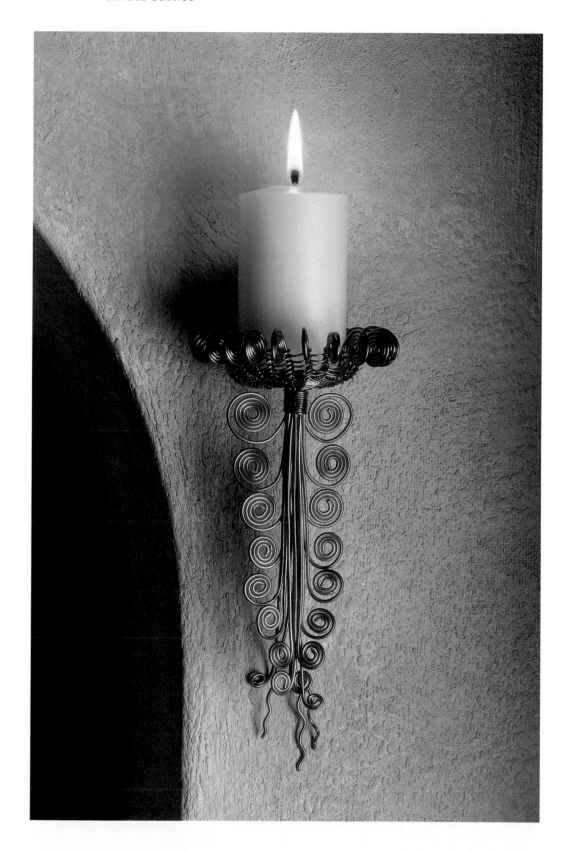

WOVEN CHAIR

YOU DON'T NEED TO HAVE DIY SKILLS TO CREATE FASHIONABLE DESIGNER FURNITURE. SECONDHAND WOODEN CHAIRS ARE CHEAP AND EASY TO FIND. BUY ONE THAT HAS A CANE OR BASKETWORK SEAT AND REMOVE IT. PAINT THE CHAIR IN ONE COLOR AND CHOOSE WIRE OF A CONTRASTING COLOR. THE CHAIR PICTURED HERE IS PAINTED MIDBLUE AND THE SEAT IS WOVEN WITH ORANGE AND BURGUNDY ENAMELED COPPER WIRE. MAKE ONE CHAIR AS A FOCAL POINT OR A WHOLE SET FOR THE DINING ROOM. MAKE SURE THE SCREW EYES ARE FIRMLY SECURED AS THEY HAVE TO TAKE THE WEIGHT OF A PERSON.

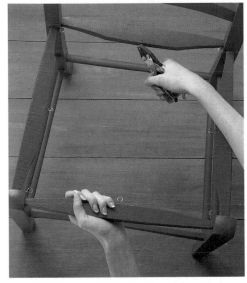

1 Screw the screw eyes into the inside of the chair frame, one in each corner and one in the middle of each side. Secure them with pliers and make sure that the rings are lying flat.

2 Attach the 0.098 in wire to one of the corner screws by threading it through the eye and twisting the end around the wire, using round-nosed pliers. Stretch it diagonally across the frame and secure it to the opposite eye. Stretch wire across the other diagonal in the same way. Squeeze all the joints.

3 Make a diamond shape between the four side screws with four more pieces of copper wire. ▶

MATERIALS AND EQUIPMENT YOU WILL NEED

WOODEN CHAIR • EIGHT SCREW EYES • ROUND-NOSED PLIERS • ENAMELED COPPER WIRE, 0.098 IN THICK AND 0.039 IN THICK IN TWO COLORS • PARALLEL (OR CHANNEL-TYPE) PLIERS • WIRE CUTTERS

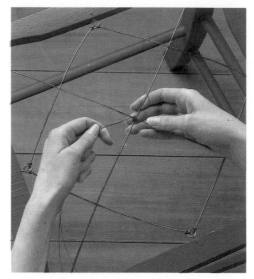

4 Cut a long length of 0.039 in enameled copper wire and fold it in half. Attach it by passing the loop under the center of the copper-wire cross and threading the end back through to secure.

5 Weave a square (see Basic Techniques) until you have covered half the distance between the center and the point where the copper wires cross. Cut off the wire, wrap it around several times and tuck in the end.

6 Weave four more squares, one at each point where the copper wires cross.

7 Attach another double length of 0.039 in enameled copper wire to one of the corner screw eyes.

8 Weave first around one side of the chair frame, then back around the diagonal copper wire and around the other side of the chair frame to make a herringbone pattern.

9 Continue weaving until you reach the square nearest to that corner. Secure the wire and cut it off. Weave the other three corners in the same way.

10 Loop a double length of 0.039 in enameled copper wire around one of the side screw eyes. Weave around the chair frame to one side of the eye, then over the eye, around the other side of the chair frame and back under the eye. Continue in this way until the eye is completely covered.

11 Continue weaving by wrapping the wire around the two diagonal copper wires as well as the chair frame.

12 Weave until you reach the two nearest squares. Secure the wire and cut it off. Weave the other three sides in the same way.

13 Stretch two lengths of copper wire across each of the spaces between the five central woven squares. Attach the ends to the corners of the squares and secure with round-nosed pliers.

14 Using 0.039 in enameled copper wire in a second color, weave a square in each space.

15 Weave the four squares so that they are smaller than the first five and there are gaps in the finished pattern.

TOASTING FORK

Toasting bread or English muffins over a fire in winter is always a pleasant activity. This fork is made from four coat hangers and is both light and strong. The bowed handle at the top prevents the wire from becoming too hot. Wire coat hangers come in different-colored finishes, so you could make a two-tone fork, as shown in the background of the picture. Before you make the fork, check that the finish on the coat hangers does not burn. Cut off the hooks and straighten the coat hangers before you start.

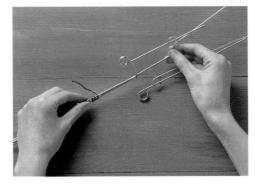

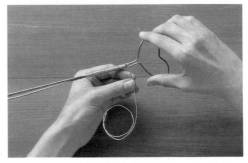

1 To make the first of the two inner struts, measure 4 in from the end of one of the straightened coat-hangers and wind it around a wooden spoon at this point to create a loop. The wire will come out of the loop at a slight angle. Measure ¾ in before bending the remaining length of wire straight. Make the second strut a mirror image of the first by winding the wire the other way around the wooden spoon. Make the two outer struts in the same way. This time allow 5 in for the prongs and bend a right angle ¾ in beyond the prong loop.

DIAGRAM 1

2 Bind the struts together temporarily with tacking wire, loosely enough to allow movement. Slide the two outer prongs through the loops of the two inner prongs, ensuring that all of the components are in the right place (see diagram 1).

3 Measure up from the prongs and mark the handle at intervals of 1½ in, 7 in, 1½ in, 8 in, 1½ in, and ¾ in. These measurements may vary depending on how much wire is left. Using the galvanized wire, bind the first two 1½ in sections. Then bind the last 1½ in section, but this time do not cut off the wire. Cut off three of the remaining wires at the last mark.

4 Make the fourth wire end into a heart shape, using pliers and bending it around a piece of copper piping (or similar tube) to create the curves. Leave ¾ in at the end and bind it in with the other three wires, continuing to use the wire from the last 1½ in section.

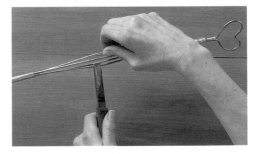

5 Using the pliers, grip each wire in turn halfway along the 8 in section. Pull the wire so that it bows out. This will be the handle of the fork, so test it in your hand for comfort and adjust if necessary. Trim the ends of the prongs so that they are even and hammer each tip flat.

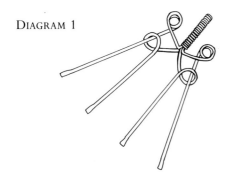

MATERIALS AND EQUIPMENT YOU WILL NEED

FOUR WIRE COAT HANGERS • WIRE CUTTERS • GENERAL-PURPOSE PLIERS • RULER • WOODEN SPOON • TACKING WIRE •
PERMANENT MARKER PEN • GALVANIZED WIRE, 0.031 IN THICK • PIECE OF COPPER PIPING • HAMMER

BOTTLE CARRIER

BOTTLE CARRIERS ARE EXTREMELY USEFUL BUT HARD TO FIND, SO MAKING YOUR OWN IS THE PERFECT SOLUTION. THIS CARRIER IS MADE FROM THICK GALVANIZED WIRE AND HOLDS THREE BOTTLES. BY ADDING THREE MORE CORE WIRES, YOU CAN MAKE ANOTHER LEAF FOR THE CLOVER SHAPE TO HOLD FOUR BOTTLES. IN THE PAST, FRENCH WIRE WINE-BOTTLE CARRIERS OFTEN INCLUDED A CANDLE HOLDER, MAKING THEM ESPECIALLY USEFUL FOR BRINGING UP BOTTLES FROM DARK WINE CELLARS. THESE CARRIERS ARE NOW QUITE HARD TO FIND AS THEY ARE MUCH SOUGHT AFTER BY COLLECTORS.

1 Cut three 32 in lengths of 0.078 in wire. Leave a 4 in allowance at the end of each wire and bend the wire at this point. Wrap the next section of wire around a bottle and bend back the wire where it meets the first bend. Make two more petals in this way. The circles will spring open to make the clover shape. Make a loop at each end of the wire and carefully close together. Cut off any excess wire. Make two more clover shapes.

2 Cut seven 32 in and two 36 in lengths of 0.078 in wire. Straighten all the wires and bundle them together so that the longest are in the center and stick out at one end. This end will form the handle.

3 Starting at the point where the longer wires stick out, bind the bundle with 0.031 in wire for 16½ in. Divide the rest of the wires into groups of three. Bend them away from the central shaft at right angles. Lay the wires in each bunch of three side by side and, bind together 1¼ in from the central bend. Bind for about ¼ in, then bend out the outer two wires at right angles. Measure 2 in from the bound section and mark each wire. Bend each wire up at a right angle so that it stands parallel to the handle. Make a hook at the end of each wire.

4 Slot the three clover shapes into the structure, and then close up the loops around the top clover shape. Bind the bottom clover in place. Bind up each strut, securing the middle clover shape halfway up. Bind over the wire ends at the top of the structure.

5 Wrap a length of 0.078 in wire around the nail to make a coil. Thread the bead on to the wires at the top of the central shaft. Apply strong glue to the coil and hammer it into the bead.

MATERIALS AND EQUIPMENT YOU WILL NEED
GALVANIZED GARDENING WIRE, 0.078 IN AND 0.031 IN THICK • RULER • WIRE CUTTERS • GENERAL-PURPOSE PLIERS • BOTTLE •
³⁄₁₆ IN NAIL • LARGE WOODEN BEAD • STRONG GLUE • HAMMER

BICYCLE TOY

An African toy was the inspiration for this project. Handmade from wire and scrap materials, it was ingeniously designed so that a little figure pedaled a bicycle when the toy was pushed along. This bicycle toy and the toys pictured in the History of Wire work on the same mechanical principle. You could adapt the figure to your liking by your choice of accessories, such as the bicycle basket, the fabrics used for the clothes and the colors of the pipe cleaners. A second toy can be dressed as a boy to make a pair.

1 To make the bicycle, cut a 40 in length of galvanized wire. Using a permanent marker pen, mark the wire at intervals of 2 in, 12¼ in, 2 in, 1¼ in, ¾ in, ¾ in, 1½ in, ¾ in, ¾ in, 1¼ in, 2 in, 12¼ in, and 2 in. Wrap both 12¼ in sections of wire around a bottle or can with a diameter of approximately 4 in to form the wheels. Using parallel (or channel-type) pliers, bend in the 2 in at each end of the wire to form a radius to the center of the circle.

2 Bend in the other two 2 in sections at right angles. Make the bicycle pedals by bending right angles in the wire at the marked points.

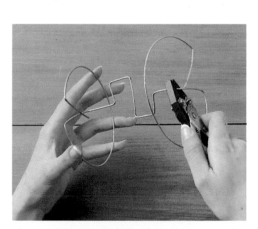

3 Bend each wheel so that it is at a right angle to the pedals.

4 Transfer the twisty wire tape to a cotton reel to make it easier to handle. Bind tape around the wheel, along the radius, across the pedals and around the second wheel. ▶

MATERIALS AND EQUIPMENT YOU WILL NEED

GALVANIZED WIRE, 0.065 IN THICK • RULER • WIRE CUTTERS • PERMANENT MARKER PENS • BOTTLE OR CAN • PARALLEL (OR CHANNEL-TYPE) PLIERS • TWISTY WIRE TAPE IN TWO COLORS • COTTON REEL • COLORED PIPE CLEANERS • SMALL CARDBOARD TUBE • PAPER FASTENERS • SELECTION OF LARGE AND SMALL WOODEN BEADS • STRONG GLUE • RIBBON • DOLL'S STRAW HAT • FABRIC IN TWO COLORS • NEEDLE AND THREAD • DOUBLE-SIDED TAPE • FREEZER-BAG TIES • DOLL'S BASKET • SILK FLOWERS • GREEN BAMBOO CANE

DIAGRAM 1

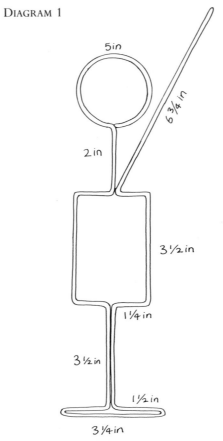

5 To make the body of the bicycle, cut a 40 in length of galvanized wire and mark it at intervals of 5 in, 2 in, 1¼ in, 3½ in, 1¼ in, 3½ in, 1½ in, 3¼ in, 1½ in, 3½ in, 1¼ in, 3½ in, 1¼ in, and 6¾ in. Cut off any excess and follow diagram 1 to shape the bicycle. Use parallel (or channel-type) pliers to bend right angles at the marked points. Bend the 5 in section into a circle to form the seat. Leave the 6¾ in section at the other end to be inserted into the bamboo cane later.

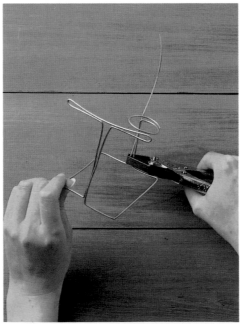

6 Bend up the handlebars, seat and stick attachment at right angles.

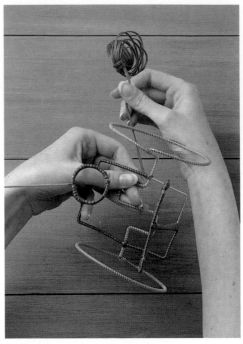

7 Bind twisty wire tape in another color around the handlebars, leaving a tiny gap near each end where you will attach the doll's hands. Bind down the neck of the handlebars and along the frame. Halfway along the frame, bind the body on to one side of the wheels. Bind the seat, leaving the projecting wire bare. Continue binding around the frame, binding on the wheels at the other side. The wheels should now rotate when you push the bicycle along gently.

8 To make the doll's body, twist together the ends of two pipe cleaners. Make a hole either side of the top and bottom of the cardboard tube. Thread the joined pipe cleaners through the holes at the top to make the arms. To make the upper legs, bend two pipe cleaners in half and twist the ends together. Attach each pipe cleaner to one of the holes at the bottom of the tube with a paper fastener. Do not fasten them too tightly as they must allow for movement.

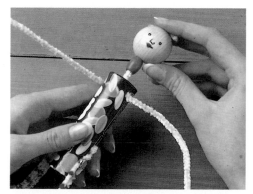

9 Draw a face in permanent marker pen on a large, plain bead. Make a hole in the end of the tube. Thread a pipe cleaner through the hole. Thread on a small bead for the neck and then the large bead. Bend the pipe cleaner over the top of the head and over the bottom edge of the tube so that the head is held on securely.

10 Bend two pipe cleaners in half to make the lower legs and thread through the upper legs. Wrap a brown pipe cleaner around the bottom of each leg and bend up to make the doll's shoes. Glue three brown pipe cleaners on to the top of the head and braid on each side to make the hair. Tie a ribbon on to the end of each braid. Glue on a doll's hat.

11 Cut a 4 in square of fabric and fray the edge. Cut a slit from one corner to the center to make the shawl. Cut a 4 x 13 in rectangle from another fabric. Sew a line of running stitch along the top edge and gather to make the skirt. Wrap a piece of strong double-sided tape around the doll's body. Dress the doll and tie a length of ribbon around the waist.

12 Attach the doll's feet to the pedals with freezer-bag ties. Wrap each arm around the handlebars, twisting the excess length around the arm. Place a little basket over one arm first and fill it with silk flowers.

13 Apply strong glue to the piece of wire projecting from the bicycle seat and insert into the hollow center of a green bamboo cane. Allow the glue to dry. Apply glue to the top end of the cane and slide on two or three beads to make a handle. Toddlers' beads are best for this as they have large holes.

COPPER BOWL

COPPER WIRE IS NATURALLY WARM IN COLOR, AND THE WRAPPING TECHNIQUE USED HERE ENHANCES ITS RICH APPEARANCE. THE BOWL LOOKS PARTICULARLY SOFT AND SUMPTUOUS WHEN DISPLAYED BY CANDLELIGHT. THE ORGANIC LOOK OF THE COILED TENDRILS MAKES THE BOWL SUITABLE FOR HOLDING FRUIT. FOR A SPECIAL DINNER PARTY, MAKE MATCHING NAPKIN RINGS FROM 24 IN LENGTHS OF WRAPPED WIRE. MAKE A CYLINDRICAL COIL IN THE MIDDLE TO HOLD THE NAPKIN AND A FLAT COIL AT EACH END. COPPER TARNISHES, SO POLISH THE BOWL REGULARLY TO KEEP IT SHINY.

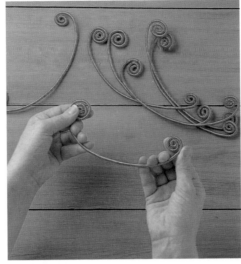

4 Bend the longer wrapped wire around the larger bowl and the shorter wrapped wire around the smaller bowl to make two wire hoops.

1 Cut eight 16½ in lengths of the 0.078 in copper wire. Wrap them with 0.031 in wire (see Basic Techniques). Make a coil with a diameter of about 1½ in at one end of each wire and one of 1 in at the other, using parallel (or channel-type) pliers.

2 Using your hands, bend each wire to form the curved side struts of the bowl. Use the first one as a model for the rest so that they all have the same shape.

3 To make the top and bottom rims of the bowl, cut two lengths of 0.104 in wire, one 32 in and the other 20 in. Wrap the longer length in 0.047 in wire and the shorter in 0.059 in wire. Pull each wire out from its coil by ¾ in. This will create a short projecting wire at one end and a length of empty coil at the other.

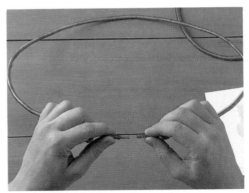

5 Insert a little quick-drying glue into the empty end of each coil and slot in the projecting end of wire. Hold it firmly in place until the glue is dry.

▶

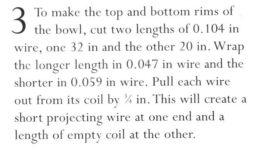

MATERIALS AND EQUIPMENT YOU WILL NEED
COPPER WIRE, 0.078 IN, 0.031 IN, 0.104 IN, 0.047 IN, 0.059 IN, AND 0.039 IN) THICK •
RULER • WIRE CUTTERS • PARALLEL (OR CHANNEL-TYPE) PLIERS • BOWLS IN TWO SIZES • QUICK-DRYING GLUE • PERMANENT MARKER PEN • GENERAL-
PURPOSE PLIERS

6 Lightly mark eight equidistant points around each of the hoops. Cut 16 5 in lengths of 0.039 in wire. Use these wires to begin binding the side struts to the hoops. Allow the struts to extend above the top rim by about 2½ in and below the bottom rim by about 1½ in.

7 Continue to bind the struts to the hoops, wiring alternate ones first. This helps to give the bowl stability as you work, although it will be a little bit wobbly at this stage.

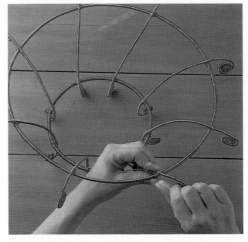

8 Bind the last four struts to the hoops, adjusting any that become misshapen in the process.

9 Make an open coil (see Basic Techniques) with a diameter of 6 in, from 0.104 in copper wire. Bind the spiral in place with two lengths of 0.039 in copper wire, leaving about 4 in spare wire at each end.

10 Attach the base coil to the bottom rim by binding the excess wire around four of the struts.

11 Twist a 2½ yd double length of 0.039 in copper wire and wrap it around the bowl (see Basic Techniques). Make a zigzag pattern between the struts at the bottom and halfway between the struts around the top rim.

ANGEL

ONCE YOU HAVE BECOME DEXTROUS AT SCULPTING WIRE, TRY MAKING THIS ELEGANT CHRISTMAS ANGEL. THE SILVER-PLATED COPPER WIRE IS SOFT AND EASY TO BEND. THE ANGEL MAKES A NOVEL ADVENT CALENDAR. HANG A DIFFERENT ORNAMENT, SUCH AS A BEAD, A STAR OR A SMALL BAUBLE, FROM HER HAND EVERY DAY. ON CHRISTMAS DAY, HANG A LITTLE PRESENT TO BE OPENED. THE ANGEL CAN ALSO BE HUNG ON THE TREE OR IN THE CENTER OF A WREATH. YOU COULD CREATE OTHER WIRE DECORATIONS FOR THE TREE. DRAW OR TRACE CHRISTMAS MOTIFS AS TEMPLATES TO SCULPT AROUND

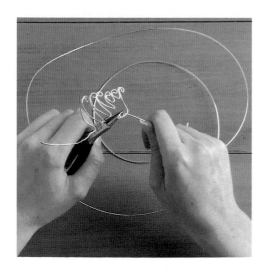

1 The template of the Angel appears on page 400. Use this as a guide for shaping the wire. You can either use it the same size or enlarge it using a photocopier. Leaving 2 in at the end start bending the wire around the template, using round-nosed pliers and your fingers. Make the hair curls and the forehead up to the eye. Make the lower lid of the eye first and then the upper lid. Halfway along the upper lid, make a loop around the end of the round-nosed pliers to form the pupil. Squeeze the corner of the eye with parallel (or channel-type) pliers.

2 Shape the nose and make a larger loop around the end of the round-nosed pliers for the nostril. Shape the mouth, closing the lips with parallel (or channel-type) pliers, then shape the chin.

4 Follow the template along the arm. Make loops with the round-nosed pliers for the fingers, and then shape the bottom line of the arm.

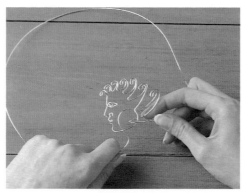

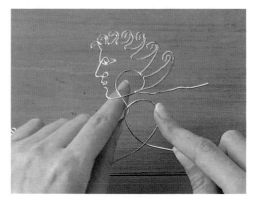

3 Loop the wire around the bottom of the hair to make the cheek. This loop will help to keep the structure flat and more manageable.

5 Make the shoulder by carefully looping the wire around the point where the arm joins the neck. ▶

MATERIALS AND EQUIPMENT YOU WILL NEED

PHOTOCOPIER AND PAPER • SILVER- OR GOLD-PLATED WIRE, 0.039 IN THICK • ROUND-NOSED PLIERS • PARALLEL (OR CHANNEL-TYPE) PLIERS • WIRE CUTTERS • NARROW RIBBON • STAR-SHAPED BEAD OR CRYSTAL DROPLET

6 At the waist, bend the wire across to form the waistband. Make a series of long horizontal loops with slightly curled ends back along the waistband. When you have made seven loops, secure with a tight twist at the bend.

8 Complete the wavy hemline and the back of the skirt. Secure by twisting the wire tightly around the waistband.

10 Loop the wire around the back of the shoulder and under the bottom of the wing. Finish off with a coil and cut off the wire.

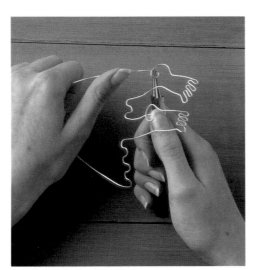

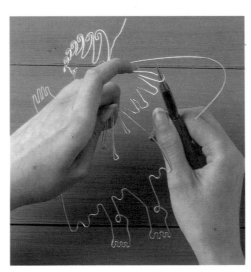

9 Make loops along the bottom of the wing and close slightly to neaten. Form the curved top of the wing.

7 Make a large curve for the lower part of the skirt. Shape a wavy hem around the thickest part of the round-nosed pliers. The legs interrupt the wavy hemline. Make the toes in the same way as the fingers, but they should be shorter and rounder. Shape the heels and make a loop at each ankle.

11 Using the 2 in of wire left at the start, bind the shoulder and wing together. Cut off the end. Thread ribbon through the loops in the waistband and hang a star-shaped bead or crystal droplet from the angel's hand.

WOVEN BOTTLE

HERE'S AN UNUSUAL WAY OF RECYCLING THOSE BEAUTIFUL BOTTLES THAT ARE TOO NICE TO THROW AWAY. THE WOVEN WIRE CASING IS NOT ONLY DECORATIVE BUT ALSO PROTECTS THE BOTTLE FROM BREAKAGE. ALTHOUGH THE TECHNIQUE IS LABOR-INTENSIVE AND REQUIRES PATIENCE, IT IS RELATIVELY EASY TO MASTER. THE FINISHED BOTTLE CAN BE USED AS A VASE, DECANTER OR CANDLE HOLDER, BUT USE NON-DRIP CANDLES. TO DISPLAY THE BOTTLE TO ITS BEST ADVANTAGE, PLACE IT IN A POSITION WHERE THE LIGHT WILL SHINE THROUGH THE WIRE TO REVEAL THE COLOR OF THE GLASS WITHIN. YOU COULD MAKE A COMPLETE SET OF BOTTLES OF VARYING SIZES, SHAPES AND COLORS, ALSO USING DIFFERENT COLORS OF WIRE.

1 Cut four pieces of 0.065 in wire 10 in longer than twice the height of the bottle. Cross the wires on the base of the bottle (you can see this in step two) and bend so that eight struts run up the sides of the bottle. Tuck the wire ends inside the neck and wrap masking tape around the body and neck of the bottle.

2 Join a doubled length of the thin wire to the point where the wires cross and start weaving (see Basic Techniques).

3 Loop the wire around each strut, creating a smooth, closely woven surface. Change the wire every so often to achieve a striped pattern.

4 Continue weaving around the sides of the bottle, twisting the wires together where you join them.

5 When you have woven to the top of the bottle, pull out the ends of the wire struts from inside the bottle. Using round-nosed pliers, make downward-curving coils.

6 Continue to weave fine enameled copper wire around the coils. You will now see the reverse pattern of the weave. Secure the last end of wire by wrapping it several times around a strut before cutting it off.

MATERIALS AND EQUIPMENT YOU WILL NEED

BOTTLE • ENAMELED COPPER WIRE, 0.065 IN AND 0.025 IN THICK IN TWO COLORS • RULER • WIRE CUTTERS • MASKING TAPE • ROUND-NOSED PLIERS

TOAST RACK

GRACE YOUR BREAKFAST TABLE WITH THIS SCULPTURAL TOAST RACK. THE TIGHT WIRE WRAPPING AND THE STAR PATTERNS ON THE HANDLE AND FEET BEADS GIVE THE PIECE AN ORIGINAL SPACE-AGE QUALITY. THE SPRINGY, ELONGATED ARCHES ARE SPACED TO ALLOW FOR THICK OR THIN SLICES OF BREAD. CHOOSE BEADS WITH QUITE LARGE HOLES, OR ENLARGE THEM BY DRILLING TO FIT THE STRUCTURAL WIRE. MATCHING EGG CUPS CAN BE MADE BY COILING WRAPPED WIRE AROUND AN EGG THEN NARROWING IT TO MAKE A NECK AND WIDENING IT AGAIN TO MAKE A BASE.

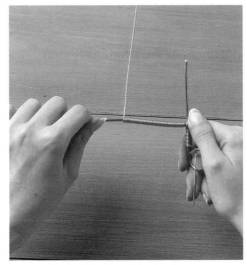

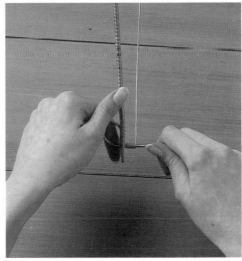

1 Cut a 4 in length of 0.104 in copper wire, and use round-nosed pliers to bend a loop in one end to make a "key". Attach the 0.047 in copper wire next to the loop and wrap for ¾ in. Do not cut off the wire.

2 Cut two 10 in lengths of 0.104 in copper wire for the main shafts. Place the key at a right angle to one of the 10 in lengths of wire, ½ in from the end. Wrap the shaft with the same length of 0.047 in wire for 9 in by turning the key.

3 Remove the key from the initial ¾ in of wrapping and place at a right angle to the other end of the 10 in piece of wire. Wrap the key for another ¾ in, making sure that this coil sticks out from the shaft wire at the same side as the first. Cut off the wrapping wire. ▶

MATERIALS AND EQUIPMENT YOU WILL NEED

COPPER WIRE, 0.104 IN AND 0.047 IN THICK • RULER • WIRE CUTTERS • ROUND-NOSED PLIERS • TACKING WIRE •
BOTTLE • FILE • PERMANENT MARKER PEN • STRONG GLUE • SILVER-PLATED COPPER WIRE 0.031 IN THICK
• FOUR MEDIUM-SIZED BEADS • LARGE BEAD • DRILL (OPTIONAL)

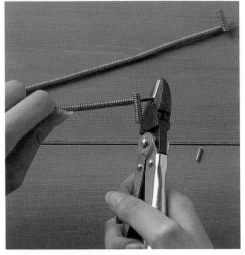

4 Remove the key from the coil and trim off the shaft wire close to the coil at each end. Wrap the second shaft wire in exactly the same way. Cut two 13¾ in lengths of 0.104 in wire. Wrap these two wires in the same way as the first two, this time leaving approximately 2¾ in unwrapped wire at each end. Do not cut off the unwrapped sections as these will form the legs later.

6 To make the handle struts, cut two 8¼ in lengths of 0.104 in wire. Make a ¼ in coil on the key as before, then begin wrapping one of the wires ½ in from the end. Wrap for 5½ in, and cut off the wrapping wire, leaving a long end. Wrap the second handle strut in the same way but, once again, do not cut off the wrapping wire.

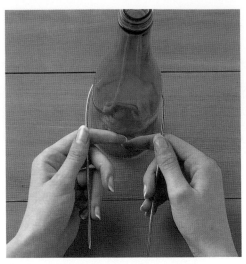

8 To make the base of the rack, cut a 20 in length of 0.104 in wire. Leave 6 in at one end and bend the next section around a small bottle measuring 2½–2¾ in in diameter. Wrap another length of 0.104 in wire for 5 in and cut off the wrapping wire. Remove the length of wire and thread the 5 in coil on to the bent wire. Move it along the wire until it sits in the bend.

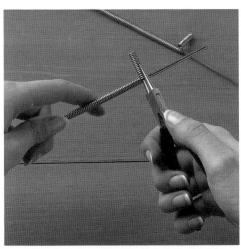

5 Using round-nosed pliers, adjust all the ¼ in coils so that they stick out from the wrapped wires at right angles and point in the same direction.

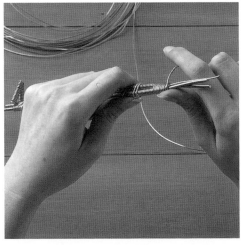

7 Tack the two handle struts together using tacking wire, checking that the coils are facing in the same direction. Wrap them together, continuing up from the 5½ in wrapped sections. Leave ¼ in at the top unwrapped.

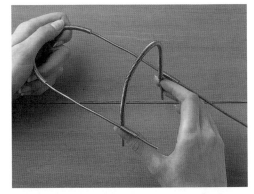

9 Bend each of the four wrapped pieces to make a curve in the center. Thread the first wrapped section on to the base. It should be one of the pieces with 2¾ in legs. If you have difficulty pushing the wires through the coils, file the ends of the base wire. Pull apart the individually wrapped struts of the handle section and bend them to make an arch shape.

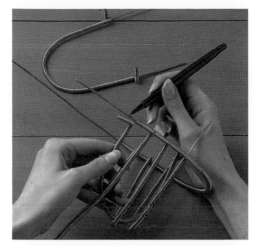

10 Thread on the next piece (with no legs), followed by the handle arch. Before threading on the next piece, mark the base wire halfway along the length of the next coil. You will cut the wire at this point later. Thread on this piece, followed by the second piece with legs. Wrap a length of 0.104 in wire for 3½ in and then remove the coil.

12 Thread the first coil on to the base wire next to the curve. Apply some strong glue to the end of the base wire and slot it into the empty section of the next coil. Allow the glue to dry.

14 Make four 2 in coils of 0.047 in wire by wrapping around a length of 0.104 in wire and then removing. Thread these coils on to the legs and then glue on bead feet. Glue the large bead on to the top of the handle. If necessary, make the hole in the bead a little larger by drilling carefully.

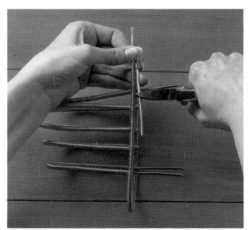

11 Thread the 3½ in coil on to the long end of the base wire. Bend the wire around the bottle to mirror the first curve and until the two wrapped sections meet. Cut off the wire where it meets the marked point on the base wire. Remove the last two coils from this side of the base wire and cut off at the marked point.

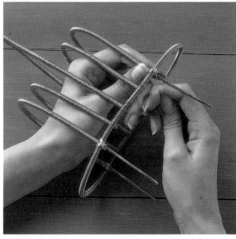

13 Using silver-plated copper wire, bind crosses around the leg joints to add stability. If you find that the rack is too springy, carefully apply a little glue to the joints.

LANTERN

CHICKEN WIRE BECOMES AN EXOTIC MATERIAL WHEN USED TO MAKE THIS LANTERN, WHICH IS PERFECT FOR HANGING IN THE GARDEN. FOR AN EVENING GARDEN PARTY, MAKE SEVERAL IN DIFFERENT SHAPES AND SIZES AND HANG THEM AROUND THE GARDEN TO CREATE A MAGICAL ATMOSPHERE. PLACE LONG-LASTING NIGHT LIGHTS IN THE JAM JARS. THE JARS PROTECT THE CANDLE FLAME FROM THE BREEZE AND FROM FALLING LEAVES. DESPITE THE HOMELY MATERIALS, THE LANTERN ALSO LOOKS VERY EFFECTIVE WHEN HUNG INDOORS. WEAR GLOVES WHEN WORKING WITH CHICKEN WIRE TO PROTECT YOUR HANDS.

1 Cut two pieces of chicken wire, measuring 7 x 24 in and 8½ x 21½ in, and two lengths of galvanized wire, one measuring 26 in, the other 24 in. Form two cylinders from the chicken wire and join the short edges together with aluminum wire (see Basic Techniques). Bend the galvanized wire to form two hoops with the same circumference as the cylinders. Bind the ends together with aluminum wire.

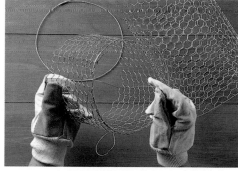

2 Use the aluminum wire to bind a hoop on to the edge of each cylinder.

3 To shape the lantern, which is the larger cylinder, bend all the holes in the chicken wire into heart shapes (see Basic Techniques). Use round-nosed pliers and your hands to mold the cylinder (see step eight for shape).

4 To make the lid, bend all the holes in the second cylinder into heart shapes, then push the wire to form a curved lid shape. You will need to squash the holes together at the top.

5 Using the hollow section in the mouth of the general-purpose pliers, carefully crimp the chicken wire in the center of each section to form a central core (see Basic Techniques).

▶

MATERIALS AND EQUIPMENT YOU WILL NEED

SMALL-GAUGE CHICKEN WIRE • GALVANIZED WIRE, 0.065 IN THICK • RULER • WIRE CUTTERS • GLOVES • ALUMINUM WIRE, 0.039 IN THICK • ROUND-NOSED PLIERS • GENERAL-PURPOSE PLIERS • BOTTLE WITH CONE-SHAPED LID • JAM JAR • LARGE BEADS • BATH PLUG CHAIN • METAL RING • FLAT-HEADED JEWELRY PINS • THIN RIBBON (OPTIONAL)

6 To form a long cone to go on the lid of the lantern, wrap the aluminum wire around the tapered top of a paint or glue bottle. The bottom of the cone must be wide enough to fit over the central core of the lid.

7 Secure a length of thin wire inside the center of the lid and push it through the core. Thread the coiled cone on to the wire and slip over the core. Leave the length of wire hanging loose from the center of the cone. Wrap another length of wire around the core of the lantern section to make a smaller coil.

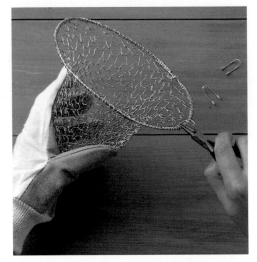

8 Cut four 4 in pieces of galvanized wire. Using round-nosed pliers, bend each piece into a loop with a hook at each end. Curve up the bend in each loop slightly. Position the loops evenly around the rim of the lantern section and close up the hooks with pliers.

9 Cut two lengths of galvanized wire and twist together around the neck of the jam jar so that the ends stick out on either side. Attach the wires to the lantern rim on either side of two opposite loops.

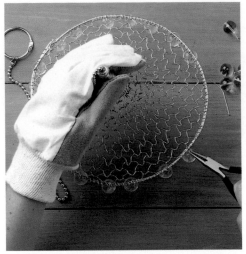

10 Thread a large metallic bead on to the wire left loose in the center of the lid. Bind the bath-plug chain to the wire and cut off the excess wire. Attach the ring to the other end of the chain for hanging. Thread beads on to flat-headed jewelry pins and hang evenly around the rim of the lid. Attach another large bead to the core of the lantern section.

11 Put the lid on the lantern and slot the four loops on the lantern rim through the chicken wire of the lid. Press them down firmly. It is very important for safety that the loops hold the bottom securely in place. Reinforce with extra pieces of wire or tie with thin ribbon.

SPICE RACK

KEEP YOUR HERB AND SPICE JARS NEAT IN THIS HEART-RIMMED RACK, WHICH IS DESIGNED TO HOLD FIVE STANDARD-SIZED SPICE JARS. IT CAN BE HUNG ON THE WALL OR USED FREE-STANDING ON A SHELF OR KITCHEN SURFACE. SCALE UP THE DESIGN AND USE THICKER WIRE TO MAKE A DISTINCTIVE WINDOW BOX. USE IT TO HOLD POTTED PLANTS OR LINE IT WITH MOSS, FILL WITH SOIL AND PLANT. IF YOU DO CHOOSE TO MAKE THE ENLARGED VERSION, MAKE SURE YOUR WORKING SPACE IS LARGE ENOUGH TO TWIST THE LONG LENGTHS OF WIRE THAT YOU WILL NEED (SEE BASIC TECHNIQUES).

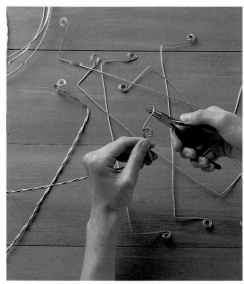

1 Cut five 18 in lengths of 0.065 in galvanized wire. Using a permanent marker pen, mark the wire at intervals of 2 in, 2 in, 10 in, 2 in, and 2 in. Using round-nosed pliers, bend the 2 in sections at the ends of each wire into coils. Using general-purpose pliers, bend up each wire at right angles at the next 2 in marks. Twist a length of wire then cut two 18 in lengths and mark these in the same way. Unravel the 2 in at either end of each wire and make four coils, two at each end, then bend right angles at the next marks.

2 Cut two 3½ in lengths of 0.065 in galvanized wire. Make the box section of the spice rack by joining together the two twisted wire struts. Twist the ends of the 3½ in lengths around the bent corners of the struts, leaving a distance of 2½ in between the two struts.

3 Cut a 41 in length of twisted wire and mark it at intervals of 8 in, 5 in, 2½ in, 10 in, 2½ in, 5 in, and 8 in. Bend a right angle at each marked point to form a rectangle. Using your hands, carefully bend the 8 in section at each end to form the two halves of a heart shape. ▶

MATERIALS AND EQUIPMENT YOU WILL NEED
GALVANIZED WIRE, 0.065 IN AND 0.025 IN THICK • RULER • WIRE CUTTERS • PERMANENT MARKER PEN
• ROUND-NOSED PLIERS • GENERAL-PURPOSE PLIERS • GALVANIZED WIRE, 0.065 IN THICK, PREVIOUSLY DOUBLED AND TWISTED
(SEE BASIC TECHNIQUES) • TACKING WIRE • BROOMSTICK

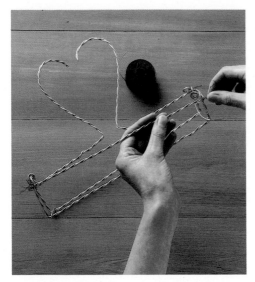

4 Attach the four corners of the heart rim to the top of the box section using tacking wire.

6 Slot the box section inside these four pieces so that the four large coils are at the back beside the heart. Tack into place where the pieces touch.

8 Wrap a long length of 0.065 in galvanized wire several times around a broomstick to make a loose coil. Position this wire coil inside the front edge of the spice rack.

5 Cut four 21½ in lengths of twisted wire and mark each at intervals of 2 in, 2 in, 2½ in, and 15 in. Unravel the 2 in end of each wire and make into two coils. Bend each wire at right angles at the next two marked points. Bend each 15 in section into a coil. Bend a curve in the wire next to two of the coils so that they will rest on the back of the spice rack.

7 Slot the plain wire struts made in step one inside the box structure. Space them evenly across the width of the box and tack into place.

9 Using 0.025 in galvanized wire, bind around the top rim of the box (see Basic Techniques), securing each piece in position and removing the tacking wire as you go. Then bind from front to back along the bottom struts. Finish by binding the heart closed at the top and bottom, and binding the decorative spirals where they touch.

HOOK RACK

A RACK OF HOOKS IS ALWAYS USEFUL, AND CAN BE HUNG IN THE HALL FOR KEYS, IN THE BATHROOM FOR TOWELS AND IN THE KITCHEN FOR UTENSILS. DURING THE NINETEENTH CENTURY, MANY TYPES OF WIRE WALL RACKS WERE MADE. THE FLATTENED COIL WAS A POPULAR DECORATIVE DEVICE, AS WAS THE CLOVER MOTIF. THE BINDING TECHNIQUE ON THE STEMS IS USEFUL TO LEARN FOR OTHER PROJECTS, SUCH AS THE TOASTING FORK AND EGG TREE. THIS IS A GOOD PROJECT TO WITH MAKE CHILDREN, AS IT IS QUITE STRAIGHT-FORWARD AND THE PLASTIC-COATED WIRE IS SAFE TO USE.

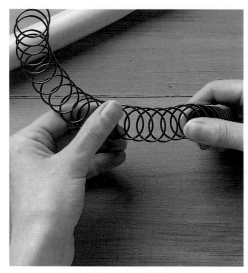

1 Tightly wrap the gardening wire 40 times around a broomstick. Leave 4 in of spare wire at each end and cut off. Flatten the coil (see Basic Techniques). The coil should be about 12 in long.

2 Cut a 22 in length of gardening wire. Mark the center point and the point 6 in from each end. Form a loop at each of the points by wrapping the wire around a pencil. Thread the wire through the flattened coil, then slot the loop at either end of the coil into the small end loops on the wire.

3 Bend the 6 in section at each end of the gardening wire around a wooden spoon to create three same size clover leaves. There should be about ¾ in left at the end to bend back down the stem. Use the 4 in of wire left at the ends of the coil to bind the stem.

MATERIALS AND EQUIPMENT YOU WILL NEED
GREEN GARDENING WIRE • BROOMSTICK • RULER • WIRE CUTTERS • PERMANENT MARKER PEN • PENCIL • WOODEN SPOON •
ROUND-NOSED PLIERS • A FRIEND

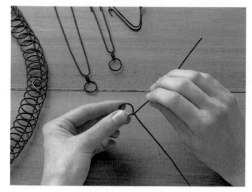

6 To finish, slot the clover hook through the middle of the coil, so that its shank lies on either side of the central loop in the bottom wire. Bend up the hook 2 in from the circle end. Screw the rack to the wall through the three loops in the bottom wire. The central screw will hold the hook firmly in place.

4 Cut four 12 in lengths of wire. Loosely bend each wire in half and wrap the bend around the wooden spoon to make a circle. Twist the circle closed. Carefully bend small hooks in the ends of the wires. Bend each wire in half to form four large hooks. Loop the ends of the hooks around the coil and bottom wire of the frame, and close tightly.

5 Cut a 79 in length of wire. Loosely bend it in half and wrap the bend around the wooden spoon to make a circle. Twist the circle closed. Mark the point 6 in up from the circle and then ask a friend to hold this point firmly while you twist the wires together. Bend the twisted wire around the broomstick to make three cloverleaves, then bind the shape closed.

MOSAICS
HELEN BAIRD

To LEARN TO MAKE A MOSAIC MAY SEEM A DAUNTING TASK, BUT IN REALITY FEW THINGS COULD BE SIMPLER. A MOSAIC CAN BE MADE OUT OF ANY MATERIAL THAT CAN BE EMBEDDED INTO OR STUCK ONTO ANOTHER.

TRADITIONAL MATERIALS SUCH AS SMALTI, VITREOUS GLASS AND STONE ARE STILL AVAILABLE, BUT MODERN ARTISTS ALSO MAKE USE OF TILES, CHINA, MIRROR AND GLASS, WHICH CAN BE BROKEN INTO REGULAR PIECES OR BROKEN HAPHAZARDLY FOR A CRAZY PAVING EFFECT. MATERIALS SUCH AS BEADS, SHELLS, STONES, SEEDS, AND FRAGMENTS OF PLASTIC, METAL AND WOOD CAN ALL BE USED. BEFORE BEGINNING TO EXPERIMENT, IT IS USEFUL TO ACQUIRE A GOOD BASIC KNOWLEDGE OF THE TECHNIQUES INVOLVED, AND IT IS IMPORTANT TO UNDERSTAND THE PROPERTIES OF THE MATERIALS YOU ARE USING. AS THESE SKILLS ARE SIMPLE TO ACQUIRE, IN VERY LITTLE TIME YOU WILL BE CREATING YOUR OWN DAZZLING PIECES.

Left: Almost any surface can be embellished with mosaics, from simple ceramic tiles to glass or wood — or even polystyrene.

HISTORY OF MOSAICS

THE WORD "MOSAIC" CONJURES UP IMAGES OF ROMAN FLOOR AND WALL DESIGNS, PICTURES MADE FROM SMALL, GEOMETRIC-SHAPED STONES. THIS IS ONLY PART OF THE STORY, HOWEVER, EVEN THOUGH THE WORD MOSAIC DOES HAVE ITS ORIGINS IN ITALY. AS A MEDIUM, MOSAIC CERTAINLY EXISTED LONG BEFORE THE ROMANS AND HAS BEEN USED IN MANY WAYS AND FOR VARIOUS PURPOSES BY SUBSEQUENT CULTURES AND CIVILIZATIONS UP THROUGH THE PRESENT DAY. MOSAIC HAS BEEN DEFINED AS "A SURFACE DECORATION MADE BY INLAYING SMALL PIECES OF VARYINGLY COLORED MATERIAL TO FORM A PATTERN OR PICTURE." WHILE THESE SMALL PIECES OF MATERIAL ARE USED TOGETHER TO FORM A WHOLE SURFACE PATTERN OR DESIGN, THEY RETAIN THEIR INDIVIDUAL IDENTITIES WITHIN THE MOSAIC. ALTHOUGH MOSAICS OFTEN HAVE A PURELY DECORATIVE FUNCTION, BECAUSE THE MATERIALS USED TO MAKE THEM ARE USUALLY VERY HARD-WEARING, THEY ARE OFTEN GIVEN A FUNCTIONAL ROLE AS FLOOR OR WALL COVERING AS WELL.

The earliest surviving mosaics were made in about 3000 BC by the Sumerians in ancient Mesopotamia, the area now known as Iraq. These consisted of arrangements of colored clay pegs that were pressed into wall surfaces. Later, the Egyptians used fragments of colored materials and semi-precious stones to decorate walls and to inlay furniture, decorative objects and items of jewelry.

Ancient Greece is the earliest civilization known to have used natural stones and pebbles in a variety of colors to create permanent designs, and was probably the originator of what we today think of as "mosaic." The Romans built on this technique, standardizing practices by cutting natural stone into regular cubes. They also used fired clay and a little glass for special effects. Another Roman innovation was the use of cements and mortars. These made their mosaics much more durable than those of their predecessors, and as a result there are many surviving examples of floor and wall mosaics throughout countries that were once part of the Roman Empire.

Right: A mosaic portrait of a Roman woman, dating from the 1st century AD. The colors and patterns of the mosaic pieces have been used to great effect in creating the contours of the features.

Left: Roman pavement mosaic depicting a banquet with musicians, 1st–2nd century AD.

Below: Detail from the church of San Vitale, Ravenna, 6th century AD, depicting the Emperor Justinian.

The Romans used an extraordinarily varied range of styles and subjects in their mosaics – from realistic, observed studies of everyday life to naive garden mosaics, from depictions of the gods in the received format to purely decorative designs and geometric borders.

These early mosaics were executed in the natural colors of the materials they were made from, such as grays, terracotta, ochre, black, white, muted blues and greens. The growth of Christianity introduced new subject matter, but techniques and colors remained broadly unchanged until the Byzantine era, usually dated as beginning with the reign of the Emperor Justinian in Ravenna, about AD 527. This was a very rich and innovative period in the history of mosaic, exemplified by the beautiful, luminous creations adorning Byzantine churches.

At this time, Ravenna was a wealthy imperial town and the main trading link between east and west. It is here that the best examples of Byzantine mosaic can be found, and the influence of Eastern art is apparent in the designs, such as the large Egyptian eyes, flattened shapes and ordered poses. This iconoclastic style was rendered with a new kind of tesserae – glass "smalti." Glass, which previously had been used sparingly for highlights, now became the main component of mosaics. It was fired with metallic oxides, copper and marble or had gold and silver leaf sandwiched in it. This new material gave mosaic artists access to a large palette of luminous colors. They also developed the technique of setting the pieces into the mortar bed at varying angles, thus achieving wonderful effects with the reflective qualities of glass.

When Ravenna ceased to be the main link between Europe and Asia, and its trade and wealth were taken over by Venice, the art of mosaic-making soon followed. Records show that a school of Venetian mosaicists was established as early as AD 979. The traditions of the Byzantine school were carried on there, then moved to Constantinople, the center of orthodox Christianity at the time. The art reached its peak in the 13th century.

With the dawning of the Renaissance, mosaicists became preoccupied with refining their technical abilities and, as did painters of the time, they tried to represent space, line and form. By the late 16th century, mosaic was imitating painting so completely that mosaicists were able to imitate brushstrokes, as, for example, in the huge mosaics created in St. Peter's Basilica in Rome.

Above: Interior of San Vitale, Ravenna, showing the apse and Byzantine columns.

During this period, the art of mosaic-making was superseded by fresco painting. The mosaics that did continue to be created tended to be copies of paintings. This tendency persisted right up to the 20th century. As a result, the mosaicist had become a master craftworker and copyist rather than an original artist.

At the beginning of the 20th century, the Art Nouveau movement gave artists a new direction, and mosaic was seen as an artistic medium that could be celebrated for its own qualities. Pure pattern re-emerged and forms were simplified and stylized.

Mosaic was freed even more with the onset of modernism. The best-known exponent of mosaic in this era was the architect Antonio Gaudí (1852–1926). He covered the large exterior surfaces of his buildings, both plain and formed, with irregularly shaped colored tiles. He also commissioned prominent modern artists of the time, including Kokoschka, Klimt and Chagall, to make designs for the mosaics which clad his buildings. Examples of his mosaics include the facade of Casa Battló, the spires of the Sagrada Familia, the serpentine benches on the terrace of Güell Park and Barcelona's cathedral.

A collaborator of Gaudí, José Maria Jujal, is also worthy of mention for the ceramic medallions he made for the ceiling of the Hypostyle Hall in Güell Park. He set brilliantly colored mosaic pieces (tesserae) against ceramic fragments such as bases of bottles, cups and dishes, arranged in patterns of stars and spirals.

But the history of mosaics is not confined to western Europe. In Central America, long before the arrival of Europeans, the Aztecs and Mayas developed mosaic techniques separately from the rest of the world. There, mosaic was not used to convey images or systematic patterns, as was the tradition in Europe.

Rather, it was simply used to embellish three-dimensional forms, very beautifully, using tesserae made from fragments of precious materials, most often turquoise and coral. These objects were often of a votive or ceremonial nature, such as skulls, weapons and carved snakes, and were encrusted with a variety of precious materials to give them color, beauty and importance.

Mosaic is an important component of Islamic art. The designs are closely related to the buildings in which they are set and seem to rise naturally from the architecture. A fine example of the Islamic mosaic tradition can be seen in the 14th-century palace of the Alhambra in Granada, Spain, and Muslim craftsmen still construct complicated geometric mosaics today.

Many cultures use mosaic-like effects to adorn buildings and objects. In African art, for example, everyday objects are often studded with tacks or covered in colored beads. The effect is that of mosaic, although the method by which the pieces are attached differs.

The handwoven carpets of India and Turkey are in many ways comparable to the medium of mosaic. The patterns are made up of individual units of color and, indeed, these can be very useful as inspiration for designs. Today mosaic artists draw their inspiration from many different cultures and traditions and combine these influences with techniques and ideas that developed in Europe.

Above: Antonio Gaudi's mosaic tiles in the garden at Belleguarde, Barcelona.

GALLERY

MOSAIC-MAKING IS AN ANCIENT CRAFT WITH A RICH HISTORY. TODAY, DESIGNERS AND CRAFTSPEOPLE ARE DRAWN TO THE MEDIUM FOR ITS DECORATIVE QUALITIES AND VERSATILITY. MOSAICS CAN BE MADE FROM ALL MANNER OF MATERIALS, FROM THE TRADITIONAL SMALTI AND TESSERAE, TO CHINA, GLASS, MIRRORS AND EVEN PLASTIC. THESE EXAMPLES OF CONTEMPORARY WORK RANGE FROM PIECES THAT REFLECT THEIR CLASSICAL ANTECEDENTS, TO MODERN ABSTRACT DESIGNS.

Above: TEMPLE
Inspired by the embroidered decorations of Rajasthan, this piece incorporates vitreous glass and broken tiles.
NIKKI GREAVES

Above right: ADAM AND EVE
This pillar is modern in its design and materials, using a "crazy paving" effect to create the pattern set into a solid concrete base, while the theme depicted reflects the historical precedents of mosaic decoration.
HELEN BAIRD

Right: STILETTOS
These sculptures were created exclusively from pieces of mirrored glass on sculpted polystyrene bases. The sinuous, almost organic shape of the shoes is enhanced by the reflective qualities of the mirror.
REBECCA NEWNHAM

Left: ABSTRACT TABLE
The perfect combination
of old and new, resulting
in a contemporary yet
pleasingly classic piece.
The tonal range and
carefully considered sizes
of the mosaic pieces create
a harmonious design.
ZOE CANDLIN

Below: PICTURE FRAMES
The artist has made great
use of contrasting textures
in these delightful picture
frames, setting jewel-
bright glass spheres and
fragments into rough
plaster backgrounds.
LUCIANA IZZI

Right: BEFORE SCHOOL
DINNER
A wonderfully quirky
piece composed of
fragments of china set on a
wok base.
CLEO MUSSI

Right: FISH PANEL
This relatively simple design makes use of the inherent pattern-making qualities of tesserae to great effect. While the background pieces are composed in a regular grid pattern, the fish are made of fragments of tiles that suggest both scales and movement.
MOSAIC WORKSHOP

Below: EMBELLISHED CABINET
This charming cabinet is made of papier-mâché, decorated with a mosaic top. Naive designs worked in pulped paper on the sides of the cabinet echo the style of the parrot design on the top.
EMMA SPRAWSON

Left: SUNFLOWER TABLE
Broken china and discarded pottery make up this delightful table design.
NORMA VONDEE

Right: THE ALLOTMENT
Whole vitreous glass tiles
are combined with
carefully shaped pieces to
make up this charming
design. The perspective is
flattened intentionally,
creating an effect
reminiscent of early folk-
art designs.
MOSAIC WORKSHOP

Above: BIRD TABLE
Here, the mosaic pattern
was inlaid into a specially
built wooden table top,
allowing the border of the
table to become part of
the design. The flowing
lines and bird patterns are
reminiscent of medieval
tapestry designs.
ELAINE GOODWIN

Left: SILVER GILT
MIRROR
For this elegant design, the
natural beauty and cool
colors of the materials are
used to great effect.
ESTITXU GARCIA

Right: FIRE
SALAMANDER
Traditional marble tiles
were used to produce this
paving slab. Movement
and interest are created by
the positioning of the
marble tesserae in the
manner of early classical
mosaicwork.
MARTIN CHEEK

Right: GREEK TABLE
Simplicity itself, this
pleasing table design is
reminiscent of Greek
friezes.
NORMA VONDEE

MATERIALS

TESSERAE IS THE TERM GIVEN TO THE INDIVIDUAL PIECES WHICH, WHEN PUT TOGETHER, MAKE A MOSAIC. THESE CAN BE MADE FROM ALMOST ANY SOLID SUBSTANCE. FOR PRACTICAL PURPOSES, ONLY THOSE MOST COMMONLY USED ARE LISTED IN THIS BOOK. THE CHOICE OF TESSERAE DEPENDS UPON THE USES OF THE MOSAIC; FOR EXAMPLE, A HARD-WEARING MATERIAL IS NEEDED FOR A MOSAIC THAT WILL BE WALKED ON. TAKE THIS INTO ACCOUNT WHEN DECIDING ON YOUR MATERIALS.

Adhesives When choosing the correct adhesive, two considerations must be taken into account. First, should the glue be waterproof? Second, is the glue suitable for sticking the tesserae to the base? White glue is most frequently used and is excellent for securing most tesserae to a wooden base. For sticking tesserae to glass, use silicone sealant. For sticking glass to metal, use epoxy resin, which should also be used with other materials when greater strength or weather resistance is required.

Bases Mosaic can be made on top of almost any surface, as long as it is rigid and correctly pre-treated and the environment in which the mosaic is to be placed is taken into account. For example, if a mosaic is being made to stand outside, it would be unwise to secure it to a base material that may warp or expand when exposed to damp conditions. One of the most popular bases for a mosaic with a flat surface, such as a table top, is plywood (exterior-grade or marine), as it is strong and warp-resistant.

Cement mortar is often used as the base for a mosaic. It can also be used to secure the mosaic to its base as well as to grout between the tesserae. It is very easy and cheap to make: three parts builder's sand mixed with one part cement and enough water to make it pliable. Cements are also available with adhesive added to them. This gives the cement extra adhesive qualities and more flexibility. Specialty dyes can also be added to cement.

China Old plates and cups can make very interesting tesserae. Often they have patterns that can be incorporated into the design of the mosaic. However, the uneven surface they create makes them unsuitable for use in some mosaics.

Grout Mosaics are often grouted with cement; however, specialty grouts are also used. These usually have a smoother texture and can be bought in a variety of colors. They can also be colored with most water-based household and acrylic paints.

Marble comes in a wide range of colors and can be bought pre-cut into small squares. It is possible to cut marble tiles into squares yourself, but special tools are needed to do this. Marble tiles can also be broken up into irregular shapes using an ordinary household hammer. When doing this, wear protective eye covering, or cover the marble with sacking.

Mirror Add shards of broken mirror to add reflective qualities to your mosaic. Cover the mirror with sacking and break with a hammer, or use tile nippers to cut more exact shapes.

Paper This is useful as a base when creating mosaics using the semi-indirect method. (See Basic Techniques)

Plastic Although not a traditional material, interesting effects can be achieved using pieces of plastic or other man-made materials as tesserae.

Shellac This can be used to seal the finished pieces.

Smalti This is opaque glass cut into regular-shaped chunks. Made by firing glass with oxides, metals and powdered marble, it has a softly reflective surface and is available in a large variety of colors. Gold and silver smalti are made by sandwiching gold and

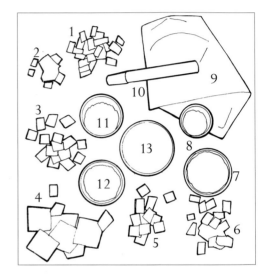

1 Glass smalti
2 Broken mirror
3 Vitreous glass
4 Broken tiles
5 Gold-leaf smalti
6 Broken china
7 Powdered cement
8 Epoxy resin
9 Brown paper
10 Paper glue
11 Powdered tile grout
12 White glue
13 Shellac

silver leaf in transparent, colored glass.

Tiles Ceramic tiles are available in an almost unlimited range of colors and textures. Most can be cut into small pieces with tile nippers, but if not, they can usually be broken with a hammer (as with marble, protect your eyes when doing this).

Vitreous glass These mosaic pieces are manufactured glass squares, flat on one side and corrugated on the other. The color range is not quite as large as that of smalti, but they are a lot cheaper and easier to cut. Also, the material is very hard-wearing.

EQUIPMENT

MANY OF THE TOOLS NEEDED TO MAKE MOSAICS ARE VERY EASY TO FIND, AND MOST CAN BE PURCHASED AT ANY GOOD HARDWARE SHOP. HOWEVER, MOST HOUSEHOLDS ALREADY HAVE THE NECESSARY EQUIPMENT, PARTICULARLY FOR DESIGNING AND CLEANING. BEFORE INVESTING A LOT OF MONEY IN SPECIALTY EQUIPMENT, IT IS A GOOD IDEA TO CHECK YOUR CUPBOARDS. YOU MAY FIND MANY OF THE TOOLS YOU NEED LURKING IN THE BACK.

Bench vice or clamps These may be useful for cutting out the wooden base material.

Bradawl Use for punching holes in wooden base materials if they require hanging.

Brushes If applying grout in powdered form, use a soft brush to spread the powder in the spaces between the tesserae and to brush off any excess. Use a stiff-bristled brush, such as an old toothbrush or nailbrush, to clean dried grout off the finished mosaic. Fine artists' paintbrushes may be used to apply adhesive to small tile pieces.

Chalk Use to sketch onto the base.

Craft knife or scalpel When making designs using the indirect or semi-indirect method, it may be necessary to cut the background paper away from the tesserae pieces. A sharp blade will help to do this.

Dust mask It is advisable to wear a dust mask when working with powdered grout or cement, or cleaning with diluted hydrochloric acid.

Diluted hydrochloric acid This can be used to clean cement-based grout from the finished mosaic but is not strictly necessary. If using, follow proper safety procedures by protecting your eyes and hands, wearing a mask and working in a well-ventilated area, if not outdoors.

Drill A good drill with hole-boring and rebating bits may be useful for some projects, particularly if you want to add mirror hooks or other hanging devices.

Hammer Use to smash ceramic or mirror tiles into shards. Cover with a piece of sacking to prevent slivers from flying out.

Felt-tipped marker Draw your design on to the base material with a marker.

Mixing containers Old mixing bowls and buckets are useful for mixing up grout and cement.

Palette knife A palette knife or flexible kitchen knife can be used to spread cement-based adhesive onto your base.

Pencil A pencil point or sharp stick may be used to apply glue to tiny pieces of tesserae.

Protective gloves Rubber gloves should be used when cleaning with diluted hydrochloric acid, and may be used to apply grouting to tesserae. Heavy work gloves should be worn whenever you are breaking tesserae with a hammer.

Rulers and tape measures Use to measure and plan designs that require accuracy.

Sacking or old cloths Use to cover tiles before smashing with a hammer to prevent small pieces from dispersing.

Safety goggles Wear when breaking tiles with a hammer or when cleaning finished mosaics with diluted hydrochloric acid.

Sandpaper Coarse-grade sandpaper can be used to sand down the edges of wooden base materials. Fine-grade sandpaper can be used in some instances for cleaning.

Saws Different types of saw are useful for cutting your wooden base material. Use a hacksaw for basic shapes, and a jigsaw for more complicated designs.

Spatula Use a spatula for spreading glue or other smooth adhesives, such as cellulose filler, onto your base material.

Sponges and old cloths Use for wiping off excess adhesive and for polishing.

Squeegee This may be used to apply grout between tesserae, particularly if the surface of the design is very flat.

1 Jigsaw
2 Vice
3 Pencil
4 Ruler
5 Felt-tipped marker
6 Hammer
7 Right-angled ruler
8 D-clamp
9 Craft knife
10 Pliers
11 Scissors
12 Trowel
13 Spatula
14 Drill
15 Soft brush

16 Fine paintbrush
17 Tape measure
18 Grout spreader
19 Flexible knife
20 Sponge
21 Dust mask
22 Sandpaper
23 Tile nippers
24 Nailbrush
25 Bradawl
26 Safety goggles
27 Plant mister
28 Chalk
29 Masking tape

Tile nippers These are invaluable for cutting tesserae to any shape required. For shapes with rounded edges, such as circles or hearts, use to nibble away the edges, a small amount at a time, until the desired shape is achieved.

Trowel or notched cement spreader Use either of these for spreading grout and cement-based adhesive.

BASIC TECHNIQUES

WHEN EMBARKING ON YOUR FIRST MOSAIC, IT IS ADVISABLE TO USE A VERY SIMPLE DESIGN. OFTEN, THESE SIMPLE DESIGNS CAN PRODUCE THE MOST EFFECTIVE MOSAICS. CONCENTRATE ON COMBINATIONS OF THE COLORS AND TEXTURES IN THE TESSERAE YOU CHOOSE. LAY THE TESSERAE SIDE BY SIDE AND LOOK AT THE EFFECT OF THE DIFFERENT ELEMENTS. WHEN YOU ARE SURE THE COMBINATIONS WORK, YOU CAN COMMIT YOURSELF TO STICKING THE TESSERAE TO THE BASE.

CUTTING TESSERAE

1 There are three basic methods for cutting tesserae. The first and most flexible method is to use tile nippers, which are very simple to operate. Hold the material to be cut between the tips of the cutting edges of the nippers. Squeeze the handles together, and the tesserae should break in two along the line of impact. Nippers are also useful for making a specific shape.

2 When breaking up larger materials such as tiles and plates, and if regular shapes are not required, the simplest technique is to break the tesserae with a hammer. When doing this, always wear a pair of goggles or cover the tesserae with an old dish cloth.

3 The third technique is to use a special piece of equipment that consists of a small tungsten-tipped anvil, which should be embedded in a log, and a curved tungsten-tipped hammer. It is generally used for cutting smalti or marble into regular shapes. Hold the material to be cut over the anvil between your thumb and forefinger, then bring down the hammer on the material, in line with the tip of the anvil. The smalti or marble should fracture cleanly along the line of impact.

SETTING TESSERAE ON THE BASE

Direct method

This method is used for most of the projects illustrated in this book. The tesserae are simply stuck, face up, onto the base. When setting a mosaic on a three-dimensional object or an uneven surface, this method may be the only feasible way of working.

1 For the direct method, simply cover the base with a layer of cement or tile adhesive and push the tesserae into it randomly.

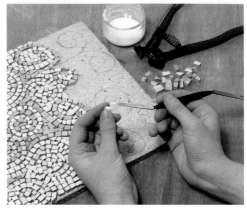

2 If you are following a more exact design, apply cement or tile adhesive to the individual tesserae and then stick them to the base. In this way, any design drawn on the base will not be obscured by having adhesive spread all over it.

3 If the tesserae have a reflective quality, the direct method allows them to be laid on the base at slightly different angles. This causes light to be reflected at different angles, and the mosaic will appear to shimmer.

Indirect method

Originally this technique was devised as a way of making large-scale mosaics off-site, so they could be transported ready-made, then laid in position. When using this method, the design is sectioned into manageable areas, and each area is formed into a mosaic slab, as described below. The slabs are transported to the chosen site and fitted together to form the finished mosaic.

1 Make a wooden frame to the desired proportions of the finished slab, attaching the corners with 1-inch screws. Grease the inside of the frame with petroleum jelly to help prevent the cement from sticking to the wood. Make a template of the slab by drawing around the inside of the frame on brown paper. Draw a simple design on the paper within the marked parameters, taking care to leave a $\frac{1}{16}$-inch margin around the outer edge.

2 Cut vitreous glass tesserae to the required shape and size. Using a water-soluble adhesive, paste them face down on the brown paper, carefully following the lines of your design. Other tesserae can be used for this method, but vitreous glass has the advantage of being the same color front and back, therefore greatly reducing the likelihood of making mistakes when positioning individual pieces.

3 When the glued tesserae have dried, place the frame carefully over them, using the guidelines to make sure the frame is in exactly the right position. Sprinkle dry sand over the design and use a soft brush to nudge the sand into the crevices between the tesserae.

4 On a board, mix three parts sand with one part cement. When this is fully mixed, pile it into a mound and make a well in the middle. Pour water into the well and mix with a trowel. Continue to add water and mix until the consistency of the resulting mortar is pliable but not runny.

5 Carefully half-fill the frame with this mortar, making sure it is pressed into the corners. Cut a square of chicken-wire a little smaller than the frame, and place this on top of the cement mortar; make sure that the wire does not touch the sides of the frame. Fill the frame with the rest of the mortar. Smooth the surface with the trowel or a straight piece of wood. Place damp newspapers, then polythene sheeting over the frame and let dry for five or six days. The drying has to be as slow as possible to let the slab dry uniformly, and to avoid the possibility of cracks forming.

6 When dry, turn over the slab and its frame and dampen the brown paper with a sponge. The paper should then peel away cleanly. Loosen the screws holding the frame together and remove the slab from the frame. To finish, the face of the slab may need grouting and cleaning.

Semi-indirect or Half-and-half

This method is a combination of the direct and indirect methods described above. As with the fully indirect method, the tesserae are glued into position away from the intended site but are actually set into cement on site. This method allows mosaics to be made up easily in irregular shapes. Their light weight is especially good for attaching the mosaics to walls. Like the indirect method, this technique is useful when a smooth, flat surface is required.

1 Draw the design on brown paper and stick the tesserae face down on it, using a water-soluble glue.

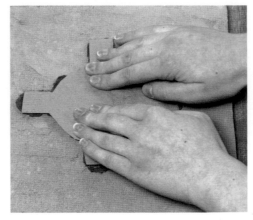

2 Spread mortar over the area designated for the mosaic. A template of the mosaic can be used to mark the exact proportions. Press the tesserae into the mortar, paper side up.

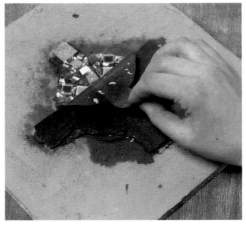

3 Let dry for 24 hours; if the mosaic is situated outside, keep it from getting wet. When it is dry, dampen the paper with a wet sponge and, once the moisture has soaked through to the glue, peel away the paper, leaving the tesserae in position. The mosaic surface is now ready to be grouted and cleaned.

4 Another method of applying a mosaic in a semi-indirect fashion is to stick the tesserae in position on netting using a white glue, but with the tesserae placed face up.

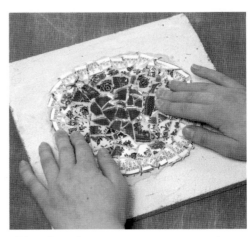

5 When the tesserae are secure on the netting, press the mosaic, face up, into cement. Let dry before grouting and cleaning. This semi-indirect method can result in an undulating surface like that created when working with the direct method.

GROUTING

Mosaics are grouted primarily to give them extra strength and a smoother finished surface. The process has the added bonus of tying the tesserae together and making the mosaic look complete. Often, mosaics are left ungrouted. This is typical when smalti are used, as the ungrouted surface is considered more expressive.

When choosing which grout to use, consider the mosaic's location and therefore whether it will need to be waterproof and/or hard-wearing. Grouts come ready-mixed or in powder form. Usually they are applied to the mosaic ready-mixed. On flat surfaces, a squeegee can be used to spread the grout over the surface and push it between the crevices.

1 When grouting three-dimensional mosaics or uneven surfaces, it is easiest to first spread the grout over the surface with a flexible knife.

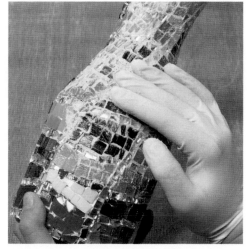

2 Then, wearing rubber gloves, rub the grout into the crevices.

3 When grouting large, flat areas, it is useful to spread the grout while it is in powder form. Use a powdered cement based adhesive and spoon it onto the surface, then spread it with a soft brush.

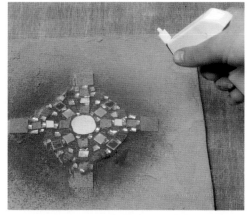

4 When all the crevices are filled, spray the mosaic with water using a household plant mister. Make sure enough water is sprayed and absorbed into the cement.

You will probably need to repeat the process, as cement shrinks when wetted.

CLEANING

It is advisable to get rid of most of the excess grout while it is still wet. Most grouts can be scrubbed from the surface using a stiff-bristled brush, such as a nailbrush, and then polished off. Cement mortars and cement-based adhesives need rougher treatment, and you will probably need to use sandpaper. A quicker alternative is to dilute hydrochloric acid and paint it onto the surface to dissolve the excess cement. This process should be done outside, as the acid gives off toxic fumes. When the excess cement has fizzed away, wash off the residue of acid from the mosaic with plenty of water.

BOTTLE

THIS BOTTLE PROJECT IS IDEAL FOR BEGINNERS WHO WANT TO EXPERIMENT WITH VITREOUS GLASS. THE DESIGN IS VERY LOOSE AND REQUIRES VIRTUALLY NO DRAWING ABILITY. IT RELIES ON THE EFFECTS CREATED BY THE JUXTAPOSITION OF COLORS AND TEXTURES. RELATIVELY INEXPENSIVE BAGS OF TESSERAE IN MIXED COLORS CAN BE BOUGHT FROM SPECIALTY MOSAIC SUPPLIERS, AND IT IS A GOOD IDEA TO EXPERIMENT WITH THESE BEFORE PURCHASING LARGER QUANTITIES OF A SINGLE COLOR. DECORATING A BOTTLE LIKE THIS IS ALSO A GOOD WAY OF USING UP BITS OF TESSERAE THAT HAVE BEEN LEFT OVER FROM OTHER PROJECTS.

1 Clean the bottle, rub off the label and dry thoroughly. Dab silicone sealant onto the bottle using a pencil or pointed stick to form a simple line drawing, such as a series of swirls.

2 Cut white vitreous glass into small pieces, about 1/16 inch and 1/8 inch, using tile nippers.

3 Stick these cut tesserae to the lines drawn in silicone sealant, then let dry overnight.

4 Choose an assortment of colors from the vitreous glass and cut them into quarters. Some of the quarters will have to be cut across the diagonal, so they can fit snugly between the white swirls. Stick these to the bottle in a series of bands of color with silicone sealant. Let dry overnight.

5 Mix up some cement-based tile adhesive. Wearing rubber gloves, rub the cement into the surface of the bottle. Make sure all the crevices between the tesserae are filled, otherwise the tesserae are liable to pull away, as silicone sealant remains rubbery. Wipe off excess cement with a dry soft cloth and let dry overnight.

6 If necessary, sand the bottle down and polish with a soft cloth.

MATERIALS AND EQUIPMENT YOU WILL NEED
WINE BOTTLE • SILICONE SEALANT • PENCIL OR POINTED STICK •
VITREOUS GLASS MOSAIC TILES, INCLUDING WHITE • TILE NIPPERS • CEMENT-BASED TILE ADHESIVE •
MIXING CONTAINER • RUBBER GLOVES • SANDPAPER (OPTIONAL) • SOFT CLOTH

LAMP STAND

THE SIMPLE SPIRAL PATTERN USED TO CREATE THIS TALL, ELEGANT LAMP STAND FOLLOWS THE ONE THAT IS ALREADY PRESENT ON THE CARDBOARD TUBE USED AS A BASE. PIECES OF MIRROR HAVE BEEN ADDED TO CATCH THE LIGHT, AND THEY SPARKLE WHEN THE LAMP IS SWITCHED ON. THE CARDBOARD BASE IS INHERENTLY LIGHT AND THEREFORE TOO UNSTABLE TO BE USED AS A LAMP STAND ON ITS OWN, SO PLASTER HAS BEEN POURED INTO THE BOTTOM TO GIVE IT MORE WEIGHT AND A LOWER CENTER OF GRAVITY. IF PLASTER SEEMS TOO MESSY, YOU COULD USE MODELING CLAY OR SAND INSTEAD.

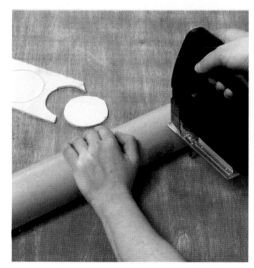

1 Draw twice around the circular end of the cardboard tube onto ⅛-inch plywood. Cut around these circles using a jigsaw and cut the cardboard tube to the length required. Drill a hole through the center of one of the plywood circles. Use a bradawl to make a hole in the cardboard tube ¾ inch from one end and large enough to take the electric flex.

2 Use wood glue to stick the plywood circle without the drilled hole to the end of the tube with the flex hole. Let dry overnight, then paint the cardboard tube with shellac.

3 Thread the flex through the hole in the cardboard tube and the hollow metal rod. Stand the metal rod inside the tube with the screw thread at the top. Mix some plaster of Paris with water and quickly pour it into the tube. Slip the second plywood circle over the metal rod and secure it with wood glue to the top of the cardboard tube. As soon as you have poured the plaster into the tube, you must ·work quickly to secure the top, as it is very important that the plaster dries with the rod in the upright position. Let dry overnight. ▶

MATERIALS AND EQUIPMENT YOU WILL NEED

PENCIL • CARDBOARD CARPET ROLL TUBE • ⅛-INCH PLYWOOD • JIGSAW • DRILL AND BIT • BRADAWL • WOOD GLUE • SHELLAC •
PAINTBRUSH • LENGTH OF FLEX • HOLLOW METAL ROD WITH A SCREW THREAD, THE LENGTH OF THE FINISHED STAND • PLASTER OF PARIS •
MIXING CONTAINER • TILES IN THREE COLORS • TILE NIPPERS • CEMENT-BASED TILE ADHESIVE • SPONGE • MIRROR • RUBBER GLOVES •
FLEXIBLE KNIFE • SANDPAPER • SOFT CLOTH • COPPER TUBING • HACKSAW • LAMP FITTINGS • PLUG • SCREWDRIVER • LAMPSHADE

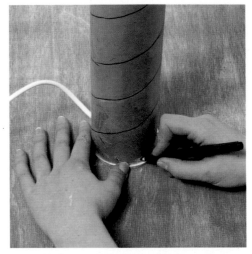

4 With a pencil, draw the design onto the tube, following the spiral lines that are already present on the cardboard tube. You can add variations and embellishments at this stage.

6 Select two colors of tile to fill the areas between the spiraling lines. Use the tile nippers to cut the tiles into various shapes and sizes. Cut the mirror into various shapes and sizes.

8 Wearing rubber gloves and using a flexible knife, apply wet cement-based tile adhesive over the whole area of the lamp stand, being sure to press it between all the tesserae. Wipe off the excess cement with a sponge and let dry overnight. Rub off any remaining surface cement with sandpaper, and polish with a soft cloth.

5 Cut the tiles for the outline color into small pieces using tile nippers. Stick these to the lines of your design using cement-based tile adhesive. Use a sponge to wipe away any large blobs of cement that seep out from under the tesserae, and let dry overnight.

7 Spread cement-based tile adhesive onto the remaining cardboard area, and apply the tesserae in separate bands of color. Work on a small area at a time, so the surface does not become too messy. Intersperse the colored tesserae with pieces of mirror as you work. Cover the whole cardboard tube, then let dry overnight.

9 Finish by attaching all the fittings. Slip copper tubing, cut to size, over the central rod, leaving the screw end exposed. Attach the lamp fittings, plug, and lampshade.

STORAGE CHEST

THIS SIMPLE STORE-BOUGHT CHEST WITH DRAWERS HAS BEEN TRANSFORMED BY MOSAIC MOTIFS INTO AN INDIVIDUAL, PLAYFUL PIECE OF FURNITURE. ALTHOUGH YOU MAY NOT BE ABLE TO FIND EXACTLY THE SAME CHEST, WITH A FEW MODIFICATIONS THE BASIC IDEAS CAN BE TRANSLATED TO ANOTHER PIECE OF FURNITURE. MANY WHITE TESSERAE ARE USED HERE, HELD TOGETHER WITH WHITE CEMENT, TO GIVE THE SHELF A FRESH, CLEAN LOOK THAT WOULD MAKE IT SUITABLE FOR A BATHROOM OR CHILD'S BEDROOM. WHEN TACKLING A PIECE OF FURNITURE THAT HAS MOVABLE PARTS SUCH AS DOORS AND DRAWERS, YOU NEED TO BE VERY CAREFUL THAT THE TESSERAE DO NOT IMPEDE THE MOVEMENT OF THE COMPONENTS ONCE THEY ARE APPLIED AND GROUTED.

1 Paint the shelf and drawers inside and out with watered-down white undercoat. Let dry.

2 Draw a simple motif on the front of each drawer. Choose motifs that have a bold outline and are easily recognizable when executed in one color.

3 Cut the tiles into unevenly shaped tesserae using tile nippers. Mix up some cement-based tile adhesive, spread it within the outline of one of the motifs, then firmly press single-colored tesserae into it.

4 Surround the motif with tesserae of a different color. Be careful not to overlap the edges of the drawer. Cover the remaining drawer fronts using a different combination of two colors each time. ▶

MATERIALS AND EQUIPMENT YOU WILL NEED
STORE-BOUGHT SHELF WITH DRAWERS • WHITE UNDERCOAT • PAINTBRUSH • PENCIL • THIN TILES IN FIVE COLORS, PLUS WHITE •
TILE NIPPERS • WHITE CEMENT-BASED TILE ADHESIVE • MIXING CONTAINER • FLEXIBLE KNIFE • RUBBER GLOVES • SPONGE •
SANDPAPER • SQUARE-BOTTOMED PAINT SCRAPER

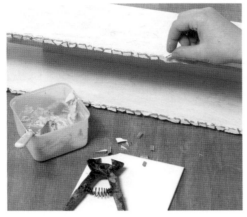

5 Cut tiny slivers of white tile. Stick these to the narrow front edges of the chest with the tile adhesive. Do this very carefully so none of the tesserae overlaps the edge.

6 Cut more white tiles into various shapes and sizes, then stick these to the large, flat outside surfaces of the shelf. When all four are covered, let the shelf and the drawers dry overnight.

7 Rub tile adhesive into the surface of the chest and drawers, wearing rubber gloves. Be especially careful when smoothing the cement into the thin edges of the shelf and the edges of the drawer fronts, making sure the cement is flush with the edges. When the gaps between the tesserae are filled, wipe off most of the excess cement with a sponge. Let the chest dry for 24 hours.

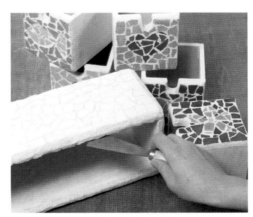

8 Sand off any remaining surface cement from the shelf and drawers. Then use an implement with a sharp, flat edge, such as a paint scraper, to scrape along the inside edge of the shelf and the sides of the drawers. Do this carefully to ensure there are no overlapping tesserae and no cement to impede the action of the drawers.

CLOCK

THIS MOSAIC CLOCKFACE IS DECORATED WITH TESSERAE MADE FROM HAND-PAINTED MEXICAN TILES IN SHADES OF BLUE, BROWN AND CREAM. PRETTY SHELLS HAVE BEEN USED HERE TO MARK THE QUARTER HOURS, ALTHOUGH THEY ARE NOT ABSOLUTELY NECESSARY. WHILE THE PAINTING ON THE TILES IS VERY FREE-STYLE AND THE TILES HAVE BEEN CUT INTO UNEVEN SHAPES, THE RESULTING TESSERAE ARE USED TO CONSTRUCT A PRECISE GEOMETRIC SHAPE. WHEN DESIGN-ING A CLOCK, YOU MUST FIRST FIND A WAY OF ACCOMMODATING THE MECHANISM THAT WORKS THE HANDS. THEN YOU MUST DESIGN THE SURFACE DECORATION TO ACCOMMODATE THE FUNCTION OF THE CLOCK. THE BASE OF THIS CLOCK IS MADE FROM TWO PIECES OF WOOD; THE THICKER PIECE AT THE BACK HAS A CIRCULAR HOLE CUT INTO IT, LARGE ENOUGH TO ACCOMMODATE THE WORKINGS AND BAT-TERIES. AS THE CLOCK MUST BE EASY TO READ, THE TESSERAE ARE LAID IN A VERY SIMPLE AND PRECISE DESIGN. IN FACT, THE PRIMARY FUNCTION OF THE DESIGN, AS WITH ANY CLOCK, IS TO DRAW ATTENTION TO THE POSITION OF THE HANDS.

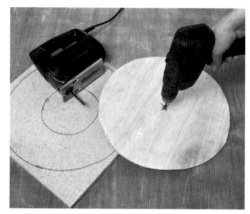

1 Using a jigsaw, cut ⅛-inch plywood and ¾-inch chipboard into circles of the same diameter; the circles shown here are 16 inches in diameter. Drill a hole through the center of the chipboard circle, large enough to take the blade of the jigsaw. Saw a hole large enough to accommodate the clock's workings. Drill a hole through the center of the plywood circle, large enough to take the pivot for the clock's hands. Prime both pieces with diluted white glue and let dry.

2 Stick the plywood and chipboard circles together with strong wood glue. Clamp the pieces together with cramps; if you don't have any cramps, use weights such as heavy books. Let dry overnight.

3 Draw a circle in the center of the plywood circle. Its radius must be the length of the longest hand of the clock. Using a felt-tipped marker or pencil, sec-tion the face into quarters and use these as a basis for your design.

MATERIALS AND EQUIPMENT YOU WILL NEED

JIGSAW • ⅛-INCH PLYWOOD • ¾-INCH CHIPBOARD • DRILL AND BITS • CLOCK FITTINGS (BATTERY-OPERATED MOTOR WITH A LONG PIVOTAL PIN, AND HANDS) • WHITE GLUE • PAINTBRUSH • STRONG WOOD GLUE • CRAMPS (AT LEAST FOUR) OR HEAVY WEIGHTS • FELT-TIPPED MARKER OR PENCIL • SELECTION OF PLAIN AND PATTERNED TILES • TILE NIPPERS • CEMENT-BASED TILE ADHESIVE • MIXING CONTAINER • FLEXIBLE KNIFE • SHELLS TO MARK QUARTER HOURS (OPTIONAL) • RUBBER GLOVES • SPONGE • SANDPAPER • SOFT CLOTH

4 Cut plain tiles into small, roughly rectangular shapes using tile nippers. Mix up some cement-based tile adhesive with water and apply to the edge using a flexible knife. Press the tesserae firmly into the cement.

5 Cut patterned tiles into small irregular shapes. This design uses three kinds of patterned tiles.

6 Tile the surface within the rotation area of the clock's arms, using cement-based tile adhesive applied to a small area at a time, so as not to obliterate the guidelines. Be careful to lay the tesserae flat, as they must not impede the rotation of the clock's hands.

7 Tile the border, marking the positions of the quarter hours. Here, shells are used, but whatever you choose, they must not overlap the area where the hands rotate. Let dry overnight.

8 Using a flexible knife, smooth cement-based tile adhesive between the tesserae around the edge of the clockface.

9 Wearing rubber gloves, rub cement-based tile adhesive over the surface of the clockface. Make sure all the gaps between the tesserae are filled, then wipe clean with a sponge. Let dry for 24 hours. ▶

10 Sand off any excess cement and polish with a soft cloth.

11 Attach the components of the clock's workings. The battery-operated workings should fit into the hole at the back. Fix the pivotal pin through the hole in the center, then fit the hands over this and secure with a nut.

POT STAND

As well as protecting your table top, this mosaic pot stand by Sarah Round will brighten up any meal. The mosaic is stuck onto a board that has been cut into a geometric shape. This shape is integral to the pattern in which the tesserae are laid. The tesserae used here are cut carefully from brightly colored tiles. Small chips are added to provide highlights to the areas of darkest color. Black tile grout is used, but if you cannot get hold of this, you could color ordinary tile grout with black ink.

1 Carefully mark the proportions of the pot stand onto a square piece of chipboard; use a ruler to make sure the lines are straight.

2 Prime both sides of the chipboard with diluted white glue and let dry. Cut around the outline of the design using a jigsaw. Sand down any rough edges and prime with diluted white glue. Let dry.

3 Decide on your color scheme. Using tile nippers, cut the tiles into small pieces that will fit inside the shapes you have drawn. Here small pieces of mirror have been added to the dark blue sections of the mosaic, and small pieces of the dark blue tiles have been included in the lighter areas. Fix them in position with tile adhesive using a flexible knife. When the surface is covered, remove any excess tile adhesive with a sponge and let dry for 24 hours.

4 Fill the gaps between the tesserae with black tile grout. Rub the grout into the sides of the stand as well, then let dry for about ten minutes. Wipe off any excess grout with a sponge, then let dry for 24 hours. Paint the sides of the pot stand with diluted white glue. Cut felt to size and stick it to the back of the stand with white glue. Finish by polishing the top surface with a soft cloth and clear glass polish.

MATERIALS AND EQUIPMENT YOU WILL NEED

½-INCH CHIPBOARD, 12 X 12 INCHES • PENCIL • RULER • WHITE GLUE • PAINTBRUSH • JIGSAW •
SANDPAPER • TILES IN THREE COLORS • TILE NIPPERS • MIRROR • TILE ADHESIVE • MIXING CONTAINER • FLEXIBLE KNIFE •
BLACK READY-MIXED TILE GROUT • GROUT SPREADER • SPONGE • FELT • SCISSORS • SOFT CLOTH • CLEAR GLASS POLISH

COAT RACK

STORAGE OF COATS IS ALWAYS A PROBLEM, BUT IF THEY HAVE TO BE HUNG IN A HALL OR ROOM, MAKE THE RACK AN INTERESTING FEATURE RATHER THAN A NECESSARY EVIL. SANDRA HADFIELD HAS DECORATED THIS HOMEMADE RACK WITH BRIGHTLY COLORED VITREOUS GLASS TESSERAE. THESE ARE CUT INTO A VARIETY OF SHAPES AND SIZES AND ATTACHED TO THE BASE USING THE DIRECT METHOD, TO FORM BOLD OUTLINES AND BLOCKS OF COLOR. THE BASE OF THE RACK CAN BE MADE FROM MEDIUM-DENSITY FIBERBOARD OR PLYWOOD, WHICH CAN BE CUT INTO ANY SIZE AND SHAPE YOU LIKE.

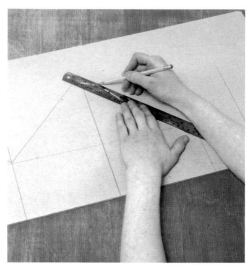

1 Cut a piece of ½-inch medium density fiberboard or plywood to the length required. Draw the outline of the top on this base using a pencil and ruler to make sure the proportions are correct. Cut around the outline using a jigsaw. Sand down any rough edges.

2 Attach two mirror plates to the back of the base, one at each end. Make sure the screw holes stick out far enough from the sides of the base; when the sides are tiled with the tesserae, the holes must remain uncovered.

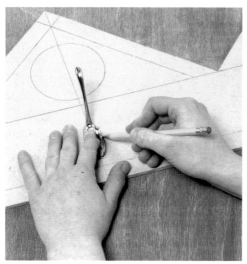

3 Draw the mosaic design on the surface of the base. Position the coat hooks and draw around them onto the base.

▶

MATERIALS AND EQUIPMENT YOU WILL NEED
½-INCH MEDIUM-DENSITY FIBERBOARD OR PLYWOOD • SAW • PENCIL • RULER • JIGSAW • SANDPAPER •
2 MIRROR PLATES • SCREWS • SCREWDRIVER • 3 COAT HOOKS • SHARP KNIFE • WHITE GLUE • MEDIUM AND FINE PAINTBRUSHES •
MIXING CONTAINER • VITREOUS GLASS MOSAIC TILES • TILE NIPPERS • RUBBER GLOVES • READY-MIXED TILE GROUT •
GROUT SPREADER • SPONGE • NAILBRUSH • SOFT CLOTH

4 Score the base with a sharp knife and prime the front, back and sides with diluted white glue.

5 Here, whole blue vitreous glass tiles are alternated with half tiles around the border. Cut the tiles using tile nippers. Attach the outlining tesserae along the outside edge of the base with white glue applied with a fine paintbrush.

6 Stick tesserae to the areas between the main outlines. Cover the entire surface, except for the areas where the hooks will be screwed in. Cut vitreous glass tiles of the same color as the outlines in half and carefully stick them along the edges of the base. Let dry for 24 hours.

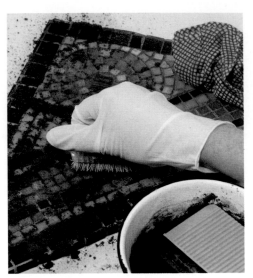

7 Wearing rubber gloves, spread grout over the surface of the mosaic, pushing it into the gaps between the tesserae. Wipe off the excess grout with a sponge and let sit for about ten minutes, so the surface dries. Then use a nailbrush to scrub off any grout that has dried on the surface of the mosaic. Let dry for 24 hours.

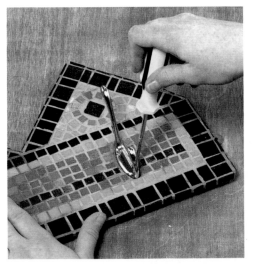

8 Sand off any remaining grout on the surface of the mosaic, then polish with a soft cloth. Screw the coat hooks into position, and hang in place.

HEART MIRROR

SARAH ROUND HAS DESIGNED A BOLD, PLAYFUL MOSAIC FRAME FOR THIS MIRROR, WITH A CROWN MOTIF ALONG THE TOP EDGE AND A MOSAIC HEART HANGING FROM THE BOTTOM. THE MAJORITY OF THE TESSERAE ARE MADE FROM WHITE TILES THAT HAVE BEEN INDIVIDUALLY FASHIONED TO FIT INTO ONE ANOTHER. THE HEART IS TILED WITH TESSERAE CUT FROM BLUE AND YELLOW TILES.

THESE COLORS ARE ALSO USED FOR THE SPOTS OF COLOR IN THE POINTS ALONG THE TOP OF THE MIRROR. THE USE OF BLACK GROUT GIVES A STIRRING EFFECT BY STRONGLY EMPHASIZING THE EDGES AND SHAPES OF THE WHITE TESSERAE. BLACK GROUT CAN BE DIFFICULT TO FIND, BUT YOU CAN MAKE YOUR OWN BY MIXING BLACK INK INTO WHITE GROUT POWDER.

1 Draw the outline of the frame and the position of the mirror on a piece of ½-inch chipboard. Draw the outline for the heart, which will hang from the bottom. Prime the chipboard with diluted white glue. Cut around the shapes using a handsaw or jigsaw. Sand any rough edges, then prime as before.

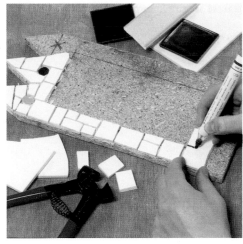

2 Cut three small circles from the tiles using tile nippers. To do this, cut the tiles into small squares, then nibble the corners away. Fix the circles in position along the top edge of the frame using tile adhesive. Lay the background tiles on the frame and mark the cutting lines with a washable marker.

3 Cut along the marked lines with the tile nippers.

4 Set the cut tiles in position with tile adhesive. Work around the frame, cutting and sticking the tesserae one at a time. In this way, you can cut the tesserae individually to fit neatly. ▶

MATERIALS AND EQUIPMENT YOU WILL NEED

½-INCH CHIPBOARD • MIRROR • PENCIL • RULER • WHITE GLUE • PAINTBRUSH • HANDSAW OR JIGSAW • SANDPAPER •
TILES IN THREE COLORS • TILE NIPPERS • TILE ADHESIVE • WASHABLE MARKER • SPONGE • EPOXY RESIN GLUE (OPTIONAL) •
BLACK READY-MIXED TILE GROUT • GROUT SPREADER • SOFT CLOTH • CLEAR GLASS POLISH • PAPER OR FELT •
HANGING CLIP (D-RING) • BRADAWL • PLIERS • THICK WIRE, SUCH AS COAT-HANGER WIRE

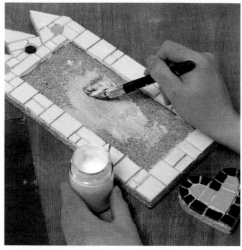

5 Remove any excess tile adhesive from the surface or sides of the mosaic with a sponge. Place the mirror in position with white or epoxy resin glue. Let dry for 24 hours.

6 Spread black tile grout over the surface of the frame and heart with a grout spreader, pushing it into all the gaps between the tesserae.

7 Spread grout onto the sides of the frame and heart.

8 Let dry for ten minutes, then wipe off any excess grout with a sponge. Let the mirror and heart dry for 24 hours, then polish the surface with a soft dry cloth and clear glass polish.

9 Paint the edges of the mirror and heart with diluted white glue. Stick either paper or felt onto the back of the mirror, and attach a hanging clip. Let dry. Using a bradawl, make a hole in the middle of the bottom edge of the mirror frame and in the center of the top edge of the heart. Use pliers to cut a piece of thick wire about 2½ inches long.

10 Apply epoxy resin glue to both ends of the wire and to the holes made in the mirror and heart. Push the wire into these holes and let dry fully before attempting to move the mirror.

BATHROOM CABINET

IN THIS WITTY VISUAL PUN, NORMA VONDEE HAS DECORATED THE DOOR OF A BATHROOM CABINET WITH A *TROMPE L'ŒIL* MOSAIC, BEHIND WHICH CAN BE HIDDEN THE CLUTTER OF BATHROOM PILLS AND POTIONS. THE SHADOWS AND HIGHLIGHTS GIVE THE BOTTLE, GLASS AND POT THE ILLUSION OF BEING THREE-DIMENSIONAL. USE THIS PROJECT TO PRACTICE CLASSIC MOSAIC TECHNIQUES.

WHEN LAYING THE MOSAIC, PAY CLOSE ATTENTION TO THE POSITION OF EACH OF THE TESSERAE AND THE PATTERNS FORMED BY THE GAPS LEFT BETWEEN THEM. THE TESSERAE USED ARE CINCA CERAMIC MOSAIC TILES, AVAILABLE IN A WIDE RANGE OF COLORS. THEY HAVE A SOFT MATTE TEXTURE AND ARE VERY EASY TO CUT AND SHAPE, SO ARE PERFECT WHEN EXPERIMENTING WITH PRECISE MOSAICS.

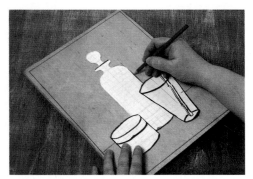

1 Remove the wooden or glass panel in the door of the bathroom cabinet. Cut a ⅛-inch plywood panel to the same size. Score the surface with a sharp knife to provide a key for the white glue. Draw your design on the plywood, using the template from the back of the book. Mark in the ellipses and areas of shadow.

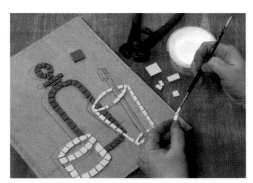

2 Cut the cinca mosaic tiles into precise shapes using tile nippers. Apply these tesserae to the main outlines, fixing them in place with white glue. Be extra careful when tiling curved areas.

3 Carefully fill the areas inside the out-lines in contrasting colors. Here, reflections and highlights are depicted using different shades of tesserae to create the illusion of a three-dimensional scene. Use tesserae a shade darker than the background to tile areas of shadow.

4 Outline the shapes with a row of tesserae in the background color. If making a larger design, you could use a double row of tesserae to outline the subjects of the mosaic.

5 Fill in the background color with tesserae arranged in straight lines and let dry overnight. Secure the panel in position on the cabinet door and mask the frame with tape. Mix three parts sand and one part cement with water and a little red cement dye. Grout the mosaic with this mixture using a squeegee. Clean the surface carefully with a soft cloth and let dry as slowly as possible.

MATERIALS AND EQUIPMENT YOU WILL NEED
WALL-MOUNTED CABINET WITH DOOR • ⅛-INCH PLYWOOD • SAW • SHARP KNIFE • PENCIL •
PAPER FOR TEMPLATE (OPTIONAL) • CINCA CERAMIC TILES • TILE NIPPERS • WHITE GLUE • FINE PAINTBRUSH •
MASKING TAPE • SAND • CEMENT • RED CEMENT DYE • MIXING CONTAINER • SQUEEGEE • SOFT CLOTH

SPLASHBACK

MOSAIC IS AN IDEAL DECORATIVE SURFACE OR WALL PROTECTOR FOR AREAS IN WHICH WATER IS PRESENT, SUCH AS THIS SPLASHBACK FOR A BATHROOM SINK. IT IS MADE BY APPLYING ROUGHLY BROKEN TILES IN SUBTLE COLORS, AND CHIPS OF GLASS TO CATCH THE LIGHT, DIRECTLY ONTO A PLYWOOD BASE.

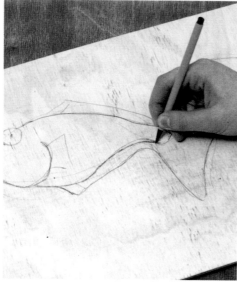

1 Measure the width of your sink and cut ⅛-inch plywood to size. Prime the surface with adhesive. When dry, draw a simple fish design on the plywood, using the template from the back of the book if required.

2 Using a bradawl, make a hole through the plywood in each corner.

3 Select the colors of the tiles to be used for tesserae; here, two similar grays are used for the fish and a muted pink for the starfish. Wear goggles or, alternatively, cover the tiles with a cloth, then, using a hammer, smash the tiles into a variety of shapes.

MATERIALS AND EQUIPMENT YOU WILL NEED
TAPE MEASURE • ⅛-INCH PLYWOOD • SAW • WHITE GLUE • PAINTBRUSH • PENCIL • BRADAWL •
TILES IN SEVERAL COLORS • GOGGLES OR CLOTH • HAMMER • TILE NIPPERS • CEMENT-BASED TILE ADHESIVE • MIXING CONTAINER •
FLEXIBLE KNIFE • THIN EDGING TILES • MIRROR • SPOON • SOFT BRUSH • PLANT MISTER • DRINKING STRAW • SCISSORS •
SANDPAPER • SOFT CLOTH • DRILL • WALL PLUGS • 4 MIRROR SCREWS • SCREWDRIVER

4 Select a suitable tile that has a soft base with a thin glaze, such as a Mexican tile. Using the tile nippers, nibble two circles for the eyes of the fish. Then use a bradawl to carefully make a hole in the center of each.

5 Mix some tile adhesive with water and spread it onto the base within the outlines of your drawing. Set the tesserae within the drawn lines, using a lighter shade for the fins and tail and the darker shade for the body of the fish. Try to find tesserae in shapes that will fit within the drawing and suggest the movement of the fish.

6 When the fish and starfish are complete, smash tiles of the background color, in this case a soft blue. Spread cement-based tile adhesive onto the base, a small area at a time. Press the background tesserae firmly into the cement. Be careful not to tile over the holes that you have made in the corners.

7 Cut thin edging tiles into short segments and attach them around the edge of the mosaic.

8 Using tile nippers, cut the mirror into small pieces. Press these tesserae into the larger gaps in the design, on top of a blob of cement to keep them level with the other tesserae. Let dry for 24 hours.

9 Spoon dry tile adhesive onto the surface of the splashback and brush it into the cracks using a soft brush. Avoid the area around the hole in each corner. ▶

10 Spray the surface with plenty of water using a plant mister.

11 Cut a drinking straw into four pieces and stand one over each hole in the corner. Mix up some tile adhesive and grout around the straws. Let dry for 12 hours.

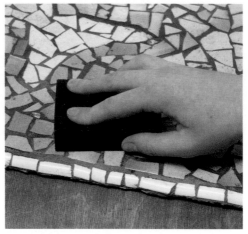

12 Remove the straws and sand off any cement remaining on the surface of the splashback, then polish with a soft cloth. Place the splashback against the wall and mark the positions of the screw holes. Drill the holes and insert wall plugs. Use mirror screws with metal caps to screw the splashback in position.

FIRE SCREEN

IN THIS PROJECT, MOSAIC IS USED TO DECORATE A READY-MADE FIRE SCREEN, WHICH CAN BE PURCHASED AT GOOD CRAFT STORES. ALTERNATIVELY, A SIMPLE SCREEN SHAPE CAN BE CUT FROM PLYWOOD USING A JIGSAW, AND SLOTTED INTO CUSTOM-MADE FEET. FOR HER BOLD DESIGN, SANDRA HADFIELD HAS USED VITREOUS GLASS MOSAIC TILES IN STRIKING COLORS. MOST OF THIS DESIGN USES WHOLE TILES, CUT DIAGONALLY INTO TRIANGLES.

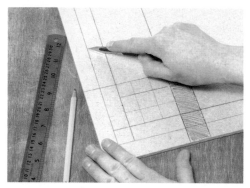

1 Draw the design on the surface of the fire screen and its feet. Calculate the amount of space needed to accommodate the tiles required and use a ruler to mark the main areas. Score the surface with a sharp knife, then prime with diluted white glue and let dry.

2 Select vitreous glass tiles in the colors you require. Cut some tiles into triangles for the border.

3 Fix the tesserae to the base with white glue. Try to make all of the gaps between the tesserae equal and leave the area that will be slotted into the feet untiled.

4 Tile the edge, then the feet, making sure they will still slot on to the screen. Let dry overnight. Wearing rubber gloves, rub grout into the surface of the mosaic, making sure all the gaps between the tesserae are filled. Let dry for about ten minutes, then remove any excess grout with a nailbrush. Allow the grout to dry for 12 more hours, then paint the back of the screen with wood primer, undercoat and finally gloss paint, allowing each coat to dry before applying the next. Polish the mosaic with a soft cloth and slot on the feet.

MATERIALS AND EQUIPMENT YOU WILL NEED
READY-MADE FIRE SCREEN BASE • PENCIL • RULER • SHARP KNIFE • WHITE GLUE • PAINTBRUSHES •
VITREOUS GLASS MOSAIC TILES • TILE NIPPERS • RUBBER GLOVES • READY-MIXED TILE GROUT • NAILBRUSH • WOOD PRIMER •
WHITE UNDERCOAT • GLOSS PAINT • SOFT CLOTH

MIRROR

MOSAIC IS A VERY EFFECTIVE WAY OF SURROUNDING A MIRROR. THE UNDULATING, FRACTURED SURFACE CREATED BY THE TESSERAE PERFECTLY SETS OFF THE SMOOTH, REFLECTIVE PLANE OF THE GLASS. THIS MIRROR, DESIGNED BY CLEO MUSSI, HAS AN ATTRACTIVE FRAME TO ADD INTEREST AND ATMOSPHERE TO A BATHROOM. SHE HAS CHOSEN TO USE CHINA WITH DELICATE PATTERNS IN COOL, FRESH COLORS AND WITH TOUCHES OF GOLD.

1 Draw the outer shape of the mirror frame onto a piece of ¾-inch plywood. Cut around this shape using a jigsaw, then sand down the rough edges. Onto this base panel, draw the desired shape of the mirror glass. Here, the shape of the mirror glass echoes the shape of the panel, but it could be a completely different shape if desired. Make sure it is a shape that glass-cutters will be able to reproduce.

2 Seal the sides and front of the base panel with diluted white glue and paint the back first with wood primer, then undercoat and finally gloss paint. Mark the position of the mirror plate on the back of the panel. Using an appropriate bit, rebate the area that will be under the keyhole-shaped opening (large enough to take a screw head). Then screw the mirror plate in position.

3 Make a cardboard template in the exact dimensions of the mirror shape you have drawn on the base. Ask your supplier to cut a piece of ⅛-inch foil-backed mirror using your template.

4 Stick the mirror in position using ready-mixed tile adhesive. Let dry overnight. ▶

MATERIALS AND EQUIPMENT YOU WILL NEED

¾-INCH PLYWOOD • PENCIL • RULER • JIGSAW • SANDPAPER • WHITE GLUE • PAINTBRUSHES • WOOD PRIMER • WHITE UNDERCOAT • GLOSS PAINT • DRILL WITH REBATING BIT • MIRROR PLATE • ¼-INCH SCREWS • SCREWDRIVER • THICK CARDBOARD • ⅛-INCH FOIL-BACKED MIRROR • TILE ADHESIVE • FLEXIBLE KNIFE • MASKING TAPE • TRACING PAPER (OPTIONAL) • TILE NIPPERS • SELECTION OF CHINA • POWDERED TILE GROUT • VINYL MATTE LATEX OR ACRYLIC PAINT (OPTIONAL) • MIXING CONTAINER • GROUT SPREADER OR RUBBER GLOVES • NAILBRUSH • SOFT CLOTH

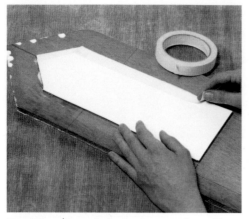

5 Trim ¹⁄₁₆ inch from the template all around the edge and cover the mirror with it, securing it in place with masking tape; this should prevent the mirror from being scratched. The mosaic will eventually overlap the ¹⁄₁₆ inches of uncovered mirror.

6 Draw the design for the frame on the dry, sealed surface surrounding the mirror; use tracing paper and a soft pencil to copy and transfer your original plan, if desired.

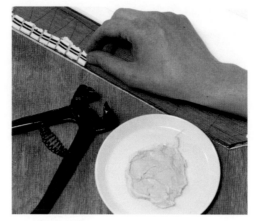

7 Using tile nippers, snip the smooth edges from the cups and plates you have collected. Use these to tile the outside edge of the base panel and to overlap the ¹⁄₁₆-inch edges of the mirror, sticking them down with ready-mixed tile adhesive. Cut the remainder of the china into small pieces and stick them to the structural lines of your design.

8 Fill in the areas of detail between the outlining tesserae. When the mirror frame is completely tiled, let it dry for 24 hours.

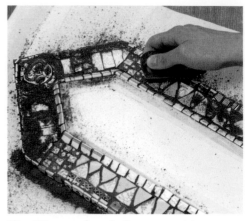

9 Mix powdered tile grout with water and, if desired, color with vinyl matte latex or acrylic paint. Spread this over the surface of the tesserae using a grout spreader, or wear rubber gloves and rub it in by hand, making sure all the gaps between the tesserae have been filled. Let the surface dry for a few minutes, then brush off the excess grout with a stiff-bristled nailbrush. Wipe clean with a soft cloth.

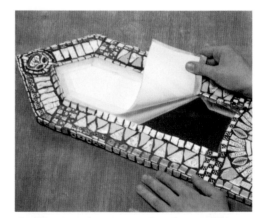

10 Let the mirror dry thoroughly overnight, then remove the protective cardboard from the mirrored glass and hang in position.

SKIRTING BOARD

A SKIRTING BOARD IS AN UNUSUAL AND DISCREET WAY OF INTRODUCING MOSAIC INTO YOUR HOME. YOU CAN USE A REPEATED ABSTRACT DESIGN, A SUCCESSION OF MOTIFS, OR A COMBINATION OF THE TWO. HERE, THE MOTIF OF A DAISY HAS BEEN REPEATED AT REGULAR INTERVALS. THE TESSERAE ARE MADE FROM MARBLE TILES THAT HAVE BEEN ROUGHLY BROKEN WITH A HAMMER. YOU WILL NEED A LARGE QUANTITY OF TILES, SO IT IS BEST TO DECORATE A SMALL ROOM.

1 Measure the room and buy lengths of skirting board to fit. Roughen the surface with coarse-grade sandpaper, then prime with diluted white glue. Let dry.

2 Mark the skirting board into small, equally spaced sections. Using a dark pencil, draw a simple motif in each section. Here, the motif is a daisy.

4 Mix up some cement-based tile adhesive and, working on a small area at a time, spread it along the lines of your drawing. Press the broken pieces of marble firmly into the cement. Choose tesserae in shapes that echo those of the design,—for example, the petal shapes of the flower. The marble can be roughly shaped by tapping the edges of larger tesserae with a hammer. When each motif is tiled, wipe off any excess cement with a sponge and let dry overnight. ▶

3 Wear goggles or cover the tiles with a cloth. Smash the marble tiles into small pieces with a hammer.

MATERIALS AND EQUIPMENT YOU WILL NEED

RULER OR TAPE MEASURE • SKIRTING BOARD • COARSE-GRADE SANDPAPER • WHITE GLUE • PAINTBRUSH • PENCIL • GOGGLES OR CLOTH • SELECTION OF MARBLE TILES • HAMMER • CEMENT-BASED TILE ADHESIVE • MIXING CONTAINER • FLEXIBLE KNIFE • SPONGE • RUBBER GLOVES OR SQUEEGEE • SANDPAPER • SOFT CLOTH

5 Break up tiles in the background color with a hammer. Working on a small area at a time, spread cement-based adhesive onto the untiled sections of skirting board and press the tesserae into it. When the surface is covered, use small pieces of the background color to tile along the top edge of the skirting, ensuring that the tesserae do not overlap the edge. Let dry for 24 hours.

7 Sand off any cement that has dried on the surface of the mosaic and polish the surface with a soft cloth. Set the skirting board in position.

6 Wearing rubber gloves or using a squeegee, rub wet cement-based adhesive into the surface of the mosaic, filling all the gaps between the tesserae. Use a flexible knife to spread the cement into the edge. Wipe off any excess with a cloth and let dry overnight.

AZTEC BOX

THE AZTECS AND MAYAS OF PRE-COLOMBIAN CENTRAL AMERICA USED TO DECORATE SKULLS, WEAPONS AND SNAKE SHAPES WITH PRECIOUS MATERIALS SUCH AS TURQUOISE, CORAL AND JADE. THIS DECORATION WAS INTENDED TO SEAL IN THE MAGICAL ENERGIES OF THE OBJECT AND WARD OFF EVIL. NORMA VONDEE WAS INSPIRED BY SUCH TREASURES TO MAKE THIS MOSAIC JEWELRY BOX. FOR THE TESSERAE SHE HAS USED VITREOUS GLASS AND CINCA TILES IN COLORS THAT ECHO THOSE USED BY THE CENTRAL AMERICAN ARTISTS. SHE HAS ALSO INCLUDED GLASS GLOBULES BACKED WITH GOLD AND SILVER LEAF.

1 Draw the design on the wooden box with a marker or dark pencil. Here, the teeth and jaws of the beast are drawn immediately below the opening edge of the lid.

2 Stick on glass globules for the eyes, holding them in place with masking tape until dry. Cut vitreous glass tiles in coral and stick onto the nose and lips. Cut vitreous glass tiles in pink and terra-cotta to line the lips. Use a paintbrush to apply glue to small pieces.

3 Cut black and white tesserae into precise shapes to fit the areas marked for the teeth, then stick them in position.

4 Select tesserae in varying shades of turquoise, blue and green, and use them to tile around the eye sockets and to delineate the snout, cutting them where necessary to fit the sides of the box. Include a few small glass globules positioned randomly. When tiling around the hinges, leave about ½ inch untiled, so the box can be opened easily. Let dry, then tile the lid in the same way.

5 Mix three parts sand with one part cement and add a little black cement dye. Add water a little at a time until the desired consistency is attained. Wearing rubber gloves, rub the cement onto the surface of the box. Scrape off the excess cement with a squeegee, then rub the box with a slightly damp sponge. Finish by polishing with a dry cloth, then cover the box with a plastic bag so it will dry as slowly as possible.

MATERIALS AND EQUIPMENT YOU WILL NEED

WOODEN BOX WITH HINGED LID • MARKER OR DARK PENCIL • GLASS GLOBULES BACKED WITH GOLD AND SILVER LEAF • WHITE GLUE • MASKING TAPE • MIXING CONTAINERS • FINE PAINTBRUSH • VITREOUS GLASS MOSAIC TILES • TILE NIPPERS • CINCA CERAMIC TILES • SAND • CEMENT • BLACK CEMENT DYE • RUBBER GLOVES • SQUEEGEE • SPONGE • SOFT CLOTH • PLASTIC BAG

GARDEN TABLE

THE BOLD DESIGN OF THIS TABLE TOP AND THE SIMPLICITY AND DELICACY OF THE METAL FRAME THAT SUPPORTS IT COMBINE TO CREATE A TABLE THAT WOULD LOOK GOOD IN THE CONSERVATORY, OR AS AN OCCASIONAL TABLE FOR A GARDEN OR PATIO ON A SUNNY DAY. THE TOP IS DECORATED WITH TESSERAE MADE FROM ROUGHLY BROKEN FLOOR TILES, WHICH HAVE A STRONG TEXTURE.

HIGHLIGHTS ARE CREATED BY THE INCLUSION OF TINY CHIPS OF GOLD-LEAF SMALTI. THE METAL FRAME USED HERE WAS MADE TO ORDER BY A LOCAL BLACKSMITH, AND THERE ARE MANY SUCH CRAFTSPEOPLE WILLING TO MAKE UNIQUE PIECES OF THIS KIND. ALTERNATIVELY, FRAMES CAN OFTEN BE FOUND AT SECONDHAND FURNITURE SHOPS.

  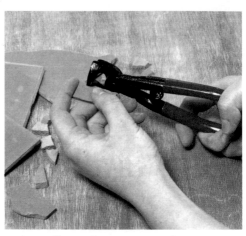

1 Draw the shape of the table top on a piece of ¾-inch plywood. Cut this out using a jigsaw and sand off any rough edges. Then prime with diluted white glue, paying special attention to the edges.

2 Draw a simple design on the table top. You may need to use a tape measure to get the proportions right, but don't be too rigid about the geometry, as a freehand approach suits this method of working.

3 Cut floor tiles in your outlining color into small pieces using tile nippers. Try to cut them into a variety of shapes; uniform shapes would jar with the crazy paving effect of the smashed tesserae used for the rest of the table.

MATERIALS AND EQUIPMENT YOU WILL NEED
¾-INCH PLYWOOD • PENCIL • JIGSAW • SANDPAPER • WHITE GLUE • PAINTBRUSH • TAPE MEASURE (OPTIONAL) •
SELECTION OF FLOOR TILES • TILE NIPPERS • CEMENT-BASED TILE ADHESIVE • MIXING CONTAINERS • FLEXIBLE KNIFE • SPONGE •
GOGGLES OR CLOTH • HAMMER • GOLD-LEAF TESSERAE • SPOON • SOFT BRUSH • PLANT MISTER • DILUTED HYDROCHLORIC ACID (OPTIONAL) •
RUBBER GLOVES (OPTIONAL) • METAL TABLE FRAME • SCREWS • SCREWDRIVER • SOFT CLOTH

4 Mix up some cement-based tile adhesive and, using a flexible knife, spread it around the edge of the table top. Firmly press the outlining tesserae into the cement, making sure they do not overlap the edges.

6 Wear goggles or cover the tiles with a cloth. Using a hammer, smash the tiles that are to fill in the areas between the outlines.

8 Using a flexible knife, smooth cement-based tile adhesive on to the edges of the table.

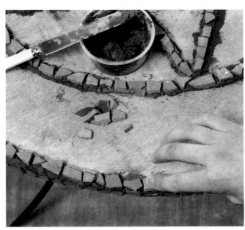

5 Apply the cement-based tile adhesive to the lines of your drawing and press in the outlining tesserae. Use a sponge to wipe away any large bits of cement that have squashed out from under the edges of the tesserae and let dry overnight.

7 Apply cement-based tile adhesive to small areas of the table top at a time and press in the tile fragments. Do this carefully as the finished surface needs to be as flat as possible. Let dry overnight.

9 Cut gold-leaf tesserae into tiny, irregular shapes using tile nippers. Place these in the larger gaps between the broken tiles on the table top. If necessary, first insert a blob of cement adhesive to ensure that the gold is at the same level as the tiles. Let dry overnight. ▶

10 Spoon dry cement-based adhesive onto the surface of the table. Smooth it over the surface with a soft brush, making sure all the gaps between the tesserae have been filled. Spray water over the table using a plant mister. When the cement has absorbed enough water, wipe away any excess with a cloth. If the cement sinks when wet, repeat the whole process. Let dry for 24 hours. Turn the table top over and rub wet cement-based tile adhesive into the plywood on the underside. Let dry overnight.

11 Clean off any excess cement with sandpaper. Alternatively, diluted hydrochloric acid can be used, but you must wear goggles and rubber gloves and apply it outside or where there is good ventilation. Wash any acid residue from the surface.

12 When clean, turn the table top face down and screw the metal frame in place using screws that are no longer than the thickness of the plywood. Polish the table top with a soft cloth.

FLOWERPOT

FOR THIS FLOWERPOT, COMBINING BOTH THE FUNCTIONAL AND DECORATIVE QUALITIES OF MOSAICS, CLEO MUSSI HAS CHOSEN A DESIGN AND COLORS THAT REFLECT THE FLOWERS TO BE PLANTED IN IT. SMALL SQUARES OF MIRROR ARE INCLUDED IN THE DESIGN, AS THEY WILL REFLECT THE DAPPLED LIGHT OF A LEAFY GARDEN OR CONSERVATORY. AS ONLY PART OF THE POT IS TO BE COVERED WITH MOSAIC, A READY-GLAZED, HIGH-FIRED TERRA-COTTA POT IS USED. THIS IS ESPECIALLY IMPORTANT IF THE POT IS TO BE LEFT OUTSIDE ALL YEAR. ALTERNATIVELY, IF THE WHOLE OUTER SURFACE OF A POT IS TO BE COVERED IN MOSAIC, A FROST-RESISTANT TERRA-COTTA POT MAY BE USED, AS LONG AS THE POT IS WATERPROOFED ON THE INSIDE BY SEALING IT WITH WHITE GLUE.

1 Draw a simple design on the pot, using chalk or a wax crayon.

2 Cut appropriate shapes from the china using tile nippers. Mix up some cement-based tile adhesive and use it to attach the tesserae to the pot with a flexible knife. Work first on the main lines and detailed areas, applying the adhesive to small areas at a time so you can follow the lines of the design.

3 Fill in the larger areas of plain color. When complete, let the pot dry for 24 hours.

4 Mix powdered grout with water and a little cement dye. Wearing rubber gloves, spread the grout over the pot, filling all the cracks between the tesserae. Let the surface dry, then brush off any excess grout with a nailbrush. Let the pot dry for at least 48 hours before polishing with a dry soft cloth.

MATERIALS AND EQUIPMENT YOU WILL NEED

FLOWERPOT • CHALK OR WAX CRAYON • SELECTION OF CHINA • TILE NIPPERS • CEMENT-BASED TILE ADHESIVE •
MIXING CONTAINER • FLEXIBLE KNIFE • POWDERED WATERPROOF TILE GROUT • CEMENT DYE •
RUBBER GLOVES • NAILBRUSH • SOFT CLOTH

DECORATIVE SPHERES

CLEO MUSSI WAS INSPIRED BY MILLEFIORI AFRICAN BEADWORK TO MAKE THESE MOSAIC SPHERES. USE THEM AS UNUSUAL GARDEN DECORATIONS, OR FILL A BOWL WITH THEM FOR A STRIKING TABLE CENTERPIECE. YOU COULD SELECT FRAGMENTS OF CHINA IN COLORS THAT REFLECT THE SEASON—FOR EXAMPLE, CITRUS COLORS FOR A FRESH SPRING FEEL; MEDITERRANEAN BLUES, WHITE AND TERRA-COTTA FOR SUMMER, GOLDS, RUSTS AND RICH BERRY COLORS FOR AUTUMN, WHITE, GRAYS AND BLACK WITH LOTS OF MIRROR FOR THE WINTER MONTHS. THE BASES USED FOR THESE SPHERES CAN BE WOOD OR POLYSTYRENE. IF POLYSTYRENE IS USED, THE SPHERES REMAIN VERY LIGHT AND WOULD MAKE EFFECTIVE HANGING DECORATIONS, SUCH AS CHRISTMAS TREE BAUBLES OR MOBILES.

1 Seal the polystyrene or wooden spheres with diluted white glue. Let dry.

2 Roughly draw a simple design onto a sphere using a pencil. A combination of circular motifs and stripes works well, but you can experiment with other geometric shapes and abstract designs.

3 Cut your china and mirror into pieces, using tile nippers; combine different sizes of tesserae. Stick the pieces to the sphere with a waterproof tile adhesive. Let dry overnight.

4 Mix grout with water and a little colored vinyl matte latex or acrylic paint. Wearing rubber gloves, rub the grout into the surface of the sphere, filling all the cracks between the tesserae.

5 Leave for a few minutes until the surface has dried, then brush off any excess grout using a stiff nailbrush.

6 Let dry overnight, then polish with a dry soft cloth. Let the spheres air for a few days before arranging.

MATERIALS AND EQUIPMENT YOU WILL NEED

10 POLYSTYRENE OR WOODEN SPHERES • WHITE GLUE • PAINTBRUSH • PENCIL •
SELECTION OF CHINA • MIRROR • TILE NIPPERS • TILE ADHESIVE • POWDERED TILE GROUT • MIXING CONTAINER •
VINYL MATTE LATEX OR ACRYLIC PAINT • RUBBER GLOVES • NAILBRUSH • SOFT CLOTH

CHINA TILES

IF YOU WOULD LIKE TO INTRODUCE MOSAIC TO AN OUTDOOR SETTING BUT ARE DAUNTED BY A LARGE PROJECT, THESE UNIQUE TILES BY CLEO MUSSI ARE THE PERFECT SOLUTION. THEY COULD BE ATTACHED TO A WALL AS AN INTERESTING FEATURE OR DISPLAYED ALONGSIDE OTHER GARDEN DECORATIONS. YOU COULD STICK A FEW TILES TO YOUR WALL, EACH IN A DIFFERENT COLOR OR DESIGN, OR REPEAT THE SAME PATTERN AT REGULAR INTERVALS. THE TILES CAN ALSO BE USED AS TABLE MATS OR COASTERS. THIS IS A GOOD PROJECT TO CHOOSE FOR YOUR FIRST ATTEMPT AT USING CHINA AS TESSERAE. DON'T BE TOO EXACTING WITH YOUR INITIAL ATTEMPTS; RATHER, THINK OF THEM AS SKETCHES OR EXPERIMENTS BEFORE EMBARKING UPON LARGER, MORE COMPLEX MOSAICS.

1 Prime the back of a plain tile with diluted white glue and let dry. Draw a simple, rough design on the back of the tile using a pencil.

2 Cut a selection of china into small pieces that will fit into your design, using tile nippers. Arrange these tesserae in groups according to color and shape.

3 Dip the tesserae into tile adhesive and press them, one by one, onto the tile, using the drawing as a guide. Make sure there is enough adhesive on the tesserae; when you press them onto the tile, glue should ooze out around the tesserae. When the tile is covered with mosaic, let dry overnight.

4 Mix acrylic paint or cement dye with powdered waterproof tile grout. Add water and mix to a dough-like consistency. Wearing rubber gloves, rub the grout into the surface of the mosaic, making sure all the gaps between the tesserae are filled. Let dry for about ten minutes.

5 Scrub the surface of the tile with a stiff nailbrush to remove all the excess grout, which should come away as powder. When clean, let the tile dry for 24 hours. Finish the tile by polishing it with a soft cloth.

MATERIALS AND EQUIPMENT YOU WILL NEED
PLAIN WHITE TILES • WHITE GLUE • PAINTBRUSH • PENCIL • SELECTION OF CHINA • TILE NIPPERS •
TILE ADHESIVE • MIXING CONTAINER • ACRYLIC PAINT OR CEMENT DYE • POWDERED WATERPROOF TILE GROUT •
RUBBER GLOVES • NAILBRUSH • SOFT CLOTH

JAM JAR NIGHT-LIGHT

WHEN LIT WITH A SMALL CANDLE, THIS STAINED GLASS NIGHT-LIGHT, DESIGNED BY TESSA BROWN, THROWS PATCHES OF COLORED LIGHT ACROSS A ROOM. ONE JAR IS USED AS THE BASE AND ANOTHER IS BROKEN INTO FRAGMENTS THAT ARE PAINTED A VARIETY OF COLORS WITH STAINED-GLASS PAINTS.

THESE FRAGMENTS ARE THEN STUCK ONTO THE BASE JAR AND THE GAPS BETWEEN THE GLASS ARE GROUTED. IDEALLY YOU SHOULD SELECT TWO JARS OF THE SAME SIZE, BUT IF YOU CANNOT FIND TWO EXACTLY THE SAME, USE THE SMALLER ONE AS THE BASE.

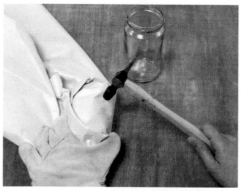

1 Wrap one of the jars in an old dish cloth. Wearing goggles and protective gloves, and covering your hair, smash the jar with a hammer. If the jars are of different sizes, smash the larger one.

3 Use reusable adhesive to pick up the broken pieces of glass and turn them over so that the sharp edges face upwards. Paint the concave surface of each fragment with stained glass paint. Here, three colors are used. Let the pieces dry.

5 Spread cellulose filler over the surface, making sure all the gaps are filled. Smooth into the top and bottom edges of the jar and wipe off most of the excess. Let dry. If the filler has settled and cracks have appeared, use more filler.

2 Pick pieces to use as tesserae. Place them on scrap paper with the sharp edges facing downwards to avoid cutting yourself. Wrap any unused glass in newspaper and dispose of it carefully.

4 Glue the painted glass fragments to the base jar, using a transparent rapid-setting epoxy resin, which must be solvent-free. Let dry thoroughly.

6 When dry, clean any excess filler with a scour pad and water. Use sandpaper to neaten the top and bottom edges. Color the filler with acrylic paint.

MATERIALS AND EQUIPMENT YOU WILL NEED

2 JAM JARS • OLD DISH CLOTH • GOGGLES • PROTECTIVE GLOVES • HAMMER • SCRAP PAPER • NEWSPAPER •
REUSABLE ADHESIVE • STAINED-GLASS PAINTS • PAINTBRUSHES • SOLVENT-FREE, RAPID-SETTING TRANSPARENT EPOXY RESIN •
WHITE CELLULOSE FILLER • GROUT SPREADER • SCOUR PAD • SANDPAPER • ACRYLIC PAINT

STAR WALL MOTIFS

THESE LITTLE WALL MOTIFS HAVE BEEN CREATED BY CLEO MUSSI TO ADD SPARKLING FOCAL POINTS TO A GARDEN. THEY ARE PARTICULARLY EFFECTIVE WHEN DISPLAYED IN CLUSTERS OR SURROUNDED BY LUSH FOLIAGE. USING TESSERAE CUT FROM CHINA AND GLASS, THEY CAN BE MADE IN ANY SHAPE, SIZE OR DESIGN AND IN AS MANY QUANTITIES AS YOU WISH. THESE STAR MOSAICS HAVE BEEN STUCK ONTO THIN PLYWOOD BASES SO THEY CAN BE MOVABLE FEATURES. HOWEVER, IF DESIRED, THEY CAN BE MADE PERMANENT SIMPLY BY STICKING THE TESSERAE DIRECTLY ONTO THE WALL SURFACE.

1 Draw a star motif on ⅛-inch plywood using a pencil and a set square, ruler and compass.

3 Make two small holes through the star using a bradawl.

5 Cut a short length of wire and bend it into a loop for hanging the star. Push the ends through the holes in the star from the painted side and secure them to the front with staples or tape. ▶

2 Cut out the star using a coping saw or an electric scroll saw. Sand down any rough edges, then seal one side with diluted white glue.

4 Paint the unsealed side with wood primer, then undercoat and finish with a coat of gloss or matte paint. Let each coat dry before applying the next.

MATERIALS AND EQUIPMENT YOU WILL NEED

⅛-INCH PLYWOOD • PENCIL • SET SQUARE • RULER • COMPASS • COPING SAW OR ELECTRIC SCROLL SAW •
SANDPAPER • WHITE GLUE • PAINTBRUSHES • BRADAWL • WOOD PRIMER • WHITE UNDERCOAT • GLOSS OR MATTE PAINT • WIRE CUTTERS •
WIRE • STAPLER OR TAPE • SELECTION OF CHINA • MIRROR • TILE NIPPERS • TILE ADHESIVE •
POWDERED TILE GROUT • CEMENT DYE • MIXING CONTAINERS • RUBBER GLOVES • NAILBRUSH • SOFT CLOTH

6 Snip the china and mirror into small pieces using tile nippers and arrange these into groups according to color and shape.

7 Stick the china and mirror fragments to the surface of the star, one piece at a time. Take each fragment and dip it into ready-mixed tile adhesive, making sure enough is on the fragment to ooze a little from under the edges when pressed onto the base. Cover the surface of the star and let dry overnight.

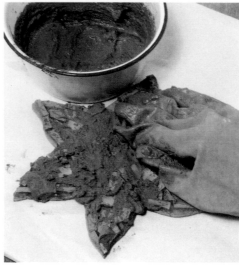

8 Mix the desired quantity of grout with cement dye. Adding a little water at a time, mix until the grout is of dough-like consistency. Wearing rubber gloves, push the grout into all the gaps between the tesserae. Let dry for a few minutes.

9 Using a nailbrush, gently remove all the excess grout. This should brush away as powder; if it does not, the grout is still too damp, so let it dry for a few more minutes before brushing again.

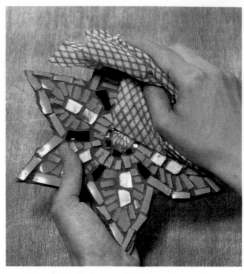

10 Polish the surface with a soft, dry cloth, then let dry for 24 hours before hanging outside.

PRINCESS WALL MOSAIC

Gardens offer the mosaic artist the opportunity to experiment with more playful wall mosaics. There is less pressure to be "tasteful," as the pieces can be softened by plants and garden bric-a-brac. This rather tongue-in-cheek princess design is applied to a wall using the semi-indirect method. This means that it can be made up in the comfort of your home or studio, then moved later, as a whole, and attached to its base. It uses tesserae of vitreous glass in vibrant colors, which will not fade when exposed to the elements.

1 Scale up the template from the back of the book or draw a simple design on brown paper.

2 Make a tracing of the outline of your drawing and cut it out. You will use this later as a template to mark the area of the wall to be covered with cement.

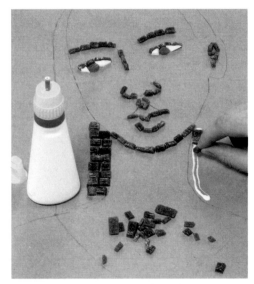

4 Stick these tesserae face down on the main lines of your drawing using water-soluble glue. Stick down any key features, such as the eyes and lips, in contrasting colors. ▶

3 Cut tiles in the outlining color into eighths, using tile nippers.

MATERIALS AND EQUIPMENT YOU WILL NEED

BROWN PAPER • PENCIL • TRACING PAPER • SCISSORS • VITREOUS GLASS MOSAIC TILES, INCLUDING PINK • TILE NIPPERS •
WATER-SOLUBLE GLUE • MIRROR • BOARD • CEMENT-BASED TILE ADHESIVE • MIXING CONTAINER • NOTCHED TROWEL • SPONGE •
SANDPAPER (OPTIONAL) • DILUTED HYDROCHLORIC ACID (OPTIONAL) • GOGGLES (OPTIONAL) • RUBBER GLOVES (OPTIONAL) • SOFT CLOTH

5 Cut pink vitreous glass tiles into quarters. Glue them face down to fill in the areas between the outlines.

6 Cut the mirror into small pieces about the same size as the quartered vitreous glass tesserae.

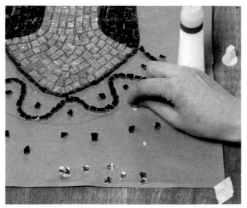

7 Stick the pieces of mirror face down onto the dress and in the crown.

8 Cut the tiles for the dress and the crown into quarters and glue them face down between the pieces of mirror. Let the paper-backed mosaic dry securely in position.

9 Transfer the mosaic to its final location, carrying it on a board to prevent any tesserae from coming loose. Cut out the tracing paper design and draw around it on the wall or floor. Spread cement-based tile adhesive over this area using a notched trowel, then press the mosaic into it, paper side up. Let dry for about two hours, then dampen the paper with a sponge and gently peel it away. Let dry overnight.

10 Using cement-based tile adhesive, grout the mosaic. Clean off any excess cement with a sponge and let the mosaic dry overnight. Remove any remaining cement with sandpaper. Alternatively, diluted hydrochloric acid can be used, but you must wear goggles and rubber gloves and apply it outside or where there is good ventilation. Wash any acid residue from the surface with plenty of water. Finish by polishing the mosaic with a soft cloth.

CRAZY PAVING CHAIR

THIS CHAIR WAS FOUND REJECTED AND BATTERED IN A JUNK SHOP. WITH A LITTLE WORK AND IMAGINATION, IT HAS BEEN TRANSFORMED INTO AN UNUSUAL, EXCITING PIECE OF FURNITURE. WHILE MOSAIC MAY NOT BE THE FIRST CHOICE FOR COVERING AN OBJECT SUCH AS A CHAIR, THIS EXAMPLE SHOWS THE EXTREMES TO WHICH THE MEDIUM CAN SUCCESSFULLY BE TAKEN. A WHOLE DINING SET DECORATED IN THIS MANNER WOULD BE A MAJOR UNDERTAKING FOR ANY INDIVIDUAL, BUT PARTS OF A CHAIR, SAY THE SEAT OR BACK-REST, COULD BE DECORATED RELATIVELY EASILY. IT IS IMPORTANT TO REALIZE THAT LARGE THREE-DIMENSIONAL OBJECTS SUCH AS THIS CHAIR, WHICH HAS BEEN COVERED WITH TESSERAE CUT FROM A SELECTION OF CHINA, REQUIRE A DECEPTIVELY LARGE AMOUNT OF MOSAIC TO COVER THEM. YOU WOULD BE LUCKY TO FIND ENOUGH OF THE SAME PATTERN TO COVER A WHOLE CHAIR. HERE, THE PROBLEM HAS BEEN SOLVED BY USING SLIGHTLY DIFFERENT PATTERNS OF CHINA TO COVER DIFFERENT SECTIONS OF THE CHAIR.

1 If the chair you have chosen has a padded seat, remove it. There may be a wooden pallet beneath the padding which you can use as a base for the mosaic. If not, cut a piece of plywood to fit in its place.

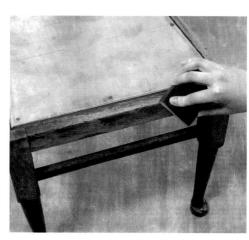

2 Strip the chair of any paint or varnish and sand down with coarse-grade sandpaper. Then paint the whole chair with diluted white glue.

3 When the surface is dry, stick the seat in place with a strong wood glue and fill any gaps around the edge with cement-based tile adhesive mixed with an admix for extra strength and flexibility.

MATERIALS AND EQUIPMENT YOU WILL NEED
CHAIR • ¾-INCH PLYWOOD (OPTIONAL) • PAINT OR VARNISH STRIPPER • COARSE-GRADE SANDPAPER • PAINTBRUSH • WHITE GLUE • WOOD GLUE • CEMENT-BASED TILE ADHESIVE • ADMIX FOR TILE ADHESIVE • MIXING CONTAINER • FLEXIBLE KNIFE • PENCIL OR CHALK • LARGE SELECTION OF CHINA • TILE NIPPERS • RUBBER GLOVES • DILUTED HYDROCHLORIC ACID (OPTIONAL) • GOGGLES (OPTIONAL) • SOFT CLOTH

4 Draw a design or motifs on any large flat surfaces of the chair with a pencil or chalk. Use simple shapes that are easy to read; this chair will have a large flower on the seat and a heart on the back-rest.

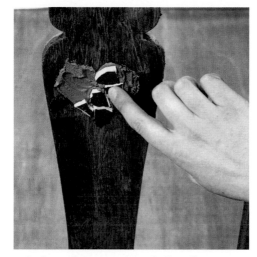

6 Spread cement-based tile adhesive, with admix, within the areas of your design and press the cut china firmly into it.

8 Working on small areas at a time, tile the rest of the chair as in step 6. Where one section of wood meets another, change the pattern of the china you are using.

5 Select china with colors and patterns to suit the motifs you have drawn. Using tile nippers, cut the china into the appropriate shapes and sizes.

7 Select china to cover the rest of the chair. As you are unlikely to have enough of the same pattern to cover the whole chair, choose two or three patterns that look good together. Cut the china into small, varied shapes.

9 Cut appropriately patterned china into thin slivers and use them to tile the edges of any thin sections of wood. Here, the edges of the back-rest are covered. Let dry for at least 24 hours.

▶

10 Mix up some more cement-based tile adhesive with the admix. Using a flexible knife, smooth this grout into the four corners of every piece of wood. Wearing rubber gloves, rub the grout over the flat surfaces. Work on a small area at a time and try to clean off most of the excess as you go. Let dry overnight.

11 Sand off the excess cement. This can be quite a difficult job, as there are many awkward angles. Alternatively, diluted hydrochloric acid can be used, but you must wear goggles and rubber gloves and apply it outside or where there is good ventilation. Wash any acid residue from the surface with plenty of water and, when dry, polish with a soft cloth.

HOUSE NUMBER PLAQUE

Hung on a door frame or fence post, this striking number plaque, designed by Sarah Round, will not be missed by the mailman. It is made with tesserae cut from brightly colored tiles and small pieces of mirror. As this piece will be left outside all year round and will have to face all weather conditions, it may be a good idea to paint the areas of grout with a transparent water sealant. If you do this, make sure you clean any sealant from the surface of the tiles. A larger plaque could be made to display a house name.

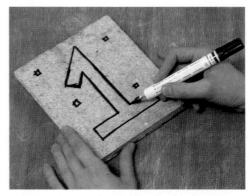

1 Cut a piece of ½-inch chipboard to size; the one used here is 7 x 6 inches. Draw the house number on the chipboard, making sure it is at least ⅜ inch wide. If you wish, you can also mark the intended positions of the mirror.

2 Paint the chipboard, front, back and sides, with diluted white glue. Let dry thoroughly.

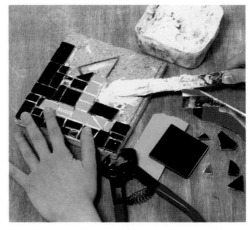

3 Cut the tiles and mirror into small pieces using tile nippers. First tile the number with the tesserae you have cut, sticking them on the base, one small area at a time, with waterproof tile adhesive. Then tile the area around the number, cutting and applying small pieces of mirror to the marked positions. Wipe off any excess tile adhesive and let the plaque dry for 24 hours.

4 Cover the surface with black outdoor tile grout, making sure all the gaps between the tesserae are well filled, as no moisture must be allowed to penetrate the chipboard base. Spread the grout along the edges of the plaque, then let dry for about ten minutes. Wipe off the excess grout with a sponge and let the plaque dry for 24 more hours. Paint the back of the plaque with an exterior paint and attach a clip for hanging. Finish by polishing the surface of the plaque with a dry, soft cloth and clear glass polish.

MATERIALS AND EQUIPMENT YOU WILL NEED

½-INCH CHIPBOARD • SAW • MARKER • WHITE GLUE • PAINTBRUSHES • TILES IN TWO CONTRASTING COLORS • MIRROR •
TILE NIPPERS • WATERPROOF TILE ADHESIVE • MIXING CONTAINER • FLEXIBLE KNIFE • BLACK READY-MIXED OUTDOOR TILE GROUT •
GROUT SPREADER • SPONGE • WATERPROOF EXTERIOR PAINT • WALL FASTENING • SCREWS • SCREWDRIVER • SOFT CLOTH • CLEAR GLASS POLISH

GARDEN URN

THIS UNUSUAL GARDEN URN IS DECORATED WITH MODERN FACES BUT HAS A LOOK THAT IS REMINISCENT OF BYZANTINE ICONS. MANY PEOPLE WILL SHY AWAY FROM ATTEMPTING TO DRAW THE HUMAN FORM, BUT IT IS WORTH A TRY; A SIMPLE AND NAIVE DRAWING CAN LOOK BETTER THAN MORE REALISTIC DEPICTIONS WHEN RENDERED IN MOSAIC. USE A FROST-RESISTANT TERRA-COTTA POT, AND IF IT IS NOT GLAZED, YOU MUST VARNISH THE INSIDE TO STOP MOISTURE FROM SEEPING THROUGH FROM THE INSIDE AND PUSHING OFF THE TESSERAE. THIS IS ESPECIALLY IMPORTANT IF THE URN IS TO BE USED FOR PLANTS LEFT OUTSIDE. AS THIS IS ONE OF THE MORE AMBITIOUS PROJECTS IN THE BOOK, IT IS BEST TACKLED AFTER YOU HAVE HAD A CHANCE TO EXPERIMENT ON SMALLER OBJECTS.

1 Paint the inside of the urn with yacht varnish. Let dry.

2 Divide the pot into quarters and draw your design on each quarter with chalk. The design used here depicts four different heads and shoulders. Keep the drawing very simple, sketching just the basic elements of the face.

3 Choose a dark color from the range of vitreous glass for the main outlines and details such as eyes and lips. Cut these into eighths using tile nippers. Mix up cement-based tile adhesive and stick the tesserae to the lines of your drawing.

4 Select a range of colors for the flesh tones and cut into quarters.

5 Working on one small area at a time, apply cement-based tile adhesive to the face and press the tesserae into it. Use a mixture of all the colors, but in areas of shade use more of the darker tesserae, and in highlighted areas use more of the lighter pieces. ▶

MATERIALS AND EQUIPMENT YOU WILL NEED
LARGE FROST-RESISTANT URN • YACHT VARNISH • PAINTBRUSH • CHALK • VITREOUS GLASS MOSAIC TILES •
TILE NIPPERS • CEMENT-BASED TILE ADHESIVE • MIXING CONTAINER • FLEXIBLE KNIFE • RUBBER GLOVES • SPONGE •
SANDPAPER • DILUTED HYDROCHLORIC ACID (OPTIONAL) • GOGGLES (OPTIONAL)

6 Choose colors for the area surrounding the heads. Spread them out on a clean table to see if they work together. A mixture of blues and whites with a little green has been chosen here. Cut the pieces into quarters.

7 Working on one small area at a time, spread tile adhesive onto the surface and press the cut vitreous glass into it, making sure the colors are arranged randomly. Cover the entire outer surface of the urn with tesserae, then let dry for 24 hours.

8 Mix up more tile adhesive and, wearing rubber gloves, spread it over the surface of the mosaic. Do this very thoroughly, making sure you fill all the gaps between the tesserae. This is especially important if the urn is going to be situated outside. Wipe off any excess cement with a sponge, then let dry for 24 hours.

9 Use sandpaper to remove any cement that has dried on the surface of the mosaic. If the cement is proving hard to remove, diluted hydrochloric acid can be used, but you must wear goggles and rubber gloves and apply it outside or where there is good ventilation. Wash any acid residue from the surface with plenty of water. Let dry.

10 Finish off the urn by rubbing tile adhesive over the lip and inside the pot. This prevents the mosaic from seeming to end abruptly and gives the urn and mosaic a more unified appearance.

MOSAIC PANEL

THIS RICHLY TEXTURED PANEL DESIGNED BY CLEO MUSSI IS COMPOSED OF TESSERAE CUT FROM A VARIETY OF PATTERNED CHINA. MOTIFS ARE CUT OUT AND USED AS FOCAL POINTS FOR THE PATTERNS; SOME ARE RAISED TO GIVE THEM EXTRA EMPHASIS. THESE ARE SURROUNDED AND SEPARATED BY TESSERAE ARRANGED TO FORM STRONG LINEAR ELEMENTS. THE DESIGN HAS BEEN STUCK ONTO A PLYWOOD BASE, RATHER THAN DIRECTLY ONTO THE WALL SURFACE, TO CREATE A MORE THREE-DIMENSIONAL EFFECT. THIS ALSO GIVES THE PANEL THE ADVANTAGE OF BEING PORTABLE.

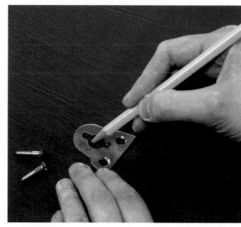

1 Draw the outer shape of the panel onto a sheet of ¾-inch plywood. If you are unsure about drawing directly onto the surface, make a stencil from thick cardboard. Cut out around this shape using a jigsaw and sand down the rough edges. Seal one side and the edges with diluted white glue. Paint the unsealed side (the back) with wood primer, undercoat and then gloss paint, letting each coat dry before applying the next.

2 Mark the position of the mirror plate on the back of the panel. Using the appropriate drill bit, rebate the area that will be under the keyhole-shaped opening, so that it is large enough to take a screw head. Screw the mirror plate in position.

3 Draw your design on the sealed top surface. If necessary, trace and transfer your original design. Tools such as rulers, set squares and compasses are helpful if your design has geometric elements. ▶

MATERIALS AND EQUIPMENT YOU WILL NEED

¾-INCH PLYWOOD • PENCIL • THICK CARDBOARD (OPTIONAL) • JIGSAW • SANDPAPER • WHITE GLUE • PAINTBRUSHES • WOOD PRIMER • WHITE UNDERCOAT • GLOSS PAINT • MIRROR PLATE • DRILL AND REBATE BIT • ¾-INCH SCREWS • SCREWDRIVER • TRACING PAPER (OPTIONAL) • RULER, SET SQUARE OR COMPASS (OPTIONAL) • SELECTION OF CHINA • TILE NIPPERS • TILE ADHESIVE • POWDERED TILE GROUT • MIXING CONTAINER • CEMENT DYE, VINYL MATTE LATEX OR ACRYLIC PAINT (OPTIONAL) • RUBBER GLOVES • SQUEEGEE OR FLEXIBLE KNIFE • NAILBRUSH • SOFT CLOTH

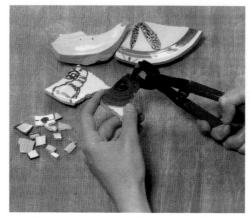

4 Sort the china into groups according to color and pattern and select interesting motifs that could be used to form the centerpieces of designs. Using the tile nippers, cut the china into the desired shapes.

5 Using smooth edges cut from cups and plates and ready-mixed tile adhesive, tile the edges of the panel. Then use small, regular-shaped tesserae to tile the structural lines of the design. Press the pieces in the adhesive first.

6 Raise small areas of the mosaic to give greater emphasis to sections of the design by setting the tesserae on a larger mound of tile adhesive. Cut more china and use it to form the patterns between the structural lines. Let the panel dry for 24 hours.

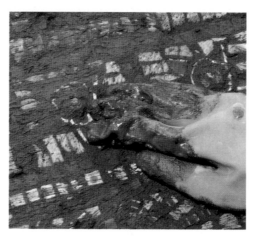

7 Mix powdered grout with water. If you wish the grout to have a color, add cement dye, vinyl matte latex or acrylic paint to the mixture (if this is to be used indoors, cement dye is not essential). Wearing rubber gloves, spread the grout over the surface using a squeegee or a flexible knife. Rub the grout into the gaps with your fingers.

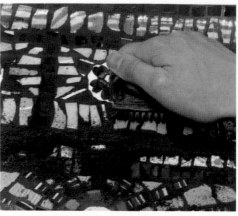

8 Let the surface dry for a few minutes, then scrub off any excess grout using a stiff nailbrush.

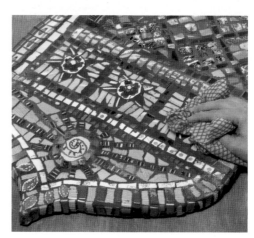

9 Let dry for 24 hours, then polish the surface with a soft cloth.

TINWORK
MARION ELLIOT

TINWARE, ONCE SEEN AS A QUAINT, OUTMODED CRAFT FORM, HAS RECENTLY ENJOYED A HUGE REVIVAL OF INTEREST. THE MARRIAGE OF SIMPLE, QUIET ELEGANCE TO SOLID UTILITY SEEMS ESPECIALLY APPEALING IN AN AGE DOMINATED BY THROWAWAY MATERIALS AND HIGH-TECH GADGETS. PUNCHED TIN KITCHENWARE IS ESPECIALLY POPULAR, EVOKING AS IT DOES AN ATMOSPHERE OF SIMPLE, HONEST LIVING IN A QUIETER AGE.

TIN REALLY IS AN EVERYDAY MATERIAL AND CAN BE OBTAINED VERY READILY. THIS SECTION WILL SHOW YOU HOW TO PREPARE AND USE DIFFERENT FORMS OF TIN, FROM CANS TO SHEET METAL, TO MAKE YOUR OWN CREATIONS. EACH PROJECT IS EXPLAINED USING STEP-BY-STEP INSTRUCTIONS, AND THE BASIC TECHNIQUES AND MATERIALS ARE DISCUSSED IN DETAIL. THE GALLERY FEATURES INSPIRATIONAL WORK MADE BY ARTISTS AND CRAFTSPEOPLE USING TIN FROM VARIOUS SOURCES.

Left: These beautifully simple items of tinware are made from galvanized tin. Each piece is made in a Greek workshop according to centuries-old traditional designs. The pieces may be left plain or embellished with a painted design.

HISTORY OF TIN

TIN HAS BEEN A POPULAR AND WIDELY USED METAL FOR MANY CENTURIES. AS LONG AGO AS 2000 BC THE ROMANS WERE MINING THE TIN-RICH LANDS AROUND CORNWALL, ENGLAND. EVEN UP TO THE MID-EIGHTEENTH CENTURY, ENGLISH TIN PLATE PRODUCTION WAS A MAJOR INDUSTRY AND AN IMPORTANT INFLUENCE ON THE WORLDWIDE DEVELOPMENT OF TINWARE. AS PRODUCTION IN VARIOUS COUNTRIES DEVELOPED, SO DIFFERENT FORMS OF TINWARE RESULTED, INCLUDING PUNCHED DESIGNS AND JAPANNED WARE OR TOLEWARE. THE MOST RECENT REVIVAL IN INTEREST IN TINWARE HAS PAVED THE WAY FOR AN UPSURGE IN DESIGNS USING RECYCLED TIN.

In the early stages of the development of tinware, Cornwall had a flourishing trade, exporting tin throughout Europe and the East. The Romans recognized the value of alloying tin with copper and experimented with the process to produce bronze in a controlled way. As well as making bronze vessels, the Romans also produced finely wrought tin artifacts.

Used both in its pure form and as an alloy, tin was also added to glazes. The Assyrians had discovered a way of rendering glaze opaque with the addition of tin oxide, possibly as early as 1000 BC. The knowledge of this process spread to Europe, and by the fourteenth century AD, there was a tin glaze industry in Spain and Italy that spread to Holland, Germany and England and resulted in the production of faience ware and majolica pottery. Tin oxide produced a white glaze that covered the body color of earthenware clay completely, leaving a bright white canvas on which to paint metal oxides, such as manganese, copper and cobalt. When fired, the oxides fused with the tin glaze to produce wonderfully bright enamel-like colors. Tin was also exported further afield to the Far East, where it was put to use in the production of pewter and also as a currency.

Because it resisted tarnishing so well, tin was commonly used to plate other metals. The tin-plating process originated in Germany, but the vast majority of tin plate was produced in England, owing to the ready availability of the raw material. By the mid-eighteenth century, English tin plate production was a major industry, exporting principally to the USA.

American and English domestic tinware production flourished and popular tinware took two main forms. There were plain domestic wares such as candle holders, sconces, sieves, boxes, food containers and trays made of unpainted metal. They were left either completely unadorned or decorated by means of punching and piercing. Punching the tin with a nail or punch left indentations and holes in the metal that could be purely decorative, or functional too. For example, items such as the classic of American tinware, the Paul Revere lantern, with its distinctive conical roof, were heavily punched with perforations that were gloriously decorative and also practical. They allowed heat and

Above: These beautiful, brightly printed toys were made in India, where millions of people are involved in the collection of scrap tin and its working into new objects. The toys are made in small workshops and commercially manufactured. The decoration may be printed on the back of recycled tin sheet or the tin may be left plain.

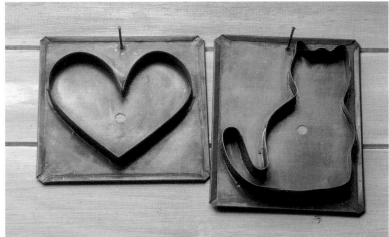

Left: These candle lanterns are contemporary versions of traditional designs. They come from Morocco, where different regions produce their own versions of the lantern. The lanterns are made of tin plate, which has been stamped and punched for decoration.

Below: These cookie cutters are made to a traditional design by Marlene Mozsak, a professional tinsmith in New York. The motifs, a heart and a cat, are commonly found in folk art. The surface of the cutters, which are made from tin plate, is distressed to give them a dark patina.

light to escape through the perforations in the tin, projecting lacy shadows on surrounding walls. Other famous examples of punched tinware were the tin panel pie safes and food cupboards that are now almost a cliché of traditional country furniture. The punched tin cabinets were not only an attractive and homey focal point, but they also kept food adequately ventilated while protecting it from flies and other pests.

While punched tinware was European in origin and was used widely in Europe, the Pennsylvania Dutch settlers of America raised tin punching to an art form, so fond were they of ornament. They decorated all sorts of domestic tinware with a dazzling array of motifs such as hearts, stars and flowers, and their designs were often of religious significance. Their tinware was in stark contrast to that of the Shaker

community, who used tin objects of great simplicity and elegance, which were beautifully designed and very functional.

The other main form of tinware was painted and was known as "japanned ware" or toleware. This was tin decorated in imitation of Japanese lacquerware, with stencils and paints. The most popular forms of toleware included trays, boxes and caddies. The tin was painted a dark color, usually black, then decorated with a stenciled and handpainted design, such as flowers or a basket of fruit. Sometimes the background was enhanced with a fine layer of bronze powder.

During the nineteenth century, various inventions appeared that helped to commercialize the production of tinware. These included a rolling machine that could mechanically turn over and wire the edges of tinware to make it safe, and a steam

hammer that could stamp out simple forms much more quickly than could be done by hand. The revolution in the tinware industry led to a gradual decline in the production of handmade pieces in Europe and the United States, and tin was itself eventually superseded by more modern materials, such as aluminum. It is now used mainly in the canning industry to plate food containers.

However, many wonderful tin artifacts, especially those made from recycled materials, are still being produced today in places such as India and Mexico, and there has been a huge revival of interest in the tinware of such groups as the Shakers and the Pennsylvania Dutch. Original pieces are much in demand, and the craft of punching and recycling tinware has been revived by designers, craftspeople and interior designers who recognize the medium's innate charm and versatility.

GALLERY

RECYCLED TIN IS A POPULAR CHOICE FOR TINWORKERS. FOOD CANS, BOXES AND OTHER FOUND OBJECTS COST NOTHING AND MAKE IDEAL BASES FOR DECORATIVE PROJECTS, AS THEIR SHAPES CAN BECOME AN INTEGRAL PART OF THE DESIGN. THE DESIGNERS FEATURED HERE HAVE TRANSFORMED OTHERWISE THROWAWAY OBJECTS INTO ARTIFACTS WHICH WE HOPE WILL INSPIRE YOU TO DEVELOP YOUR OWN DESIGNS.

Left: TIN MAN
Plain and painted tin is Adrian's preferred medium, and he uses it to make large and small objects such as these two automata. The dog and figure are mounted on a sardine can, and when operated by a simple crank mechanism, the figure's arms move and the dog appears to jump up and down.
ADRIAN TAYLOR

Above: FIERCE ANIMALS
Lucy Casson trained as a textile designer but has worked solely in tin since 1982. This example, Fierce Animals, is typical of the animated and expressive quality of her sculptural pieces. It is constructed from recycled tin plate, which Lucy purchases from a scrap merchant, and an enamel washing bowl. The sections are joined using pop rivets and solder. Lucy does not paint her work but uses the color already present on the surface of the tin as an integral part of the decoration.
LUCY CASSON

Above: SIN EATER, LANTERN AND COLLECTION BOX

Julia initially trained as an illustrator but has worked with non-precious metals since attending a jewelry-making course and has been recycling tin cans and boxes for several years. Her Sin Eater, made from tin cans and found objects, is inspired by the fictional account of a mysterious figure who eats the sins of the newly deceased, thus saving them. The lantern was inspired by temples and shrines seen during an Indian journey, and the hand is a collection box that belongs to another tin shrine, not shown.

JULIA FOSTER

Right: SARDINE TIN CHEST OF DRAWERS

Sardine tins, usually so carelessly disposed of, make perfect containers for paper clips, stamps and other small items of everyday life. These small tins are often beautifully decorated, for example with fishing scenes, and Michael feels that it is only sensible to give such lovely objects the second life that they so rightly deserve. He uses the tins as they are, rather than recycling them into different objects. The only modification to the tins in this chest is the addition of a wing nut to the end of each to make a handle.

MICHAEL MARRIOTT

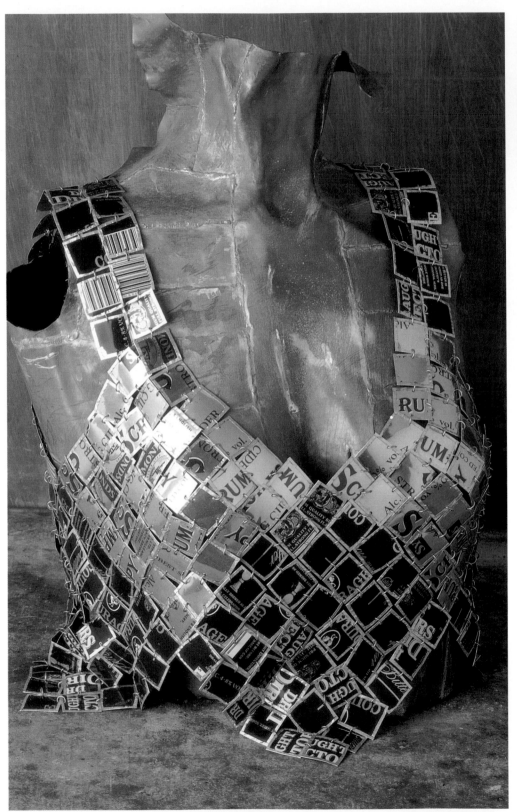

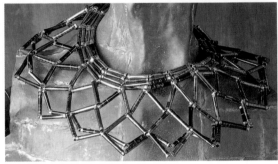

Left: BODICE
Joanne trained as a jeweler and started working with drinks cans because she was attracted to the bright colors. She makes jewelry and one-off pieces of body sculpture, such as this shimmering evening top, which is constructed from small pieces of beer and cider cans. The edges of each small section are turned over and drilled, then linked with nickel jump rings to create a material resembling chain mail that tinkles gently as it moves.
JOANNE TINKER

Above: HAT AND NECKLACE
Val trained as a jewelry maker specializing in semi-precious metals and has enthusiastically recycled beer cans for the past ten years. She rolls the aluminum into beads to create pieces like the necklace, and also forms the thin metal into amazing shapes like the hat, which is further adorned with buttons cut from iridescent compact discs. She heats the metal before using it to make it more pliable and to tone down the printed color. She has arrived at all her techniques through constant experimentation, and has developed a range of tools to work the beer cans.
VAL HUNT

Left: COWBOY MIRROR
AND SUNFLOWER
MIRROR
These two mirror frames
are constructed from pine
and decorated with tin cutouts recycled from old
cashew nut cans. The basic
shapes are cut out, filed
smooth then decorated
with enamel paints in bright
colors. The cowboy frame is
further embellished with
metal studs, which are
randomly hammered in to
create an interesting
rhinestone effect.
MARION ELLIOT

Above: THE PEACEABLE
KINGDOM
This wall decoration is
recycled from an old olive
oil drum found outside a
restaurant and is decorated
using enamel paints and
flowers cut from small
scraps of tin. The subject
matter – the peaceful co-
existence of all creatures –
appears frequently in folk
art. Marion based her
version on an allegorical
painting of the eighteenth
century.
MARION ELLIOT

Opposite: BERLIN
Andy Hazell is best known as a maker of automata, but this piece, Berlin, is static. The piece is a recollection of the city, a 360° condensed sweep of all the most striking features of the place. Andy used recycled cookie tins, car body filler tins and aerosol cans, which are soldered together using electrical solder.
ANDY HAZELL

Above: FILM PROJECTOR
This beautifully crafted film projector was brought back from India by the collector Tony Hayward. It was made by a night watchman and found in a toyshop in Mysore. Made from recycled tin and wood, the projector is wired to take a 40-watt bulb. The film is fed through the machine by turning the small handle at the side.
TONY HAYWARD COLLECTION

Right: NARCISSUS SCONCE
Nick Shinnie's sconce is made from thin steel plate that has been scored with decorative cuts and polished to a soft hue. A mirror mounted in the back of the sconce reflects and intensifies the light of the candle. Nick also makes punched steel panels for wooden cabinets and dressers.
NICK SHINNIE

MATERIALS

To complete the projects in this book, you can obtain many of the materials from hardware shops and craft suppliers. For the tin plate, metal foils and sheet metals, you will need to visit a metal supplier or hardware shop, or if you wish to opt for recycled materials, a metal merchant or scrap yard. Sheet metal, whether cut or uncut, is extremely sharp and should be handled only when protective leather gloves and a work shirt are worn.

Metal foils are thin sheet metals that usually come on rolls in 6 in and 12 in wide strips. Metal foil is so thin that it can be cut with a pair of household scissors. A variety of metal foils is available, including brass, aluminum and copper. The thinness of the foil makes it very soft, and it is easy to draw designs into the surface.

Tin plate is generally used in place of pure tin sheet, which is prohibitively expensive. Tin plate is mild sheet steel that has been coated with tin. The tin plating is very bright and will not tarnish in the open air or in humid conditions. Sheet metals come in different thicknesses, or gauges. The higher the gauge, the thinner the metal.

There are several different gauge systems in use and they vary slightly; the Brown and Sharpe gauge in the USA and the Birmingham gauge in the UK are used to measure sheet metal. At approximately 0.01 in, tin plate can be cut by hand with tin clippers and shears. The edges can then be filed and hammered over before the surface of the metal is marked with a hammer and punch for decoration.

Thin zinc sheet has a dull matte surface and is fairly soft and easy to cut. It is readily available from hardware stores.

Cookie tins are a good source of tin. Some tins have a plastic sheen to them and should be scrubbed with steel wool, if you intend to solder them.

Silicon carbide paper (wet and dry sandpaper) is very abrasive and comes in varying grades of coarseness. Fine-grade sandpaper, when dampened, is useful for finishing off filed edges to make them smooth.

During sanding, the item should be clamped in a bench vise and the paper wrapped around a small wooden block.

Fine wire is used to join pieces of metal together and as decoration.

Paint stripper can be used to remove the paint from tin cans and boxes.

Paint thinner is useful for removing excess flux after soldering.

Enamel paints are dense, opaque paints that are used to paint metal.

Glass and metal paints are translucent and allow the metal to show through the coat of paint. The paint should be applied sparingly, as otherwise it can be difficult to create a smooth coat.

Wood glue is very strong PVA glue. It is white but becomes clear once it has dried.

Epoxy resin glue comes in two parts. Mix only as much glue as you need at one time, since it dries very quickly and is wasted otherwise. Once the glue has set firm, which takes about 24 hours, the join is extremely strong.

Steel wool can be used to remove the brightness from tin plate to leave a soft, brushed surface. It is also useful for cleaning the surface of metal before soldering.

Panel pins are short nails. They should be hammered in using a tack hammer.

S-joiners and jump rings are used to join sections of an object together and to attach lengths of chain. They are very strong, and pliers are used to open and close the links.

Solder is an alloy, or mixture, of metals. Solder is used to join two pieces of metal together by providing a filler of liquid metal between the surfaces. It is most important to use a solder that has a lower melting point than the metals to be joined to avoid damaging or melting the metal. A low-melting-point solder should always be used when soldering tin, so make sure that you follow the manufacturer's instructions closely.

A flux is used during soldering to make the area to be soldered chemically clean. As the flux is heated, it runs along the metal preparing the surface so that the solder may flow smoothly and adhere properly. Some fluxes leave a corrosive residue behind which must be removed after soldering.

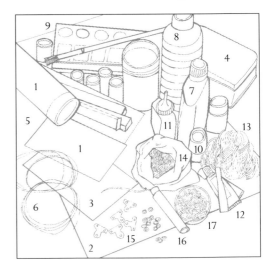

KEY
1 Metal foil
2 Tin plate
3 Thin zinc sheet
4 Cookie tin
5 Silicon carbide paper
6 Fine wire
7 Paint stripper
8 Paint thinner
9 Enamel paints
10 Glass and metal paints
11 Wood glue
12 Epoxy resin glue
13 Steel wool
14 Panel pins
15 S-joiners and jump rings
16 Solder
17 A flux

EQUIPMENT

A FAIRLY BASIC SELECTION OF TOOLS IS NEEDED TO MAKE THE PROJECTS IN THIS BOOK, AND MOST OF THEM YOU MAY ALREADY HAVE. THE MORE SPECIALIZED ITEMS SUCH AS PUNCHES, SNIPS AND SHEARS ARE READILY AVAILABLE FROM GOOD HARDWARE STORES. IT IS IMPORTANT TO HAVE GOOD PROTECTIVE CLOTHING, SUCH AS GLOVES, A WORK SHIRT AND GOGGLES, FOR THE PROJECTS USING HEAVIER TIN.

Tin shears are very strong scissors for cutting sheet metal. Shears come with straight blades to cut a straight line, or blades curved to the left or right to cut circles and curves. There are also universal shears which cut straight lines and wide curves. If possible, buy a pair of shears with a spring mechanism, as this makes it much easier to open and close the blades.

Tin clippers are a smaller version of tin shears and are good for cutting small shapes from a section of tin. Again, try to find a pair that has a spring mechanism.

A hide mallet is made from a roll of leather. It has a much softer head than an ordinary metal hammer and so will not make ugly marks in the tin.

A bench vise is very useful for clamping small metal shapes during filing and sanding, and when hammering over metal edges.

A wooden block with 90° edges and another with a 45° edge are used when turning over the sides of a piece of tin.

A sheet of ¾ in chipboard is used as a work surface when punching tin and embossing foil, as it has slightly more give than wood.

Round-nose pliers have round jaws that are good for making small circles of wire. Flat-nose pliers grip very well and are useful for turning over the edges of tin. You can also use snipe-nose pliers, which have long jaws that are useful for reaching inside narrow shapes and when working with tiny things such as jump rings.

A pair of compasses is useful for drawing out circles on tin.

A can opener is used for taking the tops off tin cans.

Hammers come in a variety of sizes. A medium ball head hammer is used with nails or a punch to make a pattern in tin. A tack hammer is used to knock panel pins into wood or medium-density fibreboard. A heavier hammer is used with a chisel to make decorative holes in a sheet of metal.

A small hand file is used to remove any burrs of metal from the tin after a shape has been cut out. Files come in varying grades of coarseness, from rough to super smooth.

A center punch is traditionally used to mark the center of a hole in a sheet of metal before it is drilled. It can be used to punch a decorative pattern into tin.

A small chisel can be used to make a decorative pattern in tin. When tapped with a ball head hammer, it will leave a short, straight mark in the surface of the metal.

A bradawl is used to make holes.

Nails in various sizes can be used to make a pattern in a piece of tin.

A soldering iron is used to heat the solder that joins two pieces of metal together. Soldering irons may be electric or gas powered. Soldering irons have a tip known as a bit, which is kept at a constant temperature during use. The bit should be cleaned with a file before use, then heated and dipped into flux. A little solder should be applied and allowed to coat the tip. This is called tinning the bit and will stop the solder sticking to the iron during soldering.

Protective leather gloves and a long-sleeved work shirt should always be worn when handling unfinished metal or sheet metal and during soldering.

A variety of fireproof soldering mats is available and may be purchased from good hardware stores and metal supply shops.

A protective mask and goggles should be worn during soldering, as the process produces fumes. Protective goggles should be worn when carrying out work that might produce small shards of metal.

Wooden pegs or masking tape can be used to hold two sections of metal together while they are soldered.

A drill is needed to make holes for screws in many of the projects. Use a metal drill bit.

Pliers are useful for holding tin steady when you are cutting it and for turning over edges.

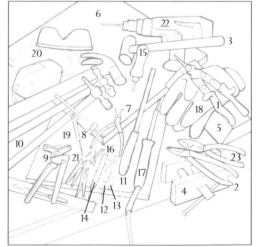

KEY

1 Tin shears	**12** Center punch
2 Tin clippers	**13** Chisel
3 Hide mallet	**14** Cold chisel
4 Bench vise	**15** Bradawl
5 45° block of wood	**16** Nails
6 Chipboard	**17** Soldering iron
7 Round-nose pliers	**18** Leather gloves
8 Pair of compasses	**19** Soldering mat
9 Can opener	**20** Mask and goggles
10 Hammers	**21** Clothes pins
11 Hand file	**22** Drill
	23 Pliers

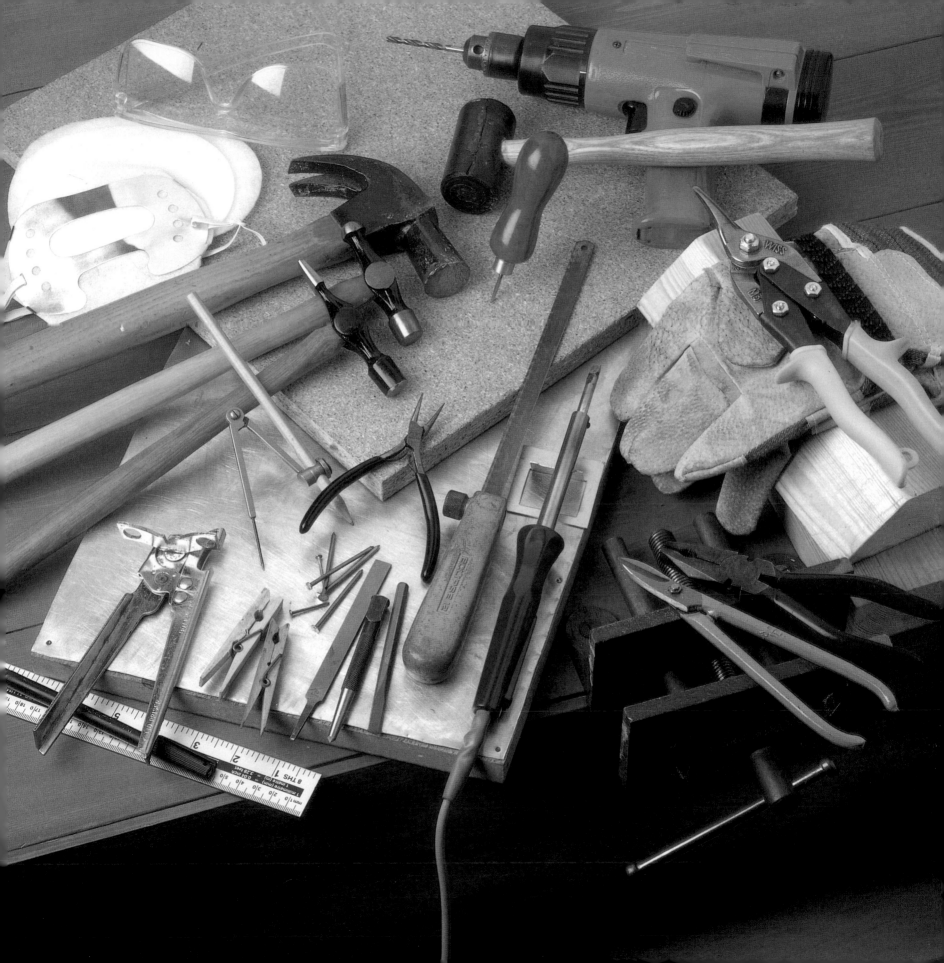

BASIC TECHNIQUES

ALTHOUGH AN EXPERT TINSMITH IS A HIGHLY SKILLED CRAFTSPERSON, THERE ARE ONLY A FEW BASIC TECHNIQUES THAT THE NOVICE TINWORKER NEEDS TO LEARN WHEN EMBARKING ON SIMPLE PROJECTS. THESE ARE CUTTING TIN, FINISHING THE EDGES, SOLDERING AND DECORATING WITH PUNCHED DESIGNS. THE MOST IMPORTANT TECHNIQUES ARE THOSE THAT RELATE TO SAFETY AND IT IS ESSENTIAL THAT THESE ARE OBSERVED EVERY TIME TO AVOID ACCIDENTS. READ THROUGH THESE TECHNIQUES BEFORE STARTING THE PROJECTS.

SAFETY ADVICE

- A heavy work shirt and protective leather gloves should always be worn when handling either cut metal pieces or uncut sheet metal.

- Tin shears and clippers are very powerful, being strong enough to cut through fairly heavy metal, and very sharp. They should be handled with respect and, like all other tools, should always be kept in a safe place well away from children during and after use.

- A protective face mask and goggles should always be worn during soldering as the hot metal, solder and flux give off fumes. Work should always be carried out on a soldering mat and the iron placed on a metal rest when not in use.

- Soldering should always be carried out in a well-ventilated area and frequent breaks should be taken when working. Don't lean too near your work during soldering to avoid close contact with fumes.

- Always wear protective gloves when soldering, as the soldering iron and metal tend to get very hot.

- Always clean up as you work. Collect any small shards of tin together as you cut and make sure you don't leave any on the floor where people and animals might walk on them.

CUTTING TIN

With proper protective clothing and tin shears or clippers, it is surprisingly easy to cut through thin sheets of tin plate, tin cans and so on. Tin shears are very powerful, and cutting tin with them is rather like cutting a sheet of paper. It is important to get used to cutting smoothly to avoid making jagged edges, so practice first on scraps of tin to get a feel for cutting metal. Cutting tin produces small shards of metal which are razor-sharp, so it is essential to collect scraps as you cut and keep them together until you can dispose of them safely.

Cutting a Section from a Sheet

1 To cut a section of tin from a large
sheet, it is necessary to use tin shears. It is important to avoid creating a jagged edge when cutting, for safety reasons, and the secret of achieving a smooth cut is never to close the blades of the shears completely. Instead, make a cut almost the length of the

blades each time, open the shears, then gently guide the metal back into the blades and continue. Keep the blades of the shears in the cut, without removing them until the line of the cutting is complete. If you are cutting a straight-sided shape, don't try to turn the shears around once you have reached a corner. Remove the shears and cut across to the corner from the edge of the sheet of metal.

Cutting a Small Shape from a Section of Tin

1 If you are cutting a small shape from a
section of tin, it is better to use a pair of tin clippers than shears. They are easier to manipulate and control, especially if you are cutting an intricate shape. Again, don't attempt to turn the clippers around in the metal: cut as much as you can, then remove the clippers and turn the metal so that you can follow the cutting line more easily.

Cutting a Panel of Metal from an Oil Drum

Oil drums are an excellent source of large areas of smooth, flat metal. It is very common to find discarded oil drums outside wholesale food importers, restaurants and cafés and they can be recycled very easily. Since many of the drums are printed with bright, highly decorative designs, it is possible to use both sides of the metal.

1 To cut a panel from an oil drum, first remove the top. Make a cut in the side of the drum using a hacksaw blade. Open the sides of the cut slightly, then insert the blades of a pair of tin clippers into the space and cut around the drum, removing the top. The metal found in oil drums is very often quite thin and springy, and so care must be taken when cutting out panels from a drum. Protect your eyes with goggles for extra safety.

2 Once you have removed the top of the drum, carefully cut down one side to within ¾ in of the base using tin shears. Gently cut around the base of the drum, carefully pushing back the panel as it is freed from the base. Once you have removed the panel completely, it may be used in the same way as a sheet of tin plate. Mop up any oil residue on the surface of the tin using tissue paper.

FINISHING THE EDGES

All tin items should be considered unfinished and unsuitable for use until all the edges have been smoothed or turned over. This should be done immediately to avoid accidents. Long, straight edges may be folded back and flattened with the aid of a hammer and wooden blocks with measured 90° and 45° edges. Irregularly shaped items may be finished with a hand file and wet and dry paper for complete smoothness. Items such as tin cans should always be filed smooth around the rims before use to remove any jagged edges.

Filing Cut Metal

1 Obviously, the raw, cut edges of a piece of tin plate are very sharp indeed, and should be immediately smoothed or finished in some way to prevent them causing harm to yourself or anyone else. Small shapes should be smoothed with a hand file while firmly clamped in a bench vise. The file should be moved forward at a right angle to the metal in one light stroke, then lifted and returned. This will remove most of the rough edges.

Finishing Rough Edges with Wet and Dry Paper

1 To make a cut edge completely smooth after filing, it should be finished with fine-grade silicon carbide paper, also known as wet and dry paper. This is dampened and wrapped around a small wooden block. Sanding with wet and dry paper will remove any remaining rough edges and leave the metal smooth to the touch.

Turning Over Cut Edges

The cut edges of straight-sided pieces of tin plate should be turned over immediately after cutting to avoid accidents. Mechanically made baking tins and boxes have their edges bent over to an angle of 45° by a folding machine. The edges are then pressed flat and made safe. It is simple to replicate this process at home using two blocks of wood.

1 First, a thick block of wood with an accurately measured 90° edge is clamped firmly in a bench vice. A border, say ½ in wide, is drawn around the cut edges of the tin plate. The piece of tin is placed on the block with the border line lying along the edge of the wooden block. The edge of the tin is then struck smartly with a hide hammer which molds the metal around the edge of the wooden block to an angle of 90°.

2 Once the edge of the metal has been folded halfway over, the piece of tin is turned over and a block of wood with a 45° edge is placed inside the fold. The wooden block is kept firmly in position with one hand and the folded edge is hammered down upon it using a hide hammer. Once the metal has been folded over to this angle, the block is removed, and the edge is then hammered completely flat using a hide hammer. Each side of the piece of tin is folded in turn and, once all the edges have been hammered flat, the corners should be filed to smooth any sharp edges. All straight edges should be finished in this way to avoid accidents, even if the panel is to be set into a recess, for example in the case of a punched panel cabinet.

DECORATING TIN

Tin may be decorated in a variety of ways. Punching, when a pattern of indentations is beaten into the surface of the metal, is one of the most common methods. A center punch or nail, plus a ball hammer, are used to produce the knobby patterns, either on the front or back of the tin. Small chisels and metal stamps are also used. Opaque and translucent enamel paints are suitable for decorating tin plate and some other metals. Any grease or dirt should be removed first before painting. Very thin metal foils, such as aluminum foil, are so soft that a design may be drawn onto the surface, to leave a raised or "embossed" pattern.

Getting the Design Right

1 Nails or punches can be used to make indentations and holes in tin. If you want to emboss a sophisticated pattern, then it is a good idea to draw the design out on a sheet of graph paper first and punch through the paper into the tin following the lines. The paper should be taped to the tin, and the tin attached to a piece of chipboard using panel pins to keep it steady as you punch.

Punching Tin from the Front

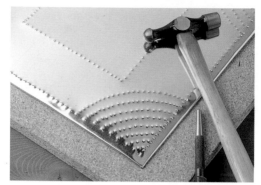

1 A design may be punched into either the front or the back of a piece of tin. If it is punched from the front, the resulting pattern will be indented. If it is punched from the back, the pattern will be raised. If an area of tin is punched from the front, and the indentations are made very close together, the punched area recedes and the unpunched area becomes slightly raised. This is a form of "chasing", where decorative patterns are punched into metal from the front and stand out in low relief.

Punching Tin from the Back

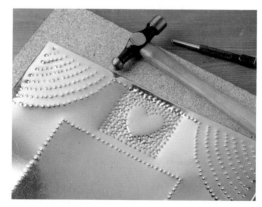

1 Punching a pattern into a piece of tin from the back leaves a very pleasing knobby effect on the surface of the tin. Pattern can be applied with nails of different sizes or punches to make a dotty texture. Short lines can be made by using a small chisel. It is also possible to buy decorative punches that have designs engraved into the tip.

Embossing Aluminum Foil

1 Aluminum foil is very soft, thin metal rather like kitchen foil. It can be easily cut with household scissors and bent or folded as desired, so it is especially useful for covering frames, books, boxes and other small items. Its softness makes it very easy to emboss and this is done by drawing onto the back of the foil using a ballpoint pen, which leaves a raised surface on the other side. It is best to use an empty ballpoint pen as it makes the process cleaner.

SOLDERING

Sections of metal may be joined together by soldering. It is essential that both surfaces to be joined are clean before they are soldered. Rubbing both areas with steel wool will help remove any dirt and grease. All soldering should be done on a soldering mat, wearing protective gloves, mask and goggles, and the soldering iron should be placed on a metal stand when not in use.

1 The two sections to be joined are placed together. They may be held in place with wooden pegs or masking tape if required. Before the joint is soldered, it is smeared with flux. This is essential, as when the metal is heated, an oxide forms on the surface which may inhibit the adhesion of the solder. The flux prevents the oxide from forming on the metal.

2 The hot soldering iron heats the metal, which causes the flux to melt. A small amount of solder is picked up on the end of the iron and starts to melt. The iron is drawn down the joint and the solder flows with it, displacing the flux. The solder then cools and solidifies, joining the two pieces of metal together.

EMBOSSED GREETING CARDS

IT IS CURRENTLY VERY FASHIONABLE TO MAKE GREETING CARDS WITH ALUMINUM FOIL MOTIFS. THE FOIL IS VERY SOFT AND EASY TO CUT WITH SCISSORS. DESIGNS CAN BE DRAWN INTO THE BACK OF THE FOIL TO MAKE A RAISED, EMBOSSED SURFACE THAT IS VERY ATTRACTIVE AND RESEMBLES STAMPED TIN. ANTIQUE ENGRAVINGS ARE A GOOD SOURCE OF INSPIRATION WHEN DECIDING ON MOTIFS, AND BOOKS CONTAINING COLLECTIONS OF OLD DESIGNS CAN BE BOUGHT. THE FOIL IS RELATIVELY CHEAP TO BUY AND CAN BE OBTAINED FROM HOBBY SHOPS AND SCULPTOR'S SUPPLIERS IN VARIOUS THICKNESSES; 0.005 IN IS EASY TO USE, MAKING IT SUITABLE FOR NEW TINWORKERS.

1 Trace the card motifs from the templates on page 403. Tape the tracing to a piece of aluminum foil and place it on top of a piece of thin card. Carefully draw over the lines of the motif with a ballpoint pen to transfer it to the foil.

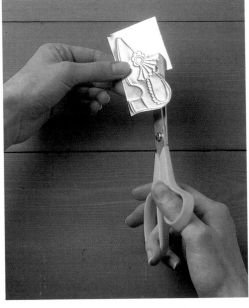

3 Turn the sheet of foil over and cut around the motif, leaving a narrow margin around the outline of the design.

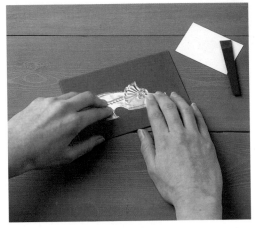

4 Cut a piece of thick colored paper and fold it in half to make a greetings card. Spread a little glue over the back of the foil motif and stick it to the card, embossed side up.

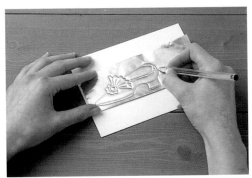

2 Remove the tracing paper from the foil and redraw over the lines of the motif to make the embossing deeper. Add detail to the design at this stage.

MATERIALS AND EQUIPMENT YOU WILL NEED
TRACING PAPER • SOFT PENCIL • MASKING TAPE • 0.005 IN ALUMINUM FOIL • THIN CARD • BALLPOINT PEN •
SCISSORS • THICK COLORED PAPER • ALL-PURPOSE GLUE

CANDLE COLLARS

ANDLE COLLARS ARE A CLEVER MEANS OF MAKING CANDLES AND CANDLESTICKS LOOK EXTREMELY DECORATIVE. THEY CAN BE USED ON A FLAT SURFACE AS A SURROUND FOR SERENE CHURCH CANDLES, OR THEY CAN SIT ATOP A PLAIN CANDLESTICK FOR A TOUCH OF RESTRAINED GLAMOUR. THESE CANDLE COLLARS ARE BASED ON FLOWER AND LEAF FORMS AND ARE EMBOSSED FROM THE BACK IN IMITATION OF VEINING. THE BEADING, THOUGH SEEMINGLY INTRICATE, IS VERY SIMPLE TO ATTACH TO THE SOFT METAL FOIL USING THIN JEWELER'S WIRE. CANDLES CAN BE A FIRE HAZARD, ESPECIALLY IF THEY ARE FREE-STANDING, AND SO THEY SHOULD NEVER BE LEFT TO BURN UNATTENDED.

1 Trace the template on page 403, enlarging it if necessary, then transfer it to thin cardboard and cut out the shape. Tape the template to a piece of copper foil. Draw around the template using a sharp pencil to transfer the shape to the foil.

3 Place the collar facedown on a sheet of thin cardboard. Redraw over the lines of the outer and inner circles using a ballpoint pen. Press a random pattern of dots into the surface of the foil between the two rings. Draw veins on each petal.

2 Remove the template and cut around the outside of the collar. Pierce the centre of the collar using a bradawl. Insert the scissors through the hole and carefully cut out the centre of the collar.

4 Place the embossed collar faceup on a block of wood. Carefully pierce a hole directly below the center of each petal using a bradawl.

5 To attach the beads to the collar, thread a length of fine wire through the first hole in the collar, from the back to the front, leaving a 1 in end. Bend the end back to keep the wire in place. Thread a large glass bead onto the wire, then a smaller bead. Loop the wire over the smaller bead, then back down through the large bead to the back of the collar and on to the next hole. When all the beads are attached, cut the wire, leaving an end. Twist the two ends of the wire together to keep the beads in place.

MATERIALS AND EQUIPMENT YOU WILL NEED

TRACING PAPER • SOFT PENCIL • THIN CARDBOARD • SCISSORS • MASKING TAPE • 0.003 IN COPPER FOIL • SHARP PENCIL • BRADAWL • BALLPOINT PEN • WOODEN BLOCK • FINE JEWELER'S WIRE • GLASS BEADS

PAINTED TIN BROOCHES

A GOOD WAY TO USE UP SMALL SCRAPS OF TIN IS TO MAKE BROOCHES. THESE CAN BE VERY SIMPLE IN CONSTRUCTION AND MADE SPECIAL WITH PAINTED DECORATION. ENAMEL PAINTS ARE VERY OPAQUE AND COVER PREVIOUS COATS OF PAINT BEAUTIFULLY, SO LIGHT COLORS CAN BE PAINTED ON TOP OF DARK VERY SUCCESSFULLY. THIS AFFORDS GREAT FREEDOM OF DESIGN AND THE ONLY RULE TO OBSERVE IS THAT PLENTY OF TIME MUST BE ALLOWED FOR ONE COAT OF PAINT TO DRY BEFORE THE NEXT IS APPLIED. THIS IS ALSO TRUE WHERE DIFFERENT COLORS ARE PAINTED CLOSE TO EACH OTHER; IT IS BEST TO LEAVE SMALL GAPS BETWEEN THE COLORS AND FILL THEM IN WHEN THE PAINT HAS DRIED.

1 To make the brooch front, draw a circle measuring 2 in in diameter freehand on a piece of tin. Wearing a work shirt and protective gloves, cut out the circle using tin clippers.

3 Draw the outline of the sun on to one side of the brooch using a chinagraph pencil. Paint around the outline with enamel paint, then fill in the design. Leave the brooch to dry thoroughly.

5 Seal the surface of the brooch with two coats of clear gloss polyurethane varnish to protect the paint from scratches. Leave the varnish to dry thoroughly before applying the second coat.

2 Clamp the circle of tin in a bench vise and file the edges. Finish off the edges with damp wet and dry sandpaper so that they are completely smooth (see Basic Techniques).

4 Paint the background and the sun's features on top of the first coat of paint, using a fine paintbrush and enamel paint. Leave the brooch to dry thoroughly.

6 Mix some epoxy resin glue and use it to attach a brooch fastener to the back. Let the glue dry thoroughly before wearing the brooch.

MATERIALS AND EQUIPMENT YOU WILL NEED

SCRAP OF 0.01 IN TIN • MAGIC MARKER • WORK SHIRT AND PROTECTIVE LEATHER GLOVES • TIN CLIPPERS • BENCH VISE • FILE • WET AND DRY SANDPAPER • CHINAGRAPH PENCIL • ENAMEL PAINTS • FINE PAINTBRUSHES • CLEAR GLOSS POLYURETHANE VARNISH • EPOXY RESIN GLUE • BROOCH FASTENER

PUNCHED PANEL CABINET

THIS CABINET, WITH ITS PUNCHED TIN PANEL, IS BASED ON THOSE MADE BY THE PENNSYLVANIA DUTCH COMMUNITIES OF AMERICA, WHICH PRODUCED A WIDE RANGE OF HOUSEHOLD ARTIFACTS USING TIN PLATE AND RAISED THE DECORATIVE PUNCHING PROCESS TO AN ART FORM. THEY PUNCHED INDENTATIONS AND HOLES INTO THE METAL FOR AESTHETIC REASONS AND ALSO FOR PRACTICALITY; TO ALLOW AIR TO CIRCULATE AND TO KEEP OUT PESTS IN THE CASE OF CABINETS, OR TO SHED LIGHT FROM TIN LANTERNS. TRADITIONAL PATTERNS SUCH AS HEARTS, TULIPS AND STARS LOOK WONDERFUL PICKED OUT ON THE SURFACE OF THE TIN, OR YOU COULD EXPERIMENT BY DESIGNING YOUR OWN PATTERNS. SIMPLE, UNCLUTTERED DESIGNS WORK BEST; ORNATE, COMPLICATED DESIGNS TEND TO BE A LITTLE CONFUSING TO "READ."

1 Measure the recess in the door of the cabinet. Mark out the dimensions of the recess on the sheet of tin using a magic marker. Draw a ½ in border around the inside of the rectangle. Measure and mark a point ¾ in from each corner of the outer rectangle. Draw diagonal lines from these points to the corners of the inner rectangle.

2 Wearing a work shirt and protective leather gloves, cut the panel from the sheet of tin using tin shears. Cut along diagonal lines at the corners.

3 Firmly clamp the 90° block of wood in the bench vise. Place the panel on the wooden block with the ruled edge of the tin resting on the edge of the block. Using a hide hammer, tap along the edge of the panel to turn it over to an angle of 90°.

▶

MATERIALS AND EQUIPMENT YOU WILL NEED
SMALL WOODEN CABINET WITH A RECESS IN THE DOOR • RULER • SHEET OF 0.01 IN TIN PLATE • MAGIC MARKER •
WORK SHIRT AND PROTECTIVE LEATHER GLOVES • TIN SHEARS • BENCH VISE • 90° AND 45° WOODEN BLOCKS • HIDE HAMMER • FILE •
GRAPH PAPER • SCISSORS • PAIR OF COMPASSES • PENCIL • MASKING TAPE • SHEET OF CHIPBOARD • PANEL PINS • TACK HAMMER •
CENTER PUNCH • BALL HEAD HAMMER • SMALL CHISEL

4 Turn the panel over. Position the 45° wooden block inside the turned edge and hammer the edge over it. Remove the block and hammer the edge completely flat. Finish the remaining three sides of the panel in the same way. Carefully file the corners of the panel to remove any sharp edges.

5 Cut a piece of graph paper the same size as the panel. Using a pair of compasses and a ruler, draw out the panel design on the paper to make a pattern.

6 Tape the paper pattern to the front of the panel. Place the panel faceup on a sheet of chipboard and secure each corner to the board with a panel pin.

7 Place the center punch on one of the lines. Tap the punch with the ball head hammer to make an indentation in the tin. Move the punch about ⅛ in along the line and tap the punch to make the next mark. Continue punching along the lines until the design is completed.

8 Unpin the panel from the board and remove the paper pattern. Pin the panel to the board again and add extra decoration to the front of the panel using a small chisel.

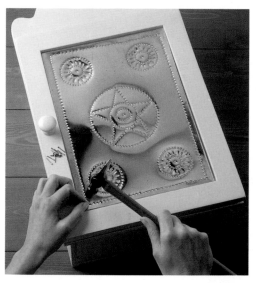

9 Unpin the panel from the board. Place the panel in the recess on the front of the cabinet and attach it to the cabinet with a panel pin at each corner.

INCENSE HOLDER

DEVOTIONAL ARTIFACTS ARE ALWAYS INSPIRATIONAL BECAUSE THEY COMBINE STURDY PRACTICALITY WITH WONDERFUL DECORATIVE DETAIL. THIS ORNATE INCENSE HOLDER IS REMINISCENT OF ECCLESIASTICAL CENSERS, WHICH ARE USED IN RELIGIOUS SERVICES AND PROCESSIONS. TWO COLORS OF METAL FOIL ARE HEAVILY EMBOSSED AND USED TO ENCASE A HUMBLE TIN CAN. TRANSLUCENT GLASS DROPS, WHICH CAN BE PURCHASED FROM HABERDASHERS AND JEWELRY SUPPLIERS, ARE SUSPENDED FROM A FOIL COLLAR TO GIVE A FEELING OF OPULENCE, WHILE THE TIN IS STUDDED WITH SMALL FLOWERS WITH CABOCHON CENTERS. THIS HOLDER IS DESIGNED TO BURN SMALL INCENSE CONES, WHICH SIT INSIDE THE CAN IN A METAL BOTTLE CAP. SMOLDERING INCENSE CAN BE A FIRE HAZARD AND SHOULD NOT BE LEFT TO BURN UNATTENDED.

1 Using a can opener, remove one end of the tin can. Carefully file around the inside top edge of the tin to remove metal burrs or rough edges. To make the covering for the tin, cut a rectangle of aluminum foil as wide as the tin and long enough to fit around it with ½ in to spare.

2 Using this pattern as a guide, draw a design on graph paper. Repeat the pattern to fit around the tin and cut it out. Tape the aluminum foil to a sheet of cardboard. Tape the pattern over the top and draw over the lines using a ballpoint pen. Press quite hard so that the pattern will be embossed onto the foil.

3 Cut a shorter, narrower rectangle of aluminum foil to make the lower section. Draw the decorative pattern for this section on graph paper. Cut out the paper pattern and transfer it to the narrower strip of aluminum foil as before, using a ballpoint pen.

▶

MATERIALS AND EQUIPMENT YOU WILL NEED

CAN OPENER • SMALL TIN CAN • FILE • 0.005 IN ALUMINUM FOIL • SCISSORS • PENCIL • GRAPH PAPER •
MASKING TAPE • THIN CARDBOARD • BALLPOINT PEN • 0.003 IN COPPER FOIL • EPOXY RESIN GLUE • WOODEN POLE •
BENCH VICE • BRADAWL • THIN METAL CHAIN • 3 CHAIN TRIANGLES • PLIERS • KEY RING • SMALL COLORED GLASS DROPS AND STONES •
CARDBOARD TUBE • METAL BOTTLE CAP

4 Draw a flower pattern on thin white cardboard and cut it out to make a template. Draw around the template on copper foil and cut out the shape. Cut as many flowers as you need to fit around the tin. Place the flowers on thin cardboard and draw lines on the petals to make a decoration.

5 Glue the covering around the tin using epoxy resin glue. When the glue is dry, firmly clamp a short length of wooden pole in a bench vise. Rest the tin on the pole and make three holes at equal distances in the top edge using a bradawl. File around the edges of the holes to make them smooth.

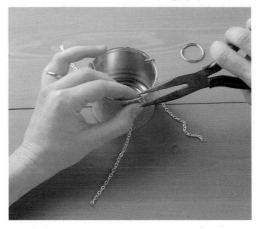

6 Cut three 5 in lengths of chain. Fix a chain triangle through each hole in the top of the tin and, using pliers, attach a length of chain to each. Attach the other ends of the chains to a key ring.

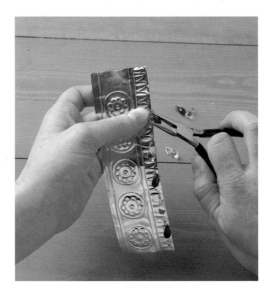

7 Make a hole every ¾ in along the bottom edge of the lower section of the burner using a bradawl. Attach a small glass drop to each hole.

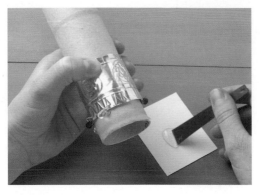

8 Snip tabs along the top edge of the lower section of the aluminum foil. Wrap it around a cardboard tube and glue the edges together. Leave to dry and remove from the tube. Bend out the tabs and glue to the underside of the tin.

9 Glue the copper flowers around the tin with the raised surfaces facing out. Glue a glass stone in the center of each flower, alternating the colors of the stones.

10 To make a holder for the incense cone, glue a metal bottle cap to the inside center of the tin.

PHOTOGRAPH FRAME

BECAUSE OF ITS SOFTNESS, FINE-GAUGE ALUMINIUM FOIL IS THE PERFECT MATERIAL FOR COVERING FRAMES. COLORED AND CLEAR GLASS NUGGETS COMBINE WITH THE SUBDUED TONES OF THE FOIL TO GIVE THIS FRAME A CELTIC AIR, FURTHER REINFORCED BY A DESIGN OF REPEATING CIRCLES, A FUNDAMENTAL ELEMENT OF CELTIC DECORATIVE ART. UNTIL RECENTLY, GLASS NUGGETS, A STAPLE MATERIAL OF STAINED GLASS ARTISTS, WERE DIFFICULT TO FIND. NOW THEY ARE POPULAR AS A DECORATIVE DEVICE IN THEIR OWN RIGHT, ESPECIALLY IN CONJUNCTION WITH FLOATING CANDLES, AND ARE WIDELY AVAILABLE IN A VARIETY OF COLORS, FINISHES AND SIZES.

1 Remove the glass and backing from the frame. Measure the four sides and cut strips of foil to cover them, making the foil long enough to wrap over and under, to the back. Mold the foil strips around the frame and glue them in place.

2 Cut pieces of foil to cover the corners. Mold these to the contours of the frame and glue them in place.

3 Draw a circle on cardboard. Cut out the circle to make a template. Draw around the cardboard onto the foil using a ballpoint pen. Cut out the foil circles. Draw a design on one side of each circle. This is now the back of the circle.

4 Turn the foil circles over so that the raised side of the embossing is faceup. Glue colored glass nuggets to the center fronts of half of the foil circles. Glue plain glass nuggets to the centers of the other half.

5 Glue the foil circles around the frame, spacing them evenly. Alternate the circles so that a colored glass center follows one with clear glass. When the glue is thoroughly dry, replace the glass and backing in the frame.

MATERIALS AND EQUIPMENT YOU WILL NEED

PHOTOGRAPH FRAME • RULER • 0.005 IN ALUMINUM FOIL • SCISSORS • EPOXY RESIN GLUE • PENCIL • THIN CARDBOARD • BALLPOINT PEN • COLORED AND CLEAR GLASS NUGGETS

LANTERN

THIS TIN CAN LANTERN IS REMINISCENT OF MOROCCAN LANTERNS THAT HAVE SIMILAR CURLICUES AND PUNCHED HOLES. A COLD CHISEL AND HEAVY HAMMER ARE USED TO CUT VENTILATION HOLES OUT OF THE METAL OF THE LANTERN ROOF. THIS ALLOWS HEAT TO ESCAPE AND PROJECTS DANCING SHADOWS ONTO WALLS AND CEILINGS. THE MATERIALS NEEDED FOR THE LANTERN ARE VERY HUMBLE: A LARGE TIN CAN, FINE WIRE AND SCRAPS OF ALUMINUM SHEET AND TIN PLATE COMBINE WONDERFULLY TO MAKE AN ATTRACTIVE LIGHT SOURCE AND FOCUS IN A ROOM. CANDLES CAN BE A FIRE HAZARD AND SHOULD NEVER BE LEFT TO BURN UNATTENDED.

1 Using a can opener, remove one end of the tin can. To make an aperture for the door of the lantern, mark out a rectangle on the front of the can. Wearing a work shirt and protective gloves, cut out the rectangle using tin shears.

2 Using pliers, turn over all the edges around the aperture to make the lantern safe. File away any remaining rough edges to make them safe.

3 To make the lantern lid, draw a semicircle on a scrap of aluminum sheet. The radius of the semicircle should be equal to the diameter of the tin can. Cut out the shape using tin shears and carefully file the edges smooth.

MATERIALS AND EQUIPMENT YOU WILL NEED

CAN OPENER • LARGE TIN CAN • MAGIC MARKER • WORK SHIRT AND PROTECTIVE LEATHER GLOVES • TIN SHEARS •
PLIERS • FILE • THIN ALUMINUM SHEET • PAIR OF COMPASSES • PENCIL • SHEET OF CHIPBOARD • PROTECTIVE GOGGLES •
COLD CHISEL • HAMMER • NAIL OR CENTER PUNCH • SCRAP OF THIN TIN • SOLDERING MAT • FLUX •
SOLDERING IRON AND SOLDER • FINE WIRE • WIRE CUTTERS

4 Lay the lid on a sheet of chipboard. Wearing goggles, cut ventilation holes in the lid using a cold chisel and hammer. File the sides of all the holes to remove any rough edges.

5 Using a hammer and nail or center punch, punch holes around the top edge of the lantern and around the bottom and the curved edge of the lid. File away all the rough edges around the holes.

6 To make a candle holder for the inside of the lantern, cut a strip of tin. File the edges of the strip and curve it around to make a circle. Place the lantern on a soldering mat. Apply flux to the join. Wearing a protective mask and goggles, solder the holder inside the lantern.

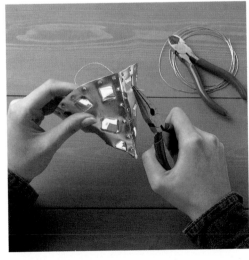

7 Gently curve the lid around to make a cone. Using a pair of pliers, thread fine wire through the holes in the lid to join the sides together.

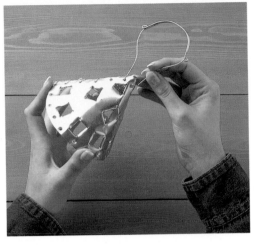

8 For the handle, cut a length of wire, then cut two shorter pieces. Make a loop in either end of the shorter pieces, then center them on either side of the longer wire and solder in place. Curve them slightly, then thread the ends through the holes in the top of the lid and twist them into tight spirals inside to secure the handle.

9 Attach the lid to the lantern using fine wire. Pull the wire tight using pliers.

►

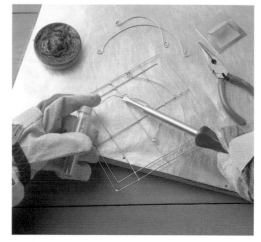

10 For the door, make a decorative rectangular frame from lengths of fine wire. The frame must be slightly taller and wider than the aperture. Lay the frame on a soldering mat and solder all the sections together. When the door is complete, gently curve it to the shape of the lantern.

12 For the latch, make a hook and a "U"-shaped catch from short lengths of wire using pliers. Solder the catch to the side of the lantern and attach the hook to the door frame.

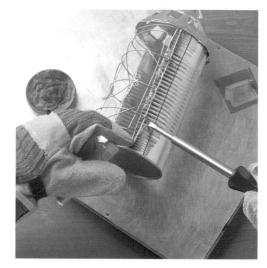

11 To make hinges for the door, use pliers to bend two short lengths of wire into "U" shapes and bend down each end of the "U" shapes at right angles. Solder one end of each hinge to the lantern. Place the door inside the hinges so that it rests on the hinges and doesn't drop down. Solder the other end of the hinges to the lantern.

CHRISTMAS DECORATIONS

THESE TWINKLY CHRISTMAS DECORATIONS ARE INSPIRED BY EASTERN EUROPEAN ARCHITECTURE AND FOLK ART. STAMPED AND DIE-CUT ARTIFACTS WERE VERY POPULAR IN MANY EUROPEAN COUNTRIES IN THE NINETEENTH CENTURY, WHEN THERE WOULD HAVE BEEN A TINWORKER IN EVERY VILLAGE. THE DECORATIONS ARE MADE OF THIN FOIL WHICH CAN BE POLISHED WITH A SOFT CLOTH AFTER EMBOSSING TO BRIGHTEN THE METAL. THERE ARE MANY TRADITIONAL FOLK ART MOTIFS THAT COULD BE USED TO CONTINUE THE SET OF DECORATIONS, SUCH AS HEARTS, BIRDS AND FLOWERS. LOOK TO EASTERN EUROPEAN EMBROIDERY, AMERICAN FOLK ART AND COUNTRY FURNITURE FOR INSPIRATION.

1 Trace the outline from the template on page 404, enlarge if necessary, and it to thin cardboard. Cut it out to make a template. Cut a small piece of aluminum foil. Place the template on the foil and draw around the outside using a sharp pencil.

3 Using the picture as a guide, carefully mark the basic lines of the design on the back of the decoration using a magic marker and ruler.

5 Using the picture as a guide, draw the details of the house on the back of the decoration using a ballpoint pen.

2 Using embroidery scissors, cut out the foil shape. Cut slowly and carefully to ensure that there are no rough edges around the decoration.

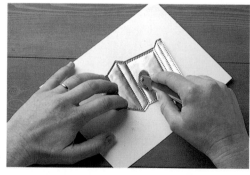

4 Place the decoration facedown on a sheet of thin cardboard. Carefully trace over the pen lines with a dressmaker's wheel to emboss a row of raised dots on the front of the decoration. Trace a second line of dots inside the first, in the center of the decoration.

6 Place the decoration faceup on a small block of wood. Using a bradawl, carefully make a hole in the top of the decoration. Tie a length of fine wire through the hole to make a hanger.

MATERIALS AND EQUIPMENT YOU WILL NEED

TRACING PAPER • SOFT PENCIL • THIN CARDBOARD • SCISSORS • 0.005 IN ALUMINUM FOIL • SHARP PENCIL •
EMBROIDERY SCISSORS • MAGIC MARKER • RULER • DRESSMAKER'S WHEEL • BALLPOINT PEN •
WOODEN BLOCK • BRADAWL • FINE WIRE

PAINTED MIRROR

PAINTED TINWARE IS PART OF THE POPULAR ART OF MANY COUNTRIES, PARTICULARLY INDIA AND LATIN AMERICA, WHERE FINE-GAUGE TIN IS STAMPED WITH DECORATIVE PATTERNS AND OFTEN HIGHLIGHTED WITH TRANSLUCENT PAINTS. THIS MIRROR FRAME FOLLOWS THE TRADITION. IT IS PUNCHED FROM BOTH THE BACK AND THE FRONT, WHICH RAISES SOME SECTIONS OF THE METAL TO MAKE A LOW RELIEF SURFACE. THE TRANSLUCENT PAINTS USED TO DECORATE THE FRAME ARE MADE PRIMARILY FOR PAINTING GLASSWARE BUT ARE SUITABLE FOR USE ON METAL AS WELL. THE PAINT SHOULD BE APPLIED SPARINGLY SO THAT THE SHEEN OF THE TIN IS STILL VISIBLE THROUGH THE COLORED SURFACE.

1 To make the mirror frame, measure out a 12 in square on a sheet of tin. Draw a ½ in border inside the square. Measure a point ¾ in from each corner of the outer square. Draw diagonal lines from these points to the corners of the smaller square. Wearing a work shirt and protective gloves, cut the square from the sheet of tin with tin shears. Cut along the diagonal lines at the corners.

2 Firmly clamp the 90° block of wood in a bench vise. Place the mirror frame on the wooden block with the ruled edge of the tin resting on the edge of the block. Using a hide hammer, tap along the edge of the tin to turn it over to an angle of 90°.

3 Turn the frame over. Hold the 45° block of wood inside the turned edge and hammer the edge over. Remove the block and hammer the edge completely flat. Finish the remaining three edges of the frame in the same way. Carefully file the corners of the mirror frame to remove any sharp edges.

▶

MATERIALS AND EQUIPMENT YOU WILL NEED
SHEET OF 0.01 IN TIN PLATE • MAGIC MARKER • RULER • WORK SHIRT AND PROTECTIVE LEATHER GLOVES • TIN SHEARS • 90° AND 45° WOODEN BLOCKS • BENCH VISE • HIDE HAMMER • FILE • GRAPH PAPER • SCISSORS • SAUCER • PENCIL • MASKING TAPE • SHEET OF CHIPBOARD • PANEL PINS • TACK HAMMER • CENTER PUNCH • BALL HEAD HAMMER • CHINAGRAPH PENCIL • SOFT CLOTH • TRANSLUCENT PAINTS • PAINTBRUSH • SQUARE MIRROR TILE • 0.005 IN ALUMINUM FOIL • EPOXY RESIN GLUE • 0.003 IN COPPER FOIL • D-RING HANGER

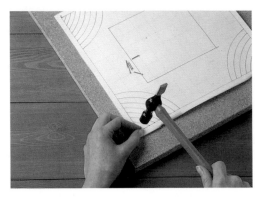

8 Lay the mirror tile on aluminum foil and draw around it. Draw a ⅜ in border around the outline. Cut out the foil, snipping the corners at right angles.

4 Cut a piece of graph paper the same size as the frame. Using a saucer as a template, draw the decorative corner lines on the paper. Draw in the central square which should be slightly larger than the mirror tile. Tape the pattern to the back of the frame. Lay the frame facedown on the chipboard and secure with a panel pins.

6 Unpin the frame from the board and remove the paper pattern. Using a chinagraph pencil, draw a square halfway along each edge between the corner decorations. Draw a heart in each square. Pin the frame to the board again and punch an outline around each square and heart. Randomly punch the border between the heart and the square to make a densely pitted surface.

9 Glue the tile to the center of the foil. Glue the edges of the foil over the tile. Cut four small squares of copper foil and glue one square in each corner of the tile.

5 Place the point of the center punch on a line of the inside square and tap it with the ball hammer to make an indentation. Move the punch about ⅛ in along the line and tap it to make the next mark. Continue punching along all the lines until the design is completed.

7 Remove the frame from the board. Wipe over the surface of the metal with a soft cloth to remove any grease. Paint the embossed areas of the frame with translucent paint. Leave the paint to dry thoroughly and apply a second coat if the first is patchy.

10 Glue the mirror to the center of the frame. Glue the hanger to the back of the frame. Allow the glue to dry thoroughly before hanging up the mirror.

SPICE RACK

THIS HANDSOME SPICE RACK IS MADE FROM A COOKIE TIN. UNWANTED FOOD CONTAINERS ARE A GOOD SOURCE OF TIN AND ARE PERFECT FOR THIS SORT OF ITEM, AS THEY ARE ALREADY PARTLY FORMED INTO THE RIGHT SHAPE. SOME TINS ARE BRIGHTLY COLORED AND, IF YOU DON'T WANT TO INCORPORATE THIS CHARACTERISTIC INTO THE DESIGN OF YOUR FINISHED ITEM, IT IS OFTEN POSSIBLE TO REMOVE THE DECORATION USING PAINT STRIPPER. WEAR PROTECTIVE CLOTHING AND WORK IN A WELL-VENTILATED AREA IF YOU DO THIS.

1 Wearing a work shirt and protective gloves, carefully cut the base of the cookie tin in half using tin shears. File all the cut edges smooth.

2 Draw the curved shape of the back panel of the spice rack on the lid of the box. Cut it out using tin shears. File all the cut edges smooth. Place the back of the spice rack in position against the cut edge of one half of the cookie tin. Hold the two together with strips of masking tape.

3 Place the spice rack on a soldering mat. Wearing a protective mask and goggles, apply flux along the join and solder the two parts together. Carefully turn over the filed edges of the back panel and the base using pliers. Squeeze the turned edges firmly between the pliers to flatten them completely. File any remaining rough edges smooth.

▶

MATERIALS AND EQUIPMENT YOU WILL NEED

WORK SHIRT AND PROTECTIVE LEATHER GLOVES • COOKIE TIN • TIN SHEARS • FILE • MAGIC MARKER • MASKING TAPE • SCISSORS • SOLDERING MAT • FLUX • PROTECTIVE MASK AND GOGGLES • SOLDERING IRON AND SOLDER • PLIERS • RULER OR TAPE MEASURE • FINE WIRE • WIRE CUTTERS • WOODEN BLOCK • BRADAWL • SCRAP OF BRASS SHIM • SUPERGLUE

4 Measure the dimensions of the inside of the spice rack. Cut lengths of fine wire and solder them together to make a grid to form compartments for the spice bottles.

6 Place the top edge of the rack on a block of wood and pierce a hole in it using a bradawl. Open the hole slightly using a pair of pliers. File away the rough edges around the inside of the hole. Turn over the edges around the hole and squeeze them flat using the pliers.

8 Cut a small circle of shim and glue it to the center back of the rack. Apply decorative blobs of solder to the shim circle, along the edges of the rack and around the wire spiral and curves.

5 Place the grid inside the spice rack and carefully solder it in place.

7 Cut a long length of fine wire and curve it into a spiral shape using pliers. Cut six lengths of wire and form two large and two small curves and two small circles. Solder the spiral to the back of the rack and the curves to the front. Shape a piece of wire to fit around the edges of the back of the tin and solder it in place.

NUMBER PLAQUE

THE RISING SUN, A VERY POPULAR DOMESTIC ART DECO MOTIF IN THE 1930s, HAS BEEN INCORPORATED INTO THE DESIGN OF THIS DOOR NUMBER PLAQUE. INDENTATIONS ARE PUNCHED INTO THE FRONT OF THE PLAQUE TO CREATE A DENSELY PITTED, DEPRESSED SURFACE IN THE TIN AND TO RAISE THE UNPUNCHED AREAS SLIGHTLY. THIS IS A SIMPLE FORM OF CHASING, AN ANCIENT METALWORKING TECHNIQUE WHERE DEFINITION IS GIVEN TO A DECORATIVE DESIGN BY RAISING AND INDENTING AREAS OF THE METAL SO THAT THE DESIGN STANDS OUT IN RELIEF. AFTER THE DESIGN HAS BEEN PUNCHED INTO THE PLAQUE, THE SURFACE OF THE TIN IS SCOURED WITH STEEL WOOL FOR A MORE MATTE FINISH.

1 Draw a rectangle on a sheet of tin. Draw a ½ in border around the inside of the rectangle. Measure a point 1 in from each corner of the outer rectangle. Draw diagonal lines across the corners. Wearing protective clothing, cut out the plaque. Cut out the corners.

3 Turn the plaque over and position the 45° wooden block inside the turned edge. Hammer the edge over it, remove the block and then hammer the edge completely flat. Finish the remaining three sides of the plaque in the same way. Carefully file the corners to make them smooth.

5 Place the center punch on a line and tap it with a ball hammer to make an indentation. Move the punch about ⅛ in along the line and tap it again to make the next mark. Continue to punch along the lines until the design is completed.

2 Firmly clamp the 90° block of wood in a bench vise. Place the plaque on the wooden block with the ruled edge of the tin resting on the edge of the block. Using a hide hammer, tap along the edge of the plaque to turn it over to an angle of 90°.

4 Cut a piece of graph paper the same size as the plaque. Draw in your pattern and desired numbers. Tape the pattern to the front of the plaque. Secure it to the chipboard with a panel pin in each corner.

6 Remove the paper pattern, then randomly punch the surface around the sunburst and inside the numbers. Scour the surface of the panel with steel wool before sealing the plaque with varnish.

MATERIALS AND EQUIPMENT YOU WILL NEED

SHEET OF 0.01 IN TIN PLATE • MAGIC MARKER • RULER • WORK SHIRT AND PROTECTIVE LEATHER GLOVES • TIN SHEARS •
90° AND 45° WOODEN BLOCKS • BENCH VISE • HIDE HAMMER • FILE • GRAPH PAPER • PENCIL • MASKING TAPE • SHEET OF CHIPBOARD • PANEL PINS •
TACK HAMMER • CENTER PUNCH • BALL HEAD HAMMER • STEEL WOOL • CLEAR POLYURETHANE VARNISH • PAINTBRUSH

REINDEER

THIS CHARMING REINDEER IS MADE FROM ZINC PLATE, THAT IS THIN ENOUGH TO CURVE AND MANIPULATE EASILY. ZINC PLATE IS STEEL THAT HAS BEEN COATED WITH A THIN LAYER OF ZINC TO PROTECT IT FROM CORROSION. THIS GIVES THE METAL AN ATTRACTIVE MATTE APPEARANCE. ZINC PLATE IS AVAILABLE FROM HARDWARE STORES, METAL MERCHANTS AND BUILDING SUPPLIERS IN VARIOUS WEIGHTS. CHOOSE A THIN GAUGE, SINCE YOU WILL NEED TO BEND THE METAL. TAKE EXTRA CARE WHEN SOLDERING THE REINDEER: ZINC CAN GIVE OFF NOXIOUS FUMES WHEN IT IS HEATED. WEAR A FACE MASK AND GOGGLES AS USUAL AND WORK IN A VERY WELL VENTILATED AREA, TAKING FREQUENT BREAKS.

1 Trace the head and body templates from from page 404, enlarge them if transfer them to thin cardboard. Cut out the shapes to make templates. Draw around each template onto a sheet of thin zinc plate using a marker pen. Wearing a work shirt and protective gloves, cut out the head and body using tin clippers. Carefully file all the edges and the corners to make them completely smooth. Draw and cut out two ears.

2 Place a paintbrush in the middle of each leg and the tail and gently tap it with a small hammer to curve the metal and make a cylinder. Curve the reindeer's body. The reindeer will now stand upright. Lay the reindeer on a soldering mat and apply flux to the joins. Wearing a protective mask and goggles, spot solder along the inside of each leg and the body.

3 Take the head piece and gently curve the reindeer's neck to make a cylinder. Hold the edges together with masking tape while you spot-solder along the join. Gently bend the head down and curve the sides to make it cylindrical.

▶

MATERIALS AND EQUIPMENT YOU WILL NEED
TRACING PAPER • SOFT PENCIL • THIN CARDBOARD • SCISSORS • THIN ZINC PLATE • MAGIC MARKER •
WORK SHIRT AND PROTECTIVE LEATHER GLOVES • TIN CLIPPERS • FILE • PAINTBRUSHES • SMALL HAMMER • SOLDERING MAT • FLUX •
PROTECTIVE MASK AND GOGGLES • SOLDERING IRON AND SOLDER • MASKING TAPE • FINE WIRE • WIRE CUTTERS •
PLIERS • ENAMEL PAINTS

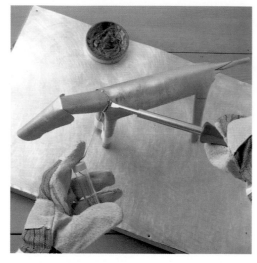

4 Place the head section inside the body. Wrap a strip of masking tape around the two front legs to pull them tightly together so that the head fits snugly inside the body. Solder along the join where the neck meets the body.

5 To make the reindeer's antlers, cut two long pieces of fine wire and 14 shorter pieces. Bend the shorter pieces into diamond shapes. Solder the wire diamonds to the two long pieces of wire. Using masking tape to keep them in place, solder the antlers to the sides of the reindeer's head. Reshape them after soldering to make them slightly irregular.

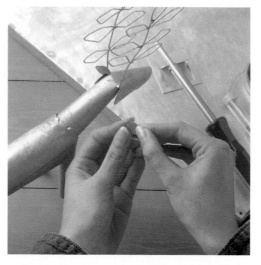

6 Gently curve the reindeer's ears and solder them to its head next to the antlers. Hold them in position with small pieces of masking tape while you work.

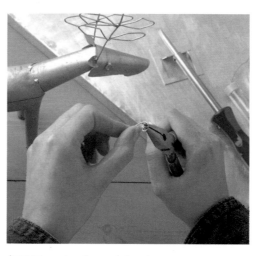

7 To make the reindeer's eyes, cut two short pieces of wire and twist them around the end of a pair of pliers to make spirals. Solder the reindeer's eyes to the sides of the head.

8 Paint the reindeer, except for its antlers, with two coats of red enamel paint, allowing the first coat to dry before adding the second.

9 When the red paint is dry, paint blue spots on the reindeer's body. Paint its ears and hooves yellow and its nose green. Paint a black line around the nose and the hooves and paint the reindeer's antlers blue.

BATHROOM SHELF

THIS CLASSIC BATHROOM SHELF IS CONSTRUCTED VERY SIMPLY FROM FIBERBOARD, WHICH CAN BE PRIMED AND PAINTED IN THE SAME WAY AS WOOD. IT IS ADORNED WITH TIN FISH AND SHELL CUTOUTS THAT HAVE BEEN PUNCHED FROM THE BACK TO GIVE A LOW-RELIEF DECORATIVE SURFACE. TIN PLATE IS SUITABLE FOR AREAS WHERE WATER IS PRESENT, AS THE TIN COATING PREVENTS THE METAL FROM TARNISHING IN DAMP, STEAMY CONDITIONS. A MIRROR IS STUCK TO THE SHELF TO ADD TO THE DECORATION. THIS SHELF IS ATTACHED TO THE BATHROOM WALL USING MIRROR PLATES AND SO SHOULD ONLY BE USED TO SUPPORT LIGHTWEIGHT OBJECTS SUCH AS TOOTHBRUSH MUGS AND SHAVING EQUIPMENT.

1 Draw out the templates for the back and ledge of the bathroom shelf on squared graph paper to make a pattern for each. The back is 16 in high at the sides and 12 in wide. The ledge is the same width as the back and 6 in deep at its widest point. Cut out the patterns and draw around them onto the sheet of fiberboard. Saw out the shapes and smooth the edges using fine sandpaper.

2 Measure the outside dimensions of the mirror tile. Cut four lengths of battening strip to make a recess for the tile. Using strong wood glue, attach the battening strips to the panel. Pin the corners with small panel pins for extra strength. Glue and pin the ledge to the bottom edge of the back panel.

3 Seal the surface of the bathroom shelf with one coat of wood primer. Lightly sand the surface of the shelf and paint it with satin-finish wood paint.

▶

MATERIALS AND EQUIPMENT YOU WILL NEED

PENCIL • GRAPH PAPER • SCISSORS • SHEET OF ½ IN MEDIUM-DENSITY FIBERBOARD • HANDSAW • FINE SANDPAPER • MIRROR TILE • RULER • 1 x ¹⁄₁₆ IN BATTENING STRIPS • WOOD GLUE • PANEL PINS • TACK HAMMER • WOOD PRIMER • PAINTBRUSH • SATIN-FINISH WOOD PAINT • TRACING PAPER • THIN CARDBOARD • WORK SHIRT AND PROTECTIVE LEATHER GLOVES • 0.01 IN TIN PLATE • FINE MAGIC MARKER • TIN CLIPPERS • BENCH VISE • SMALL FILE • WET AND DRY PAPER • WOODEN BLOCK • CHINAGRAPH PENCIL • SHEET OF CHIPBOARD • MASKING TAPE • CENTER PUNCH • BALL HEAD HAMMER • EPOXY RESIN GLUE • 2 MIRROR PLATES

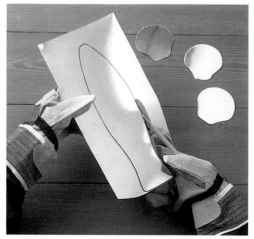

4 Trace the fish and shell templates from page 404, enlarging them if necessary. Transfer them to thin cardboard and cut them out. Wearing a work shirt and protective leather gloves, cut pieces of tin plate approximately the same size as the templates. Draw around the templates on the tin using a fine magic marker. Draw one fish and five shells. Carefully cut out the fish and shell shapes using tin clippers.

5 Clamp each shape firmly in a bench vise. Using a small file, work around each shape removing any metal burrs and rough edges. Finish off the edges with a damp piece of wet and dry paper, wrapped around a wooden block. They should be perfectly smooth with no sharp edges.

6 Draw in the decorative designs on the back of each shell and the fish with a chinagraph pencil.

7 Tape the fish and shells facedown on a sheet of chipboard. Place the center punch on a line and tap it with the ball hammer to make an indentation. Continue punching along the lines, leaving about ⅛ in between each indentation. Punch designs into the shells in the same way.

8 Lay the fish and shell shapes in position around the bathroom shelf. Attach them to the shelf using panel pins and a tack hammer.

9 Using epoxy resin glue, stick the mirror tile into the recess in the shelf back. Press the tile firmly into place. Let the glue dry thoroughly, then screw a mirror plate to either side of the shelf.

EMBOSSED BOOK JACKET

THE APPEARANCE OF A PLAIN NOTEBOOK OR PHOTOGRAPH ALBUM CAN BE DRAMATICALLY ENHANCED WITH AN EMBOSSED METAL PANEL. THE PANEL COVERING THIS BOOK IMITATES THE ORNATE LEATHER AND METAL BINDINGS ADORNING EARLY BIBLES AND PRAYER BOOKS. THESE WERE OFTEN STUDDED WITH SEMIPRECIOUS STONES, A LOOK THAT CAN BE ACHIEVED BY USING COLORED GLASS CABOCHONS, AVAILABLE FROM JEWELERS' SUPPLIERS. GOLD LACQUER PAINT HAS BEEN USED TO HIGHLIGHT SMALL AREAS OF THE EMBOSSED PATTERN TO GIVE IT A RICH, BYZANTINE FEEL. SIMPLE TEMPLATES ARE USED TO EMBOSS THE BASIC PATTERN INTO THE PANEL, THEN MORE DETAIL IS ADDED FREEHAND.

1 Cut a piece of aluminum foil the same size as the front of the book. Using a soft magic marker and a ruler, draw a ³⁄₁₆ in border all the way around the edge of the foil. Divide the rectangle into squares. Using a ruler and ballpoint pen, redraw over the lines to emboss the foil. This is now the back of the jacket.

2 Draw a circle and a rectangle on cardboard. They should be small enough to fit into the grid squares. Then draw another slightly smaller circle and square. Cut out the shapes.

3 Place the larger round template in the center of the first square. Carefully draw around it using a ballpoint pen. Repeat with the larger rectangle in the next square. Alternate the shapes to cover the whole jacket.

4 Lay the smaller round template inside the embossed circles and draw around it. Place the smaller rectangle template inside the larger rectangles and emboss all the shapes in the same way.

5 Draw a small double circle and double semicircles inside each circle. Draw a double oval and radiating lines inside each rectangle. Emboss a dotted line around each rectangle and around the edge of the jacket.

6 Turn the jacket over so that it is faceup. Using a fine brush, highlight small areas of the design with gold lacquer paint. When the paint is thoroughly dry, glue the jacket to the front of the book.

MATERIALS AND EQUIPMENT YOU WILL NEED

SHEET OF 0.005 IN ALUMINUM FOIL • SCISSORS • SOFT MAGIC MARKER • RULER • BALLPOINT PEN •
PENCIL • THIN CARDBOARD • FINE PAINTBRUSH • GOLD LACQUER PAINT • EPOXY RESIN GLUE

HERB CONTAINER

THIS BRIGHTLY PAINTED HERB CONTAINER IS MADE FROM RECYCLED TIN CANS, WHICH ARE HAMMERED FLAT AND SOLDERED TOGETHER TO MAKE A BOX. THE TOP EDGES ARE BOUND WITH FINE WIRE, AND WIRE IS ALSO USED TO MAKE SEEDS AND PETALS FOR THE FLOWERS. THE CONTAINER HAS AN APPEALING FOLK ART BRIGHTNESS AND CHARM THAT WOULD SIT WELL IN ANY KITCHEN. PUNCHED HOLES IN THE BOTTOM ALLOW FOR WATER DRAINAGE, AND THE BOX WILL HOLD THREE SMALL POTS OF HERBS QUITE COMFORTABLY. THE CONTAINER IS FOR INSIDE USE ONLY. IT IS SOMETHING THAT WOULD LOOK GOOD STANDING ON A SUNNY WINDOWSILL FOR A READY SUPPLY OF FRESH HERBS.

1 Using a can opener, remove the tops and bottoms from four tin cans. Wearing a work shirt and protective gloves, cut the tins open down one side using tin shears. Place the tin panels on a sheet of chipboard and flatten them using a hide hammer. File all the edges of the tins to make them completely smooth.

2 Use one flattened piece of tin to make the base. Bend the other three tins around the base to make a box shape. Hold all the sections of the box together with strips of masking tape. Place the box on a soldering mat, apply flux to the join and, wearing a protective mask and goggles, solder the sections together.

3 Cut four strips of thin tin plate the same length as the sides of the box base and file the edges smooth. Lay each strip along the edge of a long block of wood and hammer it over to make a right angle along its length.

MATERIALS AND EQUIPMENT YOU WILL NEED

CAN OPENER • 4 TIN CANS • WORK SHIRT AND PROTECTIVE LEATHER GLOVES • TIN SHEARS • SHEET OF CHIPBOARD • HIDE HAMMER • FILE •
MASKING TAPE • PROTECTIVE MASK AND GOGGLES • SOLDERING MAT • FLUX • SOLDERING IRON AND SOLDER • THIN TIN PLATE •
BLOCK OF WOOD • SMALL HAMMER • BRADAWL • FINE WIRE • WIRE CUTTERS • PLIERS • CLOTHESPINS • ENAMEL PAINTS • PAINTBRUSH

4 Solder the strips of tin around the base of the box and then carefully file all the corners to remove any sharp edges. Using a bradawl, punch two holes in the bottom of the box for drainage and file around the holes to remove the rough edges.

5 Cut three lengths of fine wire long enough to fit around the sides and front of the top of the box. Bend the pieces of wire to the same shape as the box and solder them together.

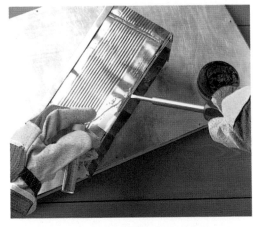

6 Solder the wires around the side and front edges of the top of the box.

7 To make the flower heads, cut three circles of thin tin about the same size as the tops of the cans. File all the edges smooth. Cut short lengths of wire and twist them around the end of a pair of pliers to make seed shapes.

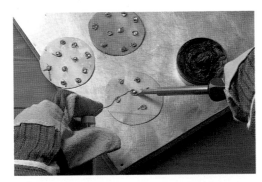

8 Place the seeds on the flower heads. Drop a dot of solder in the center of each seed to join it to the head.

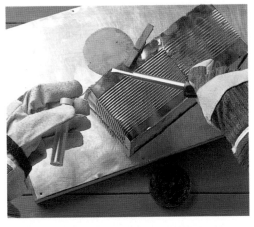

9 Solder the flower heads to the back of the box. Hold them in position using clothespins as you work.

10 Cut three lengths of wire long enough to fit around the flower heads. Using your fingers, make long loops of wire for petals. Solder the petals at equal distances along each length of wire. ▶

11 Bend the wire petals around the flower heads and solder them to the back of the box. Use clothespins to keep the petals in position while you work.

13 Solder the stems to the front and sides of the box. Paint the box using blue enamel paint.

12 To make the flower stems, cut five lengths of wire the same height as the front and sides of the container. Use your fingers to make six wire leaf shapes for each stem. Solder the leaves to the stems.

14 When the blue paint has dried, paint the stems white and the petals red. Paint the flower heads yellow and paint the seeds black. Paint the strip around the base of the box red.

WALL SCONCE

THIS SIMPLE, ELEGANT SCONCE IS MADE FROM SMALL FLUTED PUDDING MOLDS. THE SHINY RIPPLED SURFACES REFLECT AND INTENSIFY THE CANDLELIGHT BEAUTIFULLY. CATERING SUPPLIERS STOCK ALL SORTS OF MOLDS FOR CONFECTIONERY, COOKIES AND CAKES, AND LOTS OF INTERESTING SHAPES ARE AVAILABLE. THE MOLDS ARE VERY SIMPLY JOINED USING FINE WIRE AND POP RIVETS, AND A WIRE LOOP IS ADDED TO SUSPEND THE SCONCE FROM THE WALL. CANDLES CAN BE A FIRE HAZARD AND SHOULD NEVER BE LEFT TO BURN UNATTENDED.

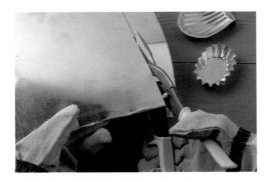

1 Wearing a work shirt and protective gloves, cut an 8 in strip of thin tin about ¼ in wider than the base of the scallop mold. Carefully turn over and flatten the long sides of the strip using pliers. File the corners smooth.

3 Line up the holes in the mold and the tin strip and pop-rivet the two together.

5 Place the mold on the shelf and mark where the edge of the mold comes to and the position of the holes. Drill two holes in the shelf and file the edges smooth. Cut off the excess tin strip and file the edge smooth. Pop-rivet the mold to the shelf.

2 Place the tin strip on a block of wood. Hold the edge with pliers and drill two holes in one end of the strip. File the holes smooth. Bend forward the lip of the scallop mold using pliers. Place the tin strip on the lip and mark where the holes are. Drill holes in the mold and file them smooth.

4 Using pliers, bend the tin strip down, then outward to make a shelf. Hold the oval mold on the block of wood with pliers and drill two holes in the bottom. File the holes smooth.

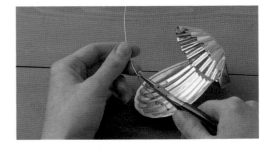

6 Pierce two holes in the back of the sconce. File the holes smooth. To make a hanger, cut a length of fine wire. Make a coil in one end, then pass the uncoiled end through the sconce. Make a loop, then pass the wire back through. Make a second coil and cut off the wire.

MATERIALS AND EQUIPMENT YOU WILL NEED

WORK SHIRT AND PROTECTIVE LEATHER GLOVES • PIECE OF 0.01 IN TIN PLATE • SCALLOP MOLD AND OVAL MOLD •
TIN SHEARS • PLIERS • FILE • WOODEN BLOCK • DRILL • POP-RIVETER AND RIVETS • MAGIC MARKER • BRADAWL • FINE WIRE •
WIRE CUTTERS • ROUND-NOSE PLIERS

REGAL COAT RACK

A COAT RACK WILL KEEP COATS, UMBRELLAS AND HATS TIDY, AVOIDING CLUTTER IN HALLS AND DOORWAYS. THE RICH PURPLE BACKGROUND AND THE SLIGHTLY MATTE TONES OF THE METAL FOILS GIVE THIS RACK A TOUCH OF MEDIEVAL SPLENDOR WITH GOTHIC OVERTONES THAT WOULD SIT WELL WITH PARQUET OR TILED FLOORING AND CAST-IRON LIGHT FITTINGS. THE BASIC SHAPE CAN EASILY BE ADAPTED TO MAKE A UTENSIL RACK FOR THE KITCHEN OR A TOWEL RAIL FOR THE BATHROOM. A KITCHEN RACK SHOULD IDEALLY HAVE LOTS OF EVENLY SPACED HOOKS TO HANG LADLES, WHISKS, SIEVES AND SO ON, WHILE A BATHROOM RACK COULD HAVE WOODEN PEGS RATHER THAN METAL HOOKS.

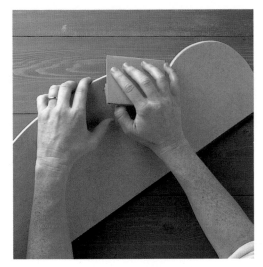

1 Draw the basic shape for the coat rack on to squared graph paper to make a pattern. This rack is 23½ in wide and 8 in high at its highest point. Cut out the pattern and draw around it on to the sheet of fiberboard. Saw out the shape and then smooth the edges using fine sandpaper.

2 Seal the surface of the coat rack with one coat of wood primer. Lightly sand the surface of the coat rack and paint it with satin-finish wood paint.

3 Trace the crown, fleur-de-lys and star templates from page 405, enlarge them necessary, then transfer them to a sheet of thin cardboard. Cut the shapes out to make templates. ►

MATERIALS AND EQUIPMENT YOU WILL NEED

PENCIL • GRAPH PAPER • SCISSORS • SHEET OF ¼ IN MEDIUM-DENSITY FIBERBOARD • HANDSAW •
FINE SANDPAPER • WOOD PRIMER • PAINTBRUSH • SATIN-FINISH WOOD PAINT • TRACING PAPER • SOFT PENCIL • THIN CARDBOARD •
0.003 IN COPPER FOIL • BALLPOINT PEN • 0.005 IN ALUMINUM FOIL • CENTER PUNCH • EPOXY RESIN GLUE •
DRILL • 3 BALL END HOOKS • 2 MIRROR PLATES

4 Lay the crown template on a piece of copper foil. Draw around the template on the foil using a ballpoint pen. Repeat to make a second crown. Draw around the fleur-de-lys and stars onto a sheet of aluminum foil. Draw two stars. Cut out all the shapes using scissors.

5 Rest each foil shape on a piece of thin cardboard. Make a line of dots around the edge of each shape by pressing into the foil using a center punch.

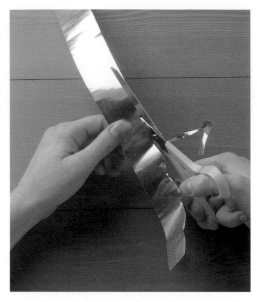

6 Cut a 2 in-wide strip of aluminum foil the same length as the bottom edge of the coat rack. Cut a wavy line along the top edge of the strip and then mark a row of dots along it with the punch.

7 Place the wavy edging and the stars, crowns and fleur-de-lys on the front of the coat rack with the raised side of the dots facing upwards. Use epoxy resin glue to stick all the pieces in position.

8 When the glue has dried thoroughly, drill three holes at equal distances 1 in from the bottom edge of the coat rack. Screw a hook into each hole. Attach a mirror plate to either side of the coat rack for hanging.

TIN CAN CHANDELIER

THIS CHANDELIER IS MADE FROM EIGHT SMALL TIN CANS AND A TIN FLAN RING. IT IS VERY SIMPLE IN CONSTRUCTION, BUT LOOKS VERY EFFECTIVE WHEN FILLED WITH FLICKERING NIGHT LIGHTS. THE TIN CANS ARE COLORED GOLD ON THE INSIDE, WHICH INTENSIFIES THE LIGHT. THE CHANDELIER IS SUSPENDED FROM STRONG BEADED CHAIN. MAKE SURE YOU BUY THE KIND WITH FORGED LINKS THAT CAN WITHSTAND THE WEIGHT OF THE CHANDELIER. GLASS NUGGETS ARE USED TO DECORATE THE OUTSIDE OF THE CHANDELIER, GIVING IT AN ECCLESIASTICAL AIR REMINISCENT OF A CORONA, A LARGE CHANDELIER THAT IS SUSPENDED FROM CHURCH CEILINGS. THE CHANDELIER IS DESIGNED TO HOLD VOTIVES AND SHOULD NOT BE USED WITH CANDLES. VOTIVES CAN BE A FIRE HAZARD AND SHOULD NEVER BE LEFT TO BURN UNATTENDED.

1 Measure and mark eight evenly spaced points around the flan ring. Rest the ring on a block of wood and pierce a hole at each point using a bradawl. File away the rough edges at the back of the holes.

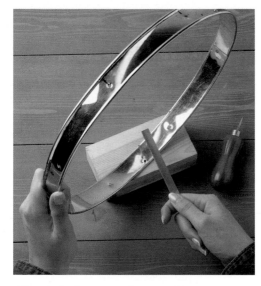

2 Mark three equally spaced points around the top of the ring. Pierce them with a bradawl as before and file away the rough edges.

3 Using a can opener, remove the top from each can and file the edges smooth. Measure and mark a point halfway down each tin can (avoiding the seam in the can). Clamp a length of wooden pole in a bench vise. Support each can on the pole and pierce a hole in the side at the marked point using a bradawl. File away the rough edges around the holes.

▶

MATERIALS AND EQUIPMENT YOU WILL NEED

TAPE MEASURE • MAGIC MARKER • TIN FLAN RING, 12 IN IN DIAMETER • WOODEN BLOCK • BRADAWL • FILE • CAN OPENER •
8 SMALL CANS • LENGTH OF WOODEN POLE • BENCH VISE • 8 NUTS AND SHORT BOLTS • SCREWDRIVER • 4 S-JOINERS • PLIERS •
STRONG BEADED CHAIN • WIRE CUTTERS • 4 JUMP RINGS • KEY RING • EPOXY RESIN GLUE • COLORED GLASS NUGGETS

4 Place each can against a hole in the flan ring. Join the cans to the ring using short bolts. Screw the nuts on to the bolts as tightly as they will go to keep the cans firmly in position.

6 Cut three 12 in lengths of beaded chain. Attach a jump ring to the end of each chain length, then attach a length to each S-joiner. Close the jump rings very tightly using pliers.

8 Glue green glass nuggets around the outside of the chandelier. Glue a red glass nugget to the outside of each tin.

5 Attach an S-joiner through each of the three holes in the top of the flan ring. Using pliers, close the joiners as tightly as they will go.

7 Hold the free ends of the chains together and join them using a jump ring. Join the jump ring to an S-joiner and close the ring very tightly. Attach a key ring to the top of the S-joiner to make a hanger.

JEWELRY BOX

THIN ZINC SHEET IS QUITE MALLEABLE AND CAN BE USED AS A DECORATIVE WRAPPING FOR ALL SORTS OF ITEMS. IT HAS A SUBTLE SHEEN RATHER LIKE PEWTER. BRASS SHIM IS A FAIRLY SOFT METAL USED MOSTLY BY SCULPTORS. IT CAN BE CUT WITH TIN SHEARS OR CLIPPERS. THE TWO METALS GO WELL TOGETHER, AND THIS JEWELRY BOX HAS A SUBTLE HERALDIC SPLENDOR, WHICH IS UNDERLINED BY THE DECORATIVE BLOBS OF SOLDER RESEMBLING METAL STUDS. LOOK OUT FOR OLD CIGAR BOXES, AS THEY HAVE PLEASING PROPORTIONS AND ARE EASILY OBTAINABLE.

1 Wearing protective clothing, cut a piece of zinc slightly larger than the lid of the cigar box using tin shears. Carefully file any rough edges or burrs of metal.

2 Draw a diamond and two different-size hearts on a sheet of thin cardboard and cut them out. Lay the templates on a piece of shim and draw around them: six small hearts, one large heart and two diamonds. Draw some small circles freehand. Draw one small heart on a scrap of zinc. Cut out all the shapes and file the edges smooth. Place them on a sheet of chipboard and stamp a line of dots around each using a hammer and nail. Do not stamp the circles and zinc heart.

3 Cut four thin strips of shim to make a border around the zinc panel. Place all the pieces on a soldering mat and, wearing a protective mask and goggles, drop a blob of liquid solder in the center of the circles, small hearts and diamonds. Cover the zinc heart with solder blobs. Add a line of blobs to each piece of the shim border.

4 Stick all the shapes and the borders on the zinc panel, leaving a small rim around the outside of the borders to turn down over the sides of the box. Turn the rim down.

5 Cut a strip of zinc as wide as the side of the box and long enough to fit all the way around. File the edges smooth. Cut circles of shim, decorate each with a blob of solder and glue them to the strip.

6 Glue the zinc strip around the sides of the box. Glue the zinc panel to the top of the lid. Gently tap along the edges of the panel to turn them over the side of the lid.

MATERIALS AND EQUIPMENT YOU WILL NEED

WORK SHIRT AND PROTECTIVE LEATHER GLOVES • THIN ZINC PLATE • TIN SHEARS • OLD CIGAR BOX • FILE • PENCIL • THIN CARDBOARD •
SCISSORS • BRASS SHIM • SHEET OF CHIPBOARD • HAMMER AND NAIL • SOLDERING MAT • PROTECTIVE MASK AND GOGGLES •
SOLDERING IRON AND SOLDER • SUPERGLUE

LUNCH BOX

WITH ITS DISTINCTIVE CURVED LID, THIS LUNCH BOX IS BASED ON TRADITIONAL AMERICAN DESIGNS. THE EXTRA SPACE UNDER THE LID MAKES A HANDY COMPARTMENT FOR STORING DRINKS FLASKS, WHICH LIE ON TOP OF THE FOOD. THE USE OF RECYCLED TIN CANS FOR HOUSEHOLD OBJECTS AND TOYS IS PREVALENT IN PARTS OF AFRICA AND INDIA, WHERE SCRAP METAL IS CAREFULLY COLLECTED AND RECYCLED.

ITEMS OF IMMENSE INGENUITY AND ELEGANCE ARE MADE BY PEOPLE OF ALL AGES, INCLUDING CHILDREN. LOOK OUTSIDE RESTAURANTS AND CAFÉS TO FIND DISCARDED OIL DRUMS AND TINS. CIRCULAR DRUMS ARE THE MOST USEFUL, AS THEY PROVIDE LARGE AREAS OF SMOOTH METAL. TRY TO FIND CONTAINERS PRINTED WITH INTERESTING TEXT OR PICTURES; SOME ARE VERY ATTRACTIVE AND WILL ENHANCE YOUR FINISHED OBJECT.

1 Wearing a work shirt and protective gloves, cut one end from an oil drum using a hacksaw (see Basic Techniques). Using tin shears, cut open the drum and remove the other end to leave a metal panel. Wipe any excess oil from the panel.

2 Mark out the dimensions of the box cover following the diagram on page 405. Using tin shears, cut out the cover. Carefully cut along the center of the cover to separate the two sections then snip up the short lines along each side to make the hinges. File away all the rough edges to make the cover safe. Make two small "V"-shaped cuts along each side as shown in the diagram.

3 Firmly clamp the 90° block of wood in the bench vise. Place the cover on the wooden block and carefully turn over one edge using a hide hammer. Turn over the cover. Position the 45° wooden block inside the turned edge and hammer the edge over it. Remove the block and hammer the edge completely flat. Repeat to turn over the other two edges. File all corners of the cover smooth. Repeat this process with the second cover section.

MATERIALS AND EQUIPMENT YOU WILL NEED

WORK SHIRT AND PROTECTIVE LEATHER GLOVES • OIL DRUM • HACKSAW • TIN SHEARS • CLOTH • MAGIC MARKER • RULER • FILE • 90° AND 45° WOODEN BLOCKS • BENCH VISE • HIDE HAMMER • PLIERS • FINE WIRE • WIRE CUTTERS • HAMMER • DRILL • G-CLAMP • ¼ IN MEDIUM-DENSITY FIBERBOARD• HANDSAWRED • RED STAIN • PAINTBRUSH • 2 CASE LOCKS • BRADAWL • NAILS • NUTS AND BOLTS • SCREWDRIVER

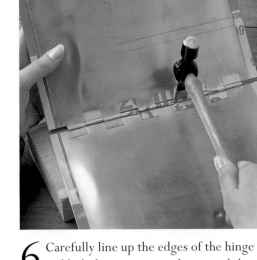

4 Using pliers, turn alternate tabs of the hinges over. Turn the tabs on each of the two covers so that each folded tab is opposite an unfolded tab. Flatten the tabs using a hammer.

6 Carefully line up the edges of the hinge and link the remaining tabs around the wire to join the two sides. Hammer the tabs firmly under the wire as before, to finish off the hinge.

8 Cut two end blocks using the template as a guide. Place the blocks in position, mark where the top of the sides of the lunch box come to then saw along this line. Stain the wood red. Fit a case lock to each pair.

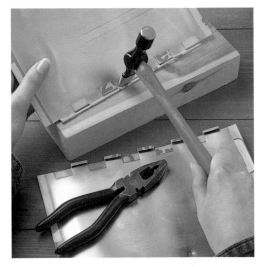

5 Bend half of each unflattened tab back using pliers. Cut a piece of fine wire the same length as the hinge and insert it through the tabs of one of the covers. Hammer the edges of the tabs on this cover firmly under the wire to secure them.

7 Place the cover on a wooden block. Hold the edge of the cover with pliers and drill a small hole 1 in in from the edge and each fold line, following the diagram. File the holes smooth. Place the 90° wooden block inside the cover along a fold line and clamp the two together. Gently bend the cover over the block to crease it. Repeat to make a crease along the other fold lines.

9 Separate the blocks and semi-circles and place the blocks inside the cover. Using a bradawl, mark the nail positions on the blocks through the holes. Nail the cover to the blocks.

▶

10 Place the semicircles of fiberboard on top of the blocks and close the catches to hold them together. Press the lid around the semicircles and nail the top and sides of the cover to the semicircles.

11 Remove the handle from the oil drum. Place it on a wooden block and drill a hole in either end of the handle. File the holes smooth.

12 Place the handle on top of the lunch box. Using a magic marker, transfer the position of the holes in the handle to the top of the lunch box and drill through. File the holes smooth, then bolt the handle in place, holding the nut firmly from the inside of the box with pliers.

ROCKET CANDLESTICK

THIS ALUMINUM CANDLESTICK HAS A CARTOONLIKE APPEARANCE THAT IS VERY APPEALING. THE SMALL SECTIONS ARE CONSTRUCTED FIRST AND THEN JOINED TOGETHER. EACH SECTION IS ATTACHED TO THE NEXT USING POP RIVETS. THESE MAKE A STRONG JOINT AS WELL AS BEING DECORATIVE. BECAUSE THE ALUMINUM IS SOFT, IT IS EASY TO SHAPE USING YOUR HANDS. THE FEET OF THE CANDLESTICK ARE MADE OF OVEN-HARDENING CLAY, WHICH CAN BE PURCHASED FROM CRAFT SHOPS. CANDLES CAN BE A FIRE HAZARD AND SHOULD NEVER BE LEFT TO BURN UNATTENDED.

1 Trace and transfer the rocket section templates on page 403 to thin card, enlarging if necessary. Cut out the templates and draw around them on to the aluminum. Draw six side sections, three fins and one top shelf. Wearing a work shirt and protective gloves, cut out all the pieces using tin clippers and file the edges smooth. Mark the drilling points on each piece and drill the holes. Hold the metal with a pair of pliers to stop it spinning around while you drill.

2 Using a pair of pliers, carefully fold down all the sides of the top shelf to make an angle of 90°.

3 Place the side sections on the edge of the wooden block and hammer over the edges. Hold each section in your hands and gently curve it outward.

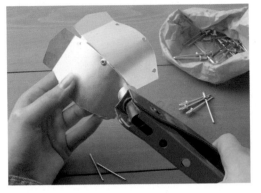

4 Hold two side sections together with the tabs to the inside. Join the sections with pop-rivets at the middle and bottom holes. Join another two sections in the same way.

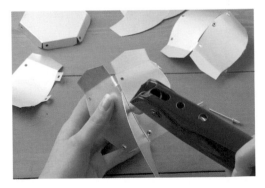

5 Place a fin section between two side sections and pop-rivet all three together at the middle and bottom holes. Pop-rivet the other fins and side sections together.

MATERIALS AND EQUIPMENT YOU WILL NEED

TRACING PAPER • SOFT PENCIL • THIN CARDBOARD • SCISSORS • THIN ALUMINUM SHEET • WORK SHIRT AND PROTECTIVE LEATHER GLOVES • TIN CLIPPERS • FILE • DRILL • PLIERS • 90° WOODEN BLOCK • HAMMER • POP-RIVETER AND RIVETS • BLACK OVEN-HARDENING CLAY • EPOXY RESIN GLUE

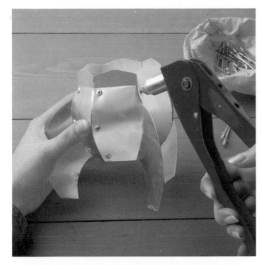

6 Position the shelf at the top of the candlestick with the sides pointing downward. Join the shelf to the base with pop rivets through the top holes.

7 To make the candlestick feet, roll three balls of black oven-hardening clay. Flatten the base of each one and make an indentation in the top. Bake the clay according to the manufacturer's instructions. When the clay is cool, glue a foot to the end of each fin.

PLANT MARKERS

THESE SIMPLE PLANT MARKERS WILL LEND AN AIR OF ELEGANT ORDER TO ANY SEED BED OR CONTAINER, AND MAKE A NICE CHANGE FROM PLASTIC MARKERS. THEY ARE VERY SIMPLE IN CONSTRUCTION AND WILL HOLD TOGETHER WITHOUT ANY GLUE. THEY ARE MADE FROM COPPER FOIL WHICH, IF THE MARKERS ARE USED OUTDOORS, WILL CHANGE COLOR TO A DELICATE VERDIGRIS AS IT REACTS TO THE ELEMENTS. LATIN PLANT NAMES ARE PUNCHED INTO EACH MARKER BUT YOU CAN USE THE COMMON NAME FOR EACH PLANT IF YOU PREFER.

1 Trace the template on page 406 and as necessary, and transfer it to thin cardboard. Cut out the template and draw around it onto a sheet of copper foil.

2 Cut the marker from the sheet of foil using a pair of scissors.

4 Cut all the way up the stem along the line directly under the flower head. Using a pair of pliers, fold back the middle sections of the marker from the center of the flower to the edges of the petals.

3 Place the copper marker on a sheet of thin cardboard on top of a sheet of chipboard. Carefully punch the design and plant name into the front of the marker using a bradawl.

5 Hold the two cut strips of the stem together so that the two halves of the bottom petal are joined. Using pliers, make a fold along the two outer lines of the stem. Wrap the stem around the cut section to hold the marker together.

MATERIALS AND EQUIPMENT YOU WILL NEED
TRACING PAPER • SOFT PENCIL • THIN CARDBOARD • SCISSORS • MAGIC MARKER • SHEET OF 0.004 IN COPPER FOIL •
SHEET OF CHIPBOARD • BRADAWL • PLIERS

PEWTER-LOOK SHELF

ALUMINUM FLASHING, TRADITIONALLY USED IN ROOFING, TAKES ON AN UNUSUAL, PITTED APPEARANCE THAT RESEMBLES PEWTER WHEN IT IS HAMMERED. IT CAN BE USED TO COVER SIMPLE SHAPES SUCH AS THIS SHELF AND IT IS VERY DIFFICULT TO GUESS WHAT THE ORIGINAL MATERIAL IS.

PRACTICE YOUR HAMMERING TECHNIQUE ON AN OFF-CUT OF FLASHING FIRST TO ACHIEVE THE RIGHT TEXTURE, AND USE A BALL HAMMER TO MAKE SMOOTH, REGULAR INDENTATIONS. ALUMINUM FLASHING MAY BE BOUGHT FROM ROOFING SUPPLIERS AND HARDWARE STORES.

1 Mark the two shelf pieces on fiberboard, using the template on page 406 as a Cut them out with the handsaw. Draw a pencil line down the center and mark two points as on the template. Mark corresponding points on the long edge of the stand. Drill holes at these points, then glue and screw the shelf and stand together.

2 Cut lengths of aluminum flashing roughly to size. Peel away the backing and stick them to the shelf front, trimming the rough edges on the side of the strips as you go.

3 Butt each new length of flashing very closely to the last, so that no fiberboard is visible beneath the covering.

4 When the front is covered, lay the shelf facedown and carefully trim away the excess flashing using a craft knife.

5 Cut lengths of flashing to cover the back and sides of the shelf, and stick them in place.

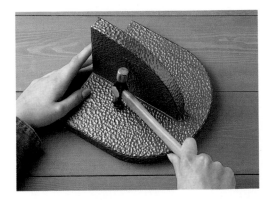

6 Using a ball head hammer, tap the surface of the flashing to make indentations close together. Vary the force with which you strike the flashing, so as to make an interesting and irregular pattern.

MATERIALS AND EQUIPMENT YOU WILL NEED

SHEET OF ¾ IN MEDIUM-DENSITY FIBERBOARD • PENCIL • RULER • HANDSAW • DRILL • WOOD GLUE • 2 SCREWS •
SCREWDRIVER • ALUMINUM FLASHING • CRAFT KNIFE • BALL HEAD HAMMER

BARBECUE

OIL DRUMS ARE A GREAT SOURCE OF METAL AND ARE OFTEN SIMPLY DISCARDED, BUT THEY CAN BE GIVEN A NEW LEASE OF LIFE BY RECYCLING. THIS IS DONE IN MANY PARTS OF THE WORLD; IN HAITI, FOR EXAMPLE, DRUMS ARE HAMMERED FLAT AND USED TO MAKE DECORATIVE PAINTED CUTOUTS. THEY ARE ALSO USED TO MAKE STEEL DRUMS, TOYS AND A WIDE VARIETY OF EVERYDAY HOUSEHOLD OBJECTS. HERE, AN OIL DRUM HAS BEEN INGENIOUSLY REUSED TO CREATE THIS BARBECUE. EVERY PART OF THE DRUM HAS BEEN USED AND A TIN CAN HAS BEEN TRANSFORMED INTO A CRAZILY ANGLED CHIMNEY STACK THAT GIVES IT THE APPEARANCE OF A SPACE ROCKET.

1 Wearing a work shirt and protective gloves, cut the oil drum in half using a hacksaw blade and tin shears. Draw two lines around the rim of the lower part of the drum, the first about ¼ in down and the second 1 in down. Place the grill on top of the drum and mark a point either side of where each bar of the grill touches the drum. As the bars of the grill run in only one direction, there will be a section on either side of the rim of the drum left unmarked. Using tin shears, cut down to the lower line from each of these points to make thin tabs.

2 Using pliers, bend the thin tabs outward. Snip them shorter using tin shears, then bend them in and down to the inside of the drum.

3 Using pliers, grip the edge of each of the wider tabs where the upper line is drawn. Bend the edges over and squeeze them firmly to flatten them.

MATERIALS AND EQUIPMENT YOU WILL NEED

WORK SHIRT AND PROTECTIVE LEATHER GLOVES • OIL DRUM AND OIL DRUM SCRAPS • HACKSAW • TIN SHEARS • MAGIC MARKER • RULER • GRILL • PLIERS • FILE • LENGTH OF 1 IN DIAMETER DOWEL • WOODEN BLOCK • BRADAWL • ANNULAR RING NAILS • HAMMER • TRACING PAPER • SOFT PENCIL • THIN CARDBOARD • SCISSORS • DRILL • POP-RIVETER AND RIVETS • TIN CAN, OPEN AT BOTH ENDS

4 The grill should rest between the tabs. To make it sit securely you will need to cut the tabs near the unmarked side sections on a diagonal. Lay the grill on top of the drum and check that it sits properly and securely on the drum.

5 To make the lid, draw a line around the other half of the drum, ½ in down from the cut edge. Cut equally spaced tabs around the rim as far as the line, using tin shears. Using pliers, bend over the tabs to the inside of the drum and flatten them.

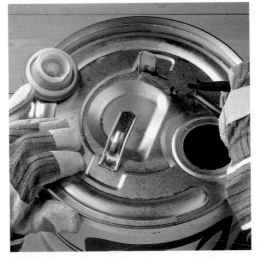

6 Remove the stopper from the top of the drum. Cut the handle in half using tin shears. Using pliers, bend both halves of the handle up at an angle of 90°. Cut the end of each half into a curve and file the edges of the handle smooth.

7 Cut a length of dowel to fit between the halves of the handle. Hold a wooden block against the side of each handle half and make a hole in each using a bradawl. File the rough edges around the holes smooth. Nail the handle halves to the dowel through the holes.

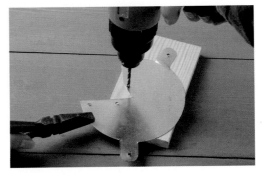

8 Draw the chimney roof pattern on a spare piece of oil drum metal as shown here. Cut out the roof using tin shears and file the edges smooth. Place the roof on a block of wood and drill holes as shown. Hold the metal with a pair of pliers to stop it spinning around as you drill.

9 Gently curve the roof around so that the holes match and pop-rivet the sides together.

10 Bend the roof tabs under. Place the tin on the tabs and mark where the edges of the tin touch them. Using pliers, bend the tabs back along the lines.

▶

11 To make the chimney, draw a line all the way around the tin to give the chimney a slanting base. Draw a second line parallel to the first and about ½ in above it. Draw four tabs at equal distances around the tin between the two lines. Cut around the upper line, leaving the tabs in place.

13 Stand the chimney on a block of wood and drill a hole in each tab. Place the chimney on top of the lid. Transfer the position of the holes in the tabs to the lid. Drill the holes and file them smooth. Pop-rivet the chimney to the lid.

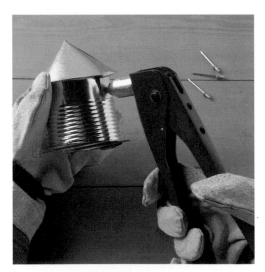

12 Place the roof on top of the chimney. Transfer the position of the holes in the tabs to the sides of the chimney. Drill holes in the side of the chimney and file away the rough edges. Pop-rivet the roof to the chimney.

14 Drill a hole every 2 in around the base of the barbecue to allow air to circulate when it is in use. File away the rough edges around the holes. When in use, the barbecue should never be left unattended.

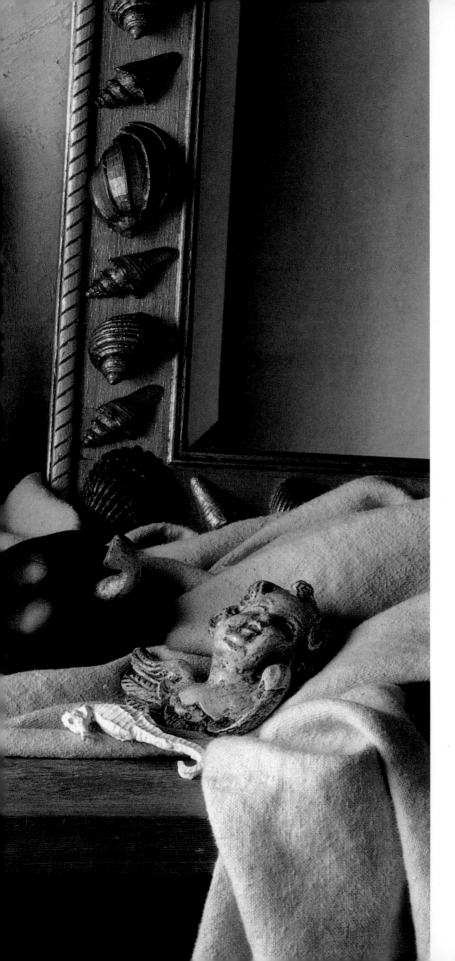

CREATIVE PLASTERWORK
STEPHANIE HARVEY

P LASTER CASTING IS A FASCINATING CRAFT AS IT ENABLES YOU TO REPRODUCE THE EXACT SHAPE OF ALL MANNER OF ITEMS, FROM NATURAL SUBJECTS SUCH AS SHELLS, ACORNS, VEGETABLES, AND FRUIT TO MANMADE OBJECTS SUCH AS WOODEN CARVINGS, MARBLE BUSTS, FABRIC TASSELS, AND EVEN BOOKS. PLASTER CASTING IS ESSENTIALLY A TWO-PART CREATIVE PROCESS: A MOLD HAS TO BE CREATED FROM AN EXISTING OBJECT BEFORE A CAST CAN BE MADE. MOLDS, ORIGINALLY MADE OF CLAY OR PLASTER, AND NOWADAYS OF SILICONE RUBBER, ARE MADE BY IMPRESSING THE PLIABLE MATERIAL WITH AN OBJECT AND THEN LEAVING IT TO HARDEN. THE OBJECT IS REMOVED AND THE "NEGATIVE" MOLD IS THEN FILLED WITH LIQUID PLASTER. WHEN THE PLASTER HAS SET, THE CAST IS REMOVED FROM THE MOLD AND THEN DECORATED, IF WISHED, USING SIMPLE PAINTING AND GILDING TECHNIQUES.

Left: Plaster casting can be used to create a wide range of decorative items, from freestanding and hanging ornaments to picture frames and wonderful decorative details which can be used to enhance furniture, frames, boxes, and fireplaces.

HISTORY OF PLASTERWORK

THE HISTORY OF PLASTER CASTING IS CLOSELY LINKED WITH THAT OF MOLD MAKING. THE ORIGINS OF MOLDING DATE BACK FAR INTO THE PREHISTORIC PAST. SOME EARLY POTTER MUST HAVE BEEN THE FIRST TO RECOGNIZE THE INTRIGUING FACT THAT HE COULD REPRODUCE A PRECISE IMPRESSION OF HIS FINGERS IN WET CLAY. VERY EARLY POTS ARE DECORATED WITH INTERWOVEN PATTERNS WHICH COULD HAVE BEEN CREATED BY PRESSING THE WET POT INTO A WICKER BASKET THAT WAS THEN DESTROYED IN FIRING. THE OLDEST SURVIVING MOLDS DATE FROM THE BRONZE AGE.

Until recently, the Bronze-Age molds that had been found had generally been used for casting metalwork. Then, in 1982, an Israeli archeologist working in the Gaza Strip found a two-part clay mold dating from 1300 BC in the shape of a small figurine – clay would have been pressed into the mold to produce a series of shaped bottles. In China, potters of the Sung dynasty (AD 960–1280) used fired clay molds as guides for carving detailed patterns in their work.

The earliest plaster molds have not survived the passage of time, for plaster is a relatively soft material which eventually dissolves in damp conditions. We know that early Mediterranean civilizations were familiar with the techniques required to calcine gypsum (plaster's main constituent), but whatever plaster they produced has long ago crumbled into dust. The first historical record of plaster being used for creating molds dates from 1554 in *The Three Books of the Potter's Art*, an Italian work intended for use by craftsmen of the period. In England, the Staffordshire potteries were using plaster molds by the mid-eighteenth century.

Decorative plasterwork for walls and ceilings, such as the work of Robert Adam, was created both by modeling and molding. The molds were sometimes carved from wood, but plaster molds were also produced by modeling the design in either clay or plaster and then impressing it in plaster. The resulting mold was soaped or coated in a film of marble dust

to prevent the plaster from sticking when the cast was formed, then held against the ceiling on a scaffold frame until it dried.

Flexible molds, made out of natural gelatin, first appeared in the middle of the nineteenth century when they were used by Italian manufacturers to satisfy the market for religious statuettes. The next

Above: The use of plaster for religious statuary is widespread. This tranquil plaster angel was made, probably, by Portuguese craftsmen for a church in Goa, which formed part of the Portuguese colony in India.

great advance in molding came with the invention of cold-curing silicone in the 1950s. Silicone combines the properties of both organic products such as rubber and inorganic minerals such as quartz. Silicone was originally developed as a grease for aircraft in the Second World War, and with the discovery of cold-curing agents, its potential as a medium for molding soon

became apparent. Its great advantage is that it offers perfect definition combined with flexibility, strength, and durability. It is also very easy to use since it does not require heat to harden it. Instead, the silicone comes in two parts, a base and a curing agent, which set hard when combined in the correct proportions.

The great advantage of plaster as a

medium for modeling and casting is that, once mixed with water, it turns into a substance without lumps, grains or knots, so that a perfectly smooth finish can be achieved. Plaster is a mineral medium primarily composed of gypsum and, as we have seen, the methods necessary for its production were known to ancient people. Indeed, gypsum mortar was used in

Above: Chiswick House in London is known for its ornate ceilings, which are richly decorated with fine plaster moldings. Lord Burlington, an amateur architect himself, commissioned William Kent to design the interiors in 1729. This shows a detail of the ceiling in the Blue Velvet Room.

Right: The all-white molded ceilings at Littlecote House provide a contrast to those at Chiswick House in their restrained geometric simplicity, more typical of seventeenth-century interiors.

building the Egyptian pyramids. Its use is supposed to have spread from Egypt eastward to India, where, by the fourth century AD, sculptors in Guadhara were making plaster models of the Buddha.

In more recent times, gypsum was mined commercially in France during the 1770s, most famously in the Parisian suburb of Montmartre, the origin of true "plaster of Paris." Once quarried, gypsum has to undergo many processes before becoming plaster. First, it must be crushed and screened of all impurities, then further pulverized prior to heating. This "calcining" removes three quarters of the chemically bound water in the gypsum.

Plasterwork today is primarily a medium for molds, ceramics and sculpture. With the revival of interest in the restoration, or creation, of period features in houses of all ages, it is also once more being used extensively to reproduce ceiling roses, cornices and other such architectural features. In this book, however, we shall chiefly be concerned with projects on a smaller and more decorative scale.

Thanks to plaster's smoothness and its weight, it is still the ideal medium for casting. With the use of molds made from cold-curing silicone, wonderfully detailed subjects can be reproduced in plaster. Many of these subjects will be found in nature, and part of the joy of molding lies in collecting them. A woodland walk or a stroll along the seashore will provide inspiration for a dozen projects – freestanding ornaments or decorative details for frames, furniture or fireplaces. However, molds can also be taken from manmade objects such as wood and stone carvings or from shapes modeled from clay or wax plasticine.

These casts can be made still more attractive by original and imaginative decoration, employing a variety of finishes. Pieces can be transformed by a

weathered "antique" look appropriate to a Doge's palace, or the natural coloring of the originals can be beautifully reproduced. No great skill is required – simply a good eye and some imagination. The result is a unique, hand-finished work of art which will give years of pleasure.

Above: This fine early nineteenth-century fireplace surround is enhanced with delicate figurative plaster decorations.

Above: The interiors of Kenwood House in London were designed by Robert Adam in the mid-eighteenth century. The plaster ceiling moldings are particularly graceful and refined. Left simply white or gilded, they are defined by the pink and green plaster ceilings.

Right: Decorative plasterwork was not just the preserve of stately homes. Plaster parqueting was a traditional craft, seen here adorning the gable end of a fifteenth-century house in Suffolk.

GALLERY

PLASTER IS AN EXTREMELY VERSATILE MEDIUM. CASTS ARE AN IDEAL WAY TO DECORATE OTHER OBJECTS, SUCH AS MIRROR FRAMES OR BOXES, AND BECAUSE OF ITS TEXTURE AND WEIGHT, PLASTER CAN ALSO BE USED TO CREATE BEAUTIFUL FREESTANDING ORNAMENTS. ITS FINE SURFACE MEANS THAT THE POSSIBILITIES FOR DECORATION ARE ENDLESS AND, GIVEN AN IMAGINATIVE DESIGN, IT CAN EVEN LOOK WONDERFUL LEFT IN ITS RAW STATE.

Right: ROMAN BUST
This plaster bust was cast from a two-part latex rubber mold supported with clay. It was covered in Dutch metal leaf. Then green paint was applied and rubbed off to give a verdigris effect.
LIZ WAGSTAFF

Left: FISHY MIRROR
The fish on this mirror were originally sculpted, then cast in plaster and decorated with aluminum Dutch metal leaf. The frame was painted a sea-green color and then overlaid with a paler wash of this color. The moldings were decorated with aluminum Dutch metal leaf and the whole frame was given a coat of acrylic varnish so that it could be used in a bathroom.
STEPHANIE HARVEY

Above: FIRESCREEN
Cast leaves, acorns and a wood carving adorn this firescreen, which is made of medium-density fiber-board (MDF). Burgundy latex paint was used as a background to the decoration, which was gilded in Dutch metal leaf. Several coats of satin-finish acrylic varnish were applied to enhance the rich color of the firescreen.
STEPHANIE HARVEY

Right: PLASTER SHOES
These exotic plaster shoes were cast from a two-part clay mold. The clay was pressed on to a pair of leather shoes, then cast separately with plaster. Once set the two halves of each plaster cast were stuck together to form the shoes. Each shoe was then lavishly decorated with broken pieces of china, beads, glass and mirror glass. Decorative bows complete the design.
IZZY MOREAU

Above: ROCOCO MIRROR
The great diversity of shell shapes is shown in this mirror. Four different kinds of shell were cast and gilded with gold Dutch metal leaf. They were then stuck on to a gilded wooden frame with a rope border, and the whole design was antiqued with a raw-umber latex wash. A shellac varnish was applied so that the gold would keep its color.
STEPHANIE HARVEY

Left: PICTURE FRAME
A carved, wooden frame was used as the basis for this design. It was gilded with Dutch metal leaf and adorned with tassels. The fleurs-de-lys and stars were cast from Christmas decorations. The casts were then painted red and wiped with gilt cream.
LIZ WAGSTAFF

Right: CARVED TASSELS
The mold for the tassels was taken from a wooden tassel made in 1820. Made in two parts, the mold was strapped together with elastic bands and plaster was poured in from the top. Dutch metal leaf was used to gild one of them. Then a green wash was painted on and rubbed off, leaving the color in the crevices. Lilac paint was then painted on to give highlights. The verdigris-effect tassel was created by using blackboard paint as a base, with green paint washed over it.
LIZ WAGSTAFF

Left: EGYPTIAN
WALL PLAQUE
The Egyptian mummy was cast by filling the inside of a two-part novelty wooden pencil box with plaster. Once removed, it was stuck together to produce a solid figure. The detail and decoration were painted in by hand. The wooden plinth was painted in blue and dragged with a brush to give a distressed effect.
LIZ WAGSTAFF

Left: SQUIGGLY
MIRROR
Thick cardboard was used as a base for this mirror with quick-setting household plaster applied on top. To create the unusual decorative effect, a cake-icing bag was filled with wet plaster and used to pipe the squiggly lines on to the plaster frame while it was still wet. Once dry, the mirror was stuck in with masking tape and the tape was obscured with more plaster.
IZZY MOREAU

Left: AUTUMNAL BOX
The molds for the decorations on this box were taken from seedheads produced by trees and flowers in the autumn. The casts were then gilded with Dutch metal leaf and antiqued with raw-umber latex paint. The color of the box is a rich terracotta, specially mixed to reflect autumnal colors. A brown wash was then rubbed on to the box so that it blended with the antiqued seedheads. The box was varnished and waxed to give it luster.
STEPHANIE HARVEY

Right: MARINE
MIRROR
This highly inventive
mirror was made from a
cardboard base spread
with quick-setting
household plaster. The sea
creatures were sculpted
from clay, then cast in
plaster, and the shells were
cast from natural shells.
All these ornaments,
though hard themselves,
were applied to the mirror
when the base plaster was
still wet.
IZZY MOREAU

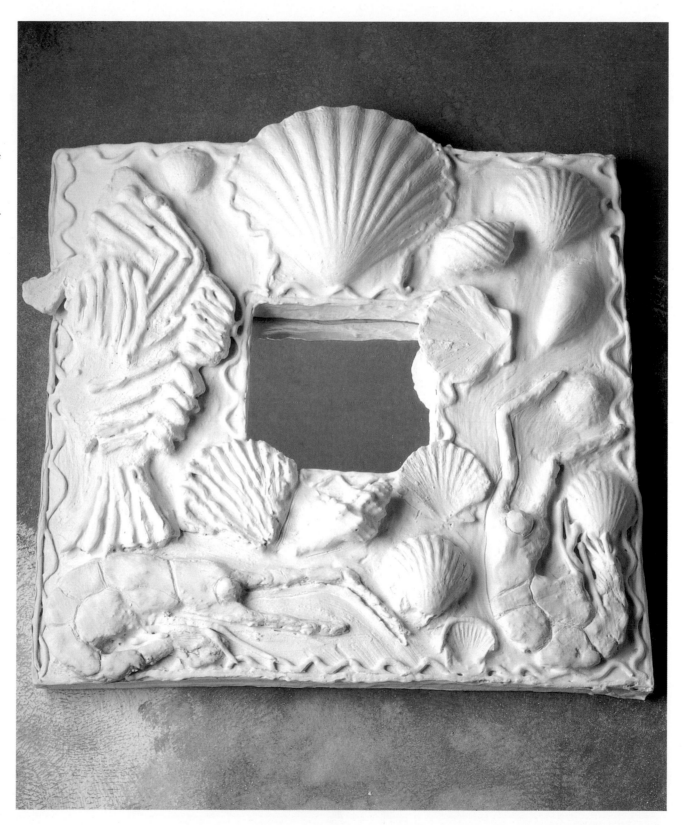

CASTING MATERIALS

ALL THE MATERIALS USED FOR PLASTER CASTING ARE AVAILABLE FROM SPECIALTY SCULPTING OR PLASTER SUPPLIERS, ADDRESSES FOR WHICH ARE LISTED AT THE BACK OF THIS BOOK. THE COMPANIES LISTED WILL SUPPLY GOODS BY MAIL ORDER SINCE YOU MAY HAVE DIFFICULTY FINDING A LOCAL SUPPLIER.

ONCE YOU HAVE MADE YOUR MOLDS, THEY CAN BE USED OVER AND OVER AGAIN, SO, ALTHOUGH THE COST OF THE COLD-CURING SILICONE RUBBER MAY SEEM EXPENSIVE, THE MATERIAL YOU CAST WITH — PLASTER — IS COMPARATIVELY CHEAP. THE MORE CASTS YOU MAKE, THE MORE WORTHWHILE THE INITIAL EXPENSE IS.

Casting plaster. There are several different types of casting plaster. They vary in strength and hardness. If you want to sand the plaster, it is important to buy one soft enough. Plaster is available from specialty sculpting or plaster suppliers. They will be able to advise you on the type you require.

Fine casting plaster. This is finer than ordinary casting powder and is a little too soft for casting the projects in this book. However, it is ideal for using as a case for supporting larger molds.

Petroleum jelly. Petroleum jelly is readily available from drugstores. In casting, it is used to prevent the silicone rubber from sticking to itself or to any other surface.

Cold-curing silicone base. Cold-curing silicone base is used to make molds for casting. It will not set unless mixed with curing agent at a ratio of 20-parts base to 1-part curing agent. It is available from specialty sculpting and plaster suppliers.

Curing agent. Curing agent is added to cold-curing silicone base so that it will set. The more curing agent you add, the quicker the silicone will set. It is available from specialty sculpting and plaster suppliers.

Thixotropic additive. Thixotropic additive is added to a mixture of silicone base and curing agent to thicken it. It is available from specialty sculpting and plaster suppliers.

Silicone colorant. Silicone colorant is normally red and is added to the first coat

of cold-curing silicone. The second coat is left white, so that you can see if the object you are molding has been covered completely by the second coat. It is available from specialty sculpting and plaster suppliers.

Elastic bands. Elastic bands are used to hold the two parts of a three-dimensional mold. (See "Basic Technique 2.")

Wax plasticine. Wax plasticine is a mixture of wax and plasticine. It is smooth and pliable and is perfect for sculpting or filling. It never hardens so it can be used again and again. It can be bought from plaster suppliers.

Clay. Clay is very inexpensive and is used for sculpting or filling. If left in the open, it will harden. It is available from pottery, sculpting or plaster suppliers.

Epoxy putty. This putty is used in casting as a filler. It sets hard within 2 hours at room temperature. It can be bought from good art-supply stores and varies in price according to the color. Any color can be used if it is going to be painted over or gilded later.

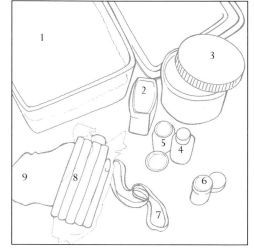

1 Casting plaster	5 Thixotropic additive
2 Petroleum jelly	6 Silicone colorant
3 Cold-curing silicone base	7 Elastic bands
4 Curing agent	8 Wax plasticine
	9 Clay

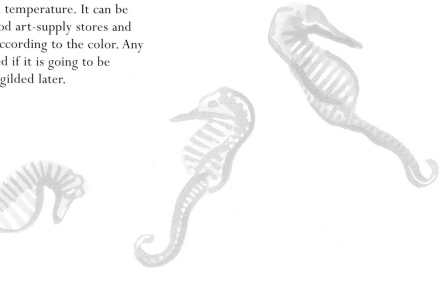

DECORATIVE MATERIALS

MOST OF THE MATERIALS ARE AVAILABLE FROM REGULAR HARDWARE STORES. SOME OF THE MORE SPECIALTY ITEMS, SUCH AS WATER-BASED GOLD SIZE, DUTCH METAL LEAF AND ACRYLIC PAINT, CAN BE BOUGHT FROM ART-SUPPLY STORES. BOTH WATER-BASED PAINTS, SUCH AS LATEX PAINTS AND ACRYLIC PAINTS, AND OIL-BASED PAINTS CAN BE APPLIED TO PLASTER. HOUSEHOLD PAINTS COME IN THREE FINISHES — MATTE, SATIN AND GLOSS — AND THERE ARE OVER A HUNDRED COLORS TO CHOOSE FROM. IT IS A GOOD IDEA TO BUY A SMALL TESTER CAN TO TEST A COLOR BEFORE PURCHASING IT IN LARGE QUANTITIES.

Latex paint. Latex paint is widely available in hundreds of different colors. It is water-based, and there are three finishes – matte, soft sheen and silk. Brushes are easily cleaned by washing with water and detergent, and the paint can be thinned with water.

Raw-umber latex paint. Raw-umber latex paint is a water-based paint which consists of pure pigment. It is used to antique gold Dutch metal leaf. It is available by mail order from specialty paint shops.

Mixture of raw-umber and black latex paint. A mixture of 50/50 raw-umber and black latex paint makes an ideal color for antiquing aluminium Dutch metal leaf.

Red latex paint. Red latex paint is painted on underneath gold Dutch metal leaf to imitate the color of bole, a pigment made from clay, which was originally used under gold leaf.

Acrylic paint. Acrylic paint can be bought from art-supply stores and comes in a variety of colors. It is water-soluble. The stronger you want the color, the less water you add. Brushes should be cleaned by washing with water and detergent.

Oil paints. Oil paints tend to be more durable than water-based paints so they are ideal for items that are to be placed outdoors.

Shellac sanding sealer. Shellac sanding sealer can be bought from hardware stores. It is ideal for sealing plaster or new wood. If you want to apply a water-based paint to an oil-based surface, such as varnish, apply a coat of shellac sanding sealer to act as a barrier. Once dry, a water-based product can be painted over the top. Brushes need to be cleaned in methylated alcohol or turpentine.

Gilt cream. Gilt cream is available from art-supply stores and good hardware stores. There are several different shades of gold, and it is also available in silver. It is easy to apply, using your finger or a cloth and is ideal for gilding small areas or, used sparingly, to highlight painted areas which catch the light.

Water-based gold size. This is ideal for all types and colors of Dutch metal leaf. It is available from large art-supply stores and by mail order. When first applied, the size is opaque. When it becomes transparent and sticky, it is ready to use. This normally takes 15–30 minutes.

Dutch metal leaf. Dutch metal leaf comes in several different shades of gold and also in aluminum. It comes either on transfer paper (in books of twenty-five sheets) or loose. It is more expensive attached to transfer paper, but it is easier to use in this form. Metal leaf is available from good art-supply stores, or you can send for it by mail order.

Felt-tipped pens. These pens are ideal for creating fine lines. They are available in all colors, including gold and silver, and with nibs of varying thickness. They are available from stationery stores or art-supply stores.

Varnishes. The best sealer for Dutch

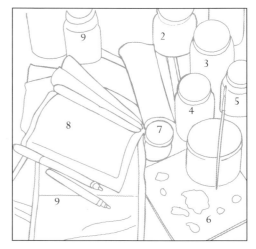

1 Latex paint
2 Raw-umber latex paint
3 Mixture of raw-umber and black latex paint
4 Red latex paint
5 Water-based gold size
6 Acrylic paint
7 Gilt cream
8 Dutch metal leaf
9 Felt-tipped pens

metal leaf is pale-shellac varnish, which is colorless, dries quickly and does not yellow with age. Oil-based varnishes are tougher and better for objects that need to be durable or are to be placed outdoors. They can take up to twenty-four hours to dry and do yellow with age. Acrylic varnishes are water-based, so they do not change with age and dry within half an hour. Acrylic floor varnish is thicker and stronger than regular acrylic varnish. Both oil and acrylic varnish come in three finishes – matte, satin and gloss.

Glues. Two-part epoxy resin glue is ideal for sticking plaster casts to other items. It is stronger than most other glues and takes twenty-four hours to dry completely.

EQUIPMENT

VERY LITTLE SPECIAL EQUIPMENT IS NEEDED FOR MOST OF THE PROJECTS IN THIS BOOK, AND YOU WILL PROBABLY HAVE MANY OF THE ITEMS AROUND THE HOUSE, ALREADY. MOST OF THE THINGS THAT YOU MAY NEED TO BUY ARE INEXPENSIVE AND EASY TO FIND. A GOOD HARDWARE STORE WILL SELL ITEMS SUCH AS DUST MASKS, TILES AND SANDPAPER. A HOME-FURNISHING STORE WILL PROVIDE AN APRON, PLASTIC POTS AND A MEASURING CUP. OTHER SPECIAL ITEMS, SUCH AS LOCATION PEGS AND A SMALL MODELING DRILL FOR SANDING, CAN BE PURCHASED FROM SPECIALTY PLASTER SUPPLIERS.

Apron. Painting and plaster casting can be a messy business, so it is best to wear an apron to protect your clothes.

Measuring cup. Use a plastic or glass cup for mixing plaster. They are available from home-furnishing stores.

Household paintbrush. Household paintbrushes come in all sizes. The $1/2$ in size is useful for painting small objects. Brushes come in different qualities, and it is advisable to buy one from the mid-range upward.

Sandpaper. Sandpaper is used to rub down any imperfections in the cast plaster. For a smooth finish, you need a sandpaper with a fine grit. It is available from hardware stores, which will give advice on a suitable type.

Plastic container. Plastic containers come in all shapes and sizes. They can be used for mixing silicone rubber or as a container for molding. They are available from home-furnishing stores.

Aluminum foil. Fold up the sides of a piece of foil to make an ideal container for molding.

Paper towels. Paper towels, being soft and absorbent, are used to rub off paint washes.

Rolling pin. A rolling pin can be used for flattening and smoothing out wax plasticine and clay.

Modeling drill. Modeling drills can be bought from specialty sculpting suppliers. They have a variety of different-sized detachable heads and are used for shaping and smoothing down cast plaster.

Sandbags. Calico cotton bags loosely filled with sand are ideal for supporting rubber molds when casting. Bags filled with rice or beans can also be used.

Tape measure. A tape measure helps to find the center of a box, frame or piece of furniture when you are attaching a plaster decoration.

Glass jar. Glass jars are useful for mixing paint and for water when you are using acrylic paints.

Spoon. A spoon is needed to stir paint, plaster and silicone rubber. Old spoons are often to be found quite cheaply in thrift shops.

Gimlet. Gimlets come in different sizes and are used to make holes in cast plaster.

Scissors. Kitchen scissors are the correct size for cutting Dutch metal leaf and picture cord.

Craft knife. Craft knives come with a variety of different handles and different-shaped blades. They are used for scraping off excess plaster. They are available from art-supply stores, which will recommend the type and size you require.

Artist's paintbrush. Available from art-supply stores, artist's paintbrushes come in a variety of sizes and qualities. The bristles may be made from sable hair, synthetic material or a combination of the two. Any of them can be used for painting.

Spatula. A small spatula is extremely useful for modeling and filling. They can be bought from sculpting suppliers.

Location pegs. Available from plaster suppliers, location pegs have a male and

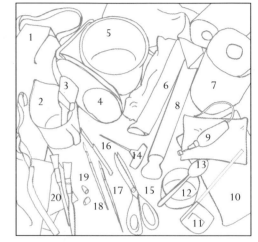

1 Apron	**11** Tape measure
2 Measuring cup	**12** Glass jar
3 Household paintbrush	**13** Spoon
4 Sandpaper	**14** Gimlet
5 Plastic container	**15** Scissors
6 Aluminum foil	**16** Craft knife
7 Paper towels	**17** Artist's paintbrush
8 Rolling pin	**18** Spatula
9 Modeling drill	**19** Location pegs
10 Sandbags	**20** White tile

female fitting and are used to align the two halves of a two-part mold.

White tile. A white tile is useful for mixing glue or paint.

Dust masks. These are available from hardware stores, and one must be worn when using gold bronze powder. It is also advisable to wear a mask when mixing plaster to avoid inhaling the dust.

Gilding brush. Available from art-supply stores, this brush can be used to press Dutch metal leaf on to gold size and to apply gold bronze powder.

BASIC TECHNIQUE 1

THIS SIMPLE TECHNIQUE IS THE BASIS FOR MANY OF THE PROJECTS IN THIS BOOK, AND IS THE IDEAL WAY FOR A BEGINNER TO START CREATING IMAGINATIVE MOLDS. IDEALLY THE SUBJECT CHOSEN SHOULD NATURALLY HAVE ONE FLAT SURFACE, ALTHOUGH THIS IS NOT ESSENTIAL. CASTS WITH A FLAT SURFACE CAN BE HUNG ON A WALL, USED AS A PAPERWEIGHT OR ORNAMENT, OR USED TO DECORATE FRAMES, BOXES, AND FURNITURE.

Casting a flat-bottomed mold

1 Cut a piece of aluminum foil approximately 2 in wider than the object you want to mold. Coat one side of the foil with petroleum jelly. Place the object on the foil, and fold up the sides to make a nest, leaving about 1 in clear all the way around.

2 Spoon cold-curing silicone base into a plastic container, counting the number of spoonfuls you use. Add curing agent at the ratio of 1 spoonful curing agent to 20-spoonfuls silicone base. Mix thoroughly. Then add enough colorant to color the mixture slightly. Spoon over the object to cover it completely. Allow to dry for twenty-four hours at room temperature.

3 Mix more silicone base, using the same ratio of curing agent as in Step 2, but do not add any colorant. Using the tip of a small spatula, add a small amount of thixotropic additive. Stir thoroughly before adding more since it does not thicken the mixture immediately. Once it is the consistency of whipped cream, spread it on the object over the first coat, using the spatula or a teaspoon. Make sure that it is completely covered with the mixture. Adding color to the first coat allows you to see if the object has been covered properly. Allow to dry for twenty-four hours at room temperature.

MATERIALS AND EQUIPMENT YOU WILL NEED

ALUMINUM FOIL • OBJECT TO BE MOLDED • PETROLEUM JELLY • SPOON • COLD-CURING SILICONE BASE • PLASTIC CONTAINER • CURING AGENT • COLORANT • SMALL SPATULA • THIXOTROPIC ADDITIVE • SMALL PAIR OF SCISSORS • WATER • JUG • CASTING PLASTER • BAG OF SAND • PICTURE-HANGING CORD (OPTIONAL)

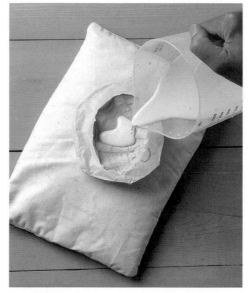

4 Remove the object from the mold. If there is any excess silicone on the bottom, snip it off with a pair of scissors. Hold the mold up to the light to see if there are any thin patches. If there are, mix some more thickened silicone and spread it over these patches.

6 Support the mold on a bag that is loosely filled with sand. Pour in the plaster mixture. When the mold is full, shake it to allow the air bubbles to rise.

8 When the plaster is dry, peel the mold away from the cast.

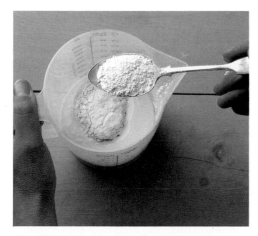

5 When the mold is dry, fill it two thirds with water. Then empty the water into a jug. Using a spoon, sprinkle casting plaster into the water until the plaster sits on top and the water no longer absorbs it. Stir thoroughly, making sure there are no lumps.

7 If you want to hang the plaster cast on the wall, cut a piece of picture cord, make a loop in it and tie a knot. Submerge the cord in the plaster, covering the knot but leaving the loop free. Allow the plaster to dry for approximately one hour at room temperature.

9 The cast seashell is almost an exact replica of the original and is now ready for decorating.

BASIC TECHNIQUE 2

MANY SUBJECTS WHICH ARE IDEAL FOR MOLDING, SUCH AS FRUIT AND VEGETABLES, DO NOT HAVE A NATURALLY FLAT SURFACE. THE TECHNIQUE SHOWN HERE WILL PRODUCE A FULLY THREE-DIMENSIONAL CAST. TO CREATE THIS EFFECT THE MOLD HAS TO BE MADE IN TWO PARTS. THIS MOLD WILL PRODUCE CASTS WHICH ARE EXACT COPIES OF THE OBJECTS USED. ONCE DECORATED, THEY MAKE WONDERFUL FREESTANDING ORNAMENTS.

Casting a three-dimensional mold

1 Use a plastic container which is slightly bigger than the object you want to cast. Grease the sides of the container with petroleum jelly.

2 Place the object in the container, and gradually add wet clay. Fill the container until the object is covered exactly halfway up. Make sure the surface is smooth.

3 At regular intervals, insert pairs of location pegs. Push the pegs into the clay until they are also half submerged.

4 In a plastic container or glass jar, mix cold-curing silicone base with curing agent at a ratio of 20-parts base to 1-part curing agent. Stir well. Pour the silicone mixture over the clay and the object, covering them completely to a thickness of about 1/2–3/4 in above the object. Allow to dry for twenty-four hours.

5 Slide a knife down between the silicone and the container, and push the silicone out of the container. Grease the silicone with petroleum jelly, but not the location pegs or the object.

6 Put the whole piece back into the original container, facing upward. Roll two pieces of wax plasticine into sausage shapes, and place them on top of the object. This will give you two channels for pouring in the plaster.

MATERIALS AND EQUIPMENT YOU WILL NEED

PLASTIC CONTAINER • OBJECT TO BE MOLDED • PETROLEUM JELLY • CLAY • LOCATION PEGS • PLASTIC CONTAINER OR GLASS JAR • COLD-CURING SILICONE BASE • CURING AGENT • KNIFE • WAX PLASTICINE • TWO THICK, ELASTIC BANDS • JUG • WATER • SPOON • CASTING PLASTER

7 Mix some more silicone base and curing agent, using the same ratio as in Step 4. Pour in the silicone, supporting the plasticine with your finger. Cover the object to a thickness of about ¹/₂—³/₄ in. Allow to dry for twenty-four hours.

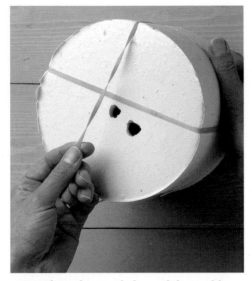

9 Place the two halves of the mold together, and secure with two thick, elastic bands. Place the half with the two holes facing up.

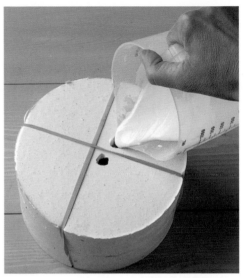

11 Pour the plaster into the mold through one of the holes. The other will act as an escape route for air. Fill the mold with plaster until both holes are full.

8 Remove the silicone from the container in the same way as described in Step 5. Pull the mold apart, and remove the object.

10 Fill a jug with water. Using a spoon, sprinkle plaster into the jug. Repeat until the water stops absorbing the plaster and the plaster no longer sinks. Stir well.

12 Leave the plaster to dry for two hours. Pull the mold apart and remove the plaster cast.

FINISHING TECHNIQUES

Flat-bottomed casts are generally smooth and require very little finishing work to get them ready for decorating. Air holes may have been captured in the plaster, and if these appear on the surface of the cast, they will need filling. This is easily done with a small amount of casting plaster mixed with water. Three-dimensional casts require a little more work to disguise the marks left by the casting process.

Basic technique 1

1 If there are any air holes, mix a small amount of plaster with water until it is the consistency of putty. Using a spatula, fill the holes with plaster, and rub smooth with your finger.

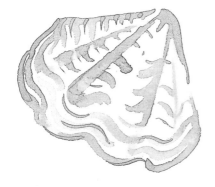

Basic technique 2

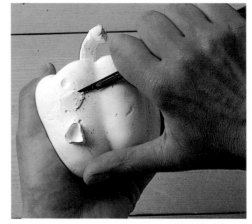

1 Using a craft knife, remove the two plaster "stalks" left by the pouring channels.

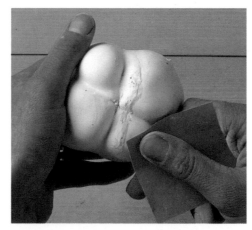

2 Rub down the joint and any other imperfections with sandpaper until perfectly smooth.

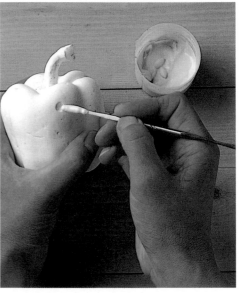

3 Mix some more plaster with water in a small plastic container until it is the consistency of putty. Using a spatula, fill any air holes, and smooth the plaster down with your finger.

MATERIALS AND EQUIPMENT YOU WILL NEED

CRAFT KNIFE • SANDPAPER • CASTING PLASTER • WATER • SPOON • SMALL PLASTIC CONTAINER • SPATULA

TEDDY BEARS

SIMPLE REPEAT DESIGNS CAN BE ACHIEVED WITH PASTRY CUTTERS. YOU CAN STICK THEM ON TO PICTURE OR MIRROR FRAMES, OR FURNITURE, OR USE THEM TO MAKE A FRIEZE. THERE ARE MANY DESIGNS SUITABLE FOR CHILDREN'S ROOMS, AND CHILDREN ENJOY CUTTING OUT SHAPES AND CASTING THEM IN PLAS-TER. THIS PROJECT USES A PRODUCT WHICH COMBINES WAX AND PLASTICINE. THE RESULT IS A VERY SMOOTH AND PLIABLE MATERIAL THAT IS IDEAL FOR THIS KIND OF WORK. HOWEVER, CLAY COULD BE USED, INSTEAD. PAINT THE CAST SHAPES TO COMPLEMENT THE ROOM'S COLOR SCHEME.

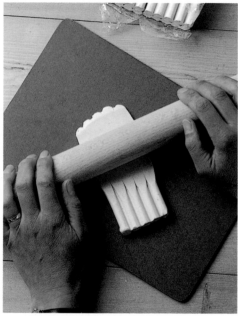

1 Roll out the wax plasticine with a rolling pin to a thickness of about ¼ in.

2 Using a pastry cutter, cut out teddy-bear shapes.

3 Mold and cast the teddy-bear shapes as described in Basic Technique 1, omitting Step 7. Paint the casts with yellow acrylic paint.

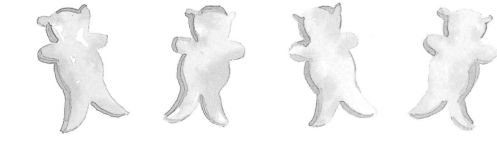

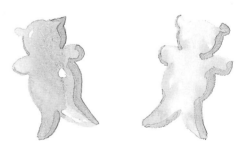

MATERIALS AND EQUIPMENT YOU WILL NEED
WAX PLASTICINE • ROLLING PIN • PASTRY CUTTER IN TEDDY-BEAR SHAPE • MATERIALS LISTED FOR BASIC TECHNIQUE 1 •
YELLOW ACRYLIC PAINT • ½ IN HOUSEHOLD PAINTBRUSH

STARS

E VEN THE PLAINEST PIECE OF FURNITURE, BOX OR FRAME CAN BE TRANS-FORMED WITH THE ADDITION OF SOME SIMPLE DECORATED PLASTER SHAPES. A STAR-SHAPED PASTRY CUTTER IS USED IN THIS PROJECT. CUTTERS ARE AVAILABLE IN A WIDE VARIETY OF DIFFERENT SHAPES AND ARE QUICK AND EASY TO USE. HOWEVER, YOU COULD MAKE CARDBOARD TEMPLATES OF THE SHAPES YOU WANT TO USE, AND CUT AROUND THEM WITH A CRAFT KNIFE TO PRODUCE THE SAME EFFECT.

1 Roll the wax plasticine out with a rolling pin to a thickness of about $^1/_4$ in.

2 Using a pastry cutter, cut out star shapes.

3 Mold and cast the shapes as described in Basic Technique 1, omitting Step 7. Paint with dark-blue, dark-red and olive-green latex paint.

MATERIALS AND EQUIPMENT YOU WILL NEED
WAX PLASTICINE • ROLLING PIN • PASTRY CUTTER IN STAR SHAPE • MATERIALS LISTED FOR BASIC TECHNIQUE 1 •
LATEX PAINT: DARK BLUE, DARK RED AND OLIVE GREEN • $^1/_2$ IN HOUSEHOLD PAINTBRUSH

FACE MASK

THIS PROJECT IS UNUSUAL BECAUSE THE MOLD IS PLASTIC AND IS IN TWO PARTS. THE LARGER PART IS FILLED WITH PLASTER, AND THE SMALLER PART IS PRESSED INTO IT, PRODUCING A THIN, HOLLOW FACE MASK. IT CAN BE HUNG ON THE WALL AS A DECORATIVE ITEM OR USED AS A FACE MASK. FOR A FACE MASK, CUT OUT THE EYES WITH A SHARP CRAFT KNIFE, DRILL A HOLE IN EACH SIDE OF THE MASK AND KNOT RIBBON THROUGH THE HOLES TO ACT AS TIES.

1 Support the larger part of the mold on a bag that is loosely filled with sand. Cast, following the instructions provided with the mold. While the plaster is still wet, press the smaller part of the mold down on top of the larger part, and weigh down with a second bag of sand. Allow eave to dry for approximately half an hour at room temperature.

2 Remove the mold by pressing your fingers on to the forehead and chin of the face, and pulling the mold apart. Break off the outside edges. Mix red and white acrylic paint together on a white tile or saucer to make pink. Then paint the skin. Paint the eye mask in black acrylic paint. Paint the lips red. Mix a darker pink color and paint around the eyes, nose and the outside of the eye mask to create a shaded effect.

3 Finally, decorate the eye mask with a gold pen.

MATERIALS AND EQUIPMENT YOU WILL NEED

TWO-PART PLASTIC MOLD OF FACE MASK (SEE LIST OF SUPPLIERS) • TWO BAGS OF SAND • CASTING PLASTER • WATER •
ACRYLIC PAINT: RED, WHITE AND BLACK • ARTIST'S PAINTBRUSH • WHITE TILE OR SAUCER • GOLD FELT-TIPPED PEN •
CRAFT KNIFE TO CUT OUT EYES (OPTIONAL) • RIBBON TIES (OPTIONAL)

SCULPTED GRAPES

BEING ABLE TO SCULPT YOUR OWN DESIGNS OPENS UP ENDLESS POSSIBILITIES. IN THIS PROJECT, A BUNCH OF GRAPES IS USED TO DECORATE A WASTEPAPER BIN MADE OF MEDIUM-DENSITY FIBERBOARD (MDF). THE BIN IS PAINTED WITH BURGUNDY OIL-BASED GLOSS PAINT, AND BLACK GLOSS PAINT INSIDE. CLAY IS THE TRADITIONALLY USED FOR SCULPTING, BUT HERE, WAX PLASTICINE IS USED. THIS DOES NOT DRY OUT OR GO HARD, SO YOU CAN LEAVE IT BEFORE MAKING A MOLD.

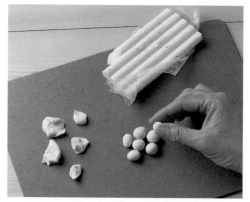

1 To make the grapes, roll small pieces of wax plasticine into oval balls. Place the grapes together in a cluster.

2 Using a craft knife, cut out five-pointed leaves. Score in vein lines.

3 Place the leaves on top of the grape cluster. Fill in any gaps using a spatula and extra wax plasticine. Cast as described in Basic Technique 1, omitting Step 7.

4 Mix green and yellow acrylic paint together on a white tile or saucer to make a yellowish green color. Paint the grapes. Mix green and blue paint to make a bluish-green color. Paint the leaves. Allow to dry for one hour.

5 Dip your finger into a jar of gilt cream. Using a small amount, rub lightly on to the leaves to highlight them. Using a small spatula and two-part epoxy resin glue, stick the bunch of grapes on to the side of the wastepaper bin.

MATERIALS AND EQUIPMENT YOU WILL NEED

WAX PLASTICINE • CRAFT KNIFE • MATERIALS LISTED FOR BASIC TECHNIQUE 1 • ACRYLIC PAINT: GREEN, YELLOW AND BLUE • WHITE TILE OR SAUCER • ARTIST'S PAINTBRUSH • GILT CREAM • WASTEPAPER BIN • TWO-PART EPOXY RESIN GLUE

SILVERING A SHELL

IN AFRICA, SEVERAL KINDS OF LARGE LAND SNAILS HAVE BEAUTIFUL SHELLS. NATURE GIVES US SHAPES WHICH JUST CRY OUT TO BE USED. SILVER IS PARTICULARLY APPROPRIATE SINCE IT OFFERS BOTH LIGHTNESS AND SHINE SO THAT EACH LAYER CATCHES THE LIGHT. TO CREATE THE RIGHT LUSTER, ALUMINUM DUTCH METAL LEAF IS APPLIED TO THE SHELL, THEN DISTRESSED WITH BLACK AND RAW-UMBER LATEX PAINT TO GIVE AN ANTIQUE LOOK.

1 Cast the shell as described in Basic Technique 1, omitting Step 7.

2 Paint the shell with two coats of black latex paint, allowing the paint to dry for two hours after each coat. Paint water-based gold size on to the shell, smoothing out any air bubbles with the brush. Allow to dry for about half an hour. When it is ready, the size will become transparent.

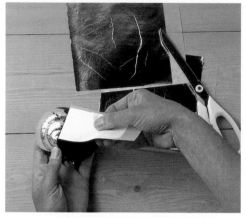

3 Cut the sheet of aluminum Dutch metal leaf into four pieces. Place them one at a time on top of the size, and press down with your finger. Once the metal leaf has stuck to the size, remove the transfer paper. Each piece should slightly overlap the last one. If there are any gaps, fill them in with smaller pieces of metal leaf. When the shell is covered, brush it lightly with a dry brush to remove any excess metal leaf. Using a household paintbrush, paint on pale-shellac varnish to seal the metal leaf. (Clean the brush with methylated alcohol.) Allow to dry for half an hour.

4 Mix together equal amounts of black and raw-umber latex paint. Thin to the consistency of heavy cream, and stir well. Paint on top of the metal leaf, covering it completely.

5 Wipe off the paint immediately with a paper towel. Make sure you use a clean part of the paper towel each time you rub, or you will put the paint back on the shell.

MATERIALS AND EQUIPMENT YOU WILL NEED

LAND SHELL • MATERIALS LISTED FOR BASIC TECHNIQUE 1 • LATEX PAINT: BLACK AND RAW UMBER •
TWO ½ IN HOUSEHOLD PAINTBRUSHES • WATER-BASED GOLD SIZE • ALUMINUM DUTCH METAL LEAF ON TRANSFER PAPER • BRUSH •
PALE-SHELLAC VARNISH • METHYLATED ALCOHOL • PAPER TOWELS

COLOR-WASHED SHELL

W HEN YOU ARE CHOOSING AN OBJECT TO DECORATE, IT IS IMPORTANT TO LOOK AT BOTH SHAPE AND TEXTURE. THE SHELL USED IN THIS PROJECT IS JUST A SIMPLE CLAM SHELL, BUT IT HAS A VERY INTRICATE SURFACE. A COLOR WASH, RUBBED OFF WHEN WET, ALLOWS THE BASE COLOR OF THE OBJECT TO SHOW THROUGH ON THE RAISED AREAS WHILE THE COLOR WASH STAYS IN THE NOOKS AND CRANNIES, GIVING A WONDERFULLY WEATHERED LOOK.

1 Cast the shell as described in Basic Technique 1.

3 Mix dark-green latex paint with white in a 50/50 ratio. Add 1-part water to 2-parts latex paint, and mix thoroughly. Cover the shell all over with this watered-down color.

4 While the paint is still wet, rub off some of the color with a paper towel. Rub only the raised areas, leaving the color in the crevices. Allow to dry for one hour. Thread the ribbon through the picture cord loop for hanging.

2 Paint the shell all over with dark-green latex paint. Let dry for one hour at room temperature. Paint on a second coat of the same color and allow to dry for one hour.

MATERIALS AND EQUIPMENT YOU WILL NEED

SEASHELL • MATERIALS LISTED FOR BASIC TECHNIQUE 1 • LATEX PAINT: DARK GREEN AND WHITE • $^{1}/_{2}$ IN HOUSEHOLD PAINTBRUSH •
PAPER TOWELS • RIBBON

BRONZED OAK DECORATION

WE CANNOT ALL BE GOOD SCULPTORS, BUT NATURE SUPPLIES AN ABUN-
DANCE OF INTERESTING SHAPES TO COPY. THESE ACORNS ARE CAST FROM
REAL ACORNS, AND THE OAK LEAVES ARE COPIED IN WAX PLASTICINE. BRONZE CAR
PAINT AND A SOFT-GREEN WASH MAKE THEM LOOK AS IF THEY ARE CAST IN ANCIENT
BRONZE. IN THIS PROJECT, AN OLD BOX FROM A THRIFT SHOP IS TOTALLY TRANS-
FORMED WITH A LITTLE DECORATION.

1 Cast the acorns as described in Basic
Technique 1, omitting Step 7.

2 Using thin, white cardboard, draw
around two oak leaves. Cut out with a
small pair of scissors.

3 Roll out the wax plasticine with a
rolling pin to a thickness of about $1/4$ in.

MATERIALS AND EQUIPMENT YOU WILL NEED

ACORNS AND OAK LEAVES • MATERIALS LISTED FOR BASIC TECHNIQUE 1 • THIN, WHITE CARDBOARD • PENCIL OR BALLPOINT PEN • WAX PLAS-
TICINE • ROLLING PIN • CRAFT KNIFE • SPATULA • BRONZE CAR PAINT • DARK-GREEN LATEX PAINT • ARTIST'S PAINTBRUSH • PAPER TOWELS •
WOODEN BOX • SHELLAC SANDING SEALER (OPTIONAL) • $1/2$ IN HOUSEHOLD PAINTBRUSH • SATIN-FINISH ACRYLIC VARNISH •
TWO-PART EPOXY RESIN GLUE

4 Place the cut-out leaf shapes on the plasticine. Using a craft knife, cut around the shapes.

6 Place the cast acorns on top of the plasticine leaves. Using a spatula, fill in any gaps with extra wax plasticine.

8 Spray the cast with bronze car paint, covering it completely. Allow to dry for one hour.

5 Score the plasticine leaves with the sharp end of a spatula to make veins.

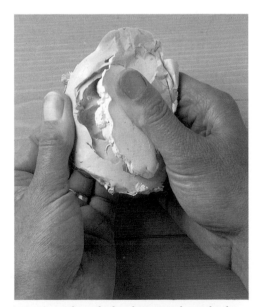

7 Cast the whole object as described in Basic Technique 1, omitting Step 7. Once it is cast in plaster, leave for at least two hours before removing from the mold. Make sure you remove the cast as a whole or you may break the leaves.

9 Thin dark-green latex paint with water in a 50/50 ratio. Paint it over the bronze paint with an artist's paint-brush, and rub off with a paper towel while still wet. Leave some dark-green paint in the crevices. ▶

10 If the box has been varnished, coat it with shellac sanding sealer. Allow to dry for half an hour. Paint on two coats of dark-green latex paint, allowing the box to dry for two hours at room temperature after each coat.

12 Using a spatula and two-part epoxy resin glue, stick the oak decoration to the top of the box.

11 Paint the box with two coats of satin-finish acrylic varnish. Allow to dry for one hour after each coat.

"IVORY" CHERUB

THE USE OF REAL IVORY IS NOW ILLEGAL, BUT SINCE PLASTER IS COLD TO THE TOUCH, IT MAKES A CONVINCING SUBSTITUTE. ALL THAT IS REQUIRED TO CREATE THE "IVORY" FINISH IS A SIMPLE PROCESS OF SEALING AND COLOR-WASHING. THIS CHERUB WAS ORIGINALLY CARVED IN WOOD, PROBABLY TO DECORATE A FIREPLACE SURROUND OR A PIECE OF FURNITURE. IT WOULD LOOK VERY ATTRACTIVE HANGING ON THE WALL.

1 Cast the cherub as described in Basic Technique 1.

2 Paint shellac sanding sealer all over the cherub. Use an artist's paintbrush to make sure the shellac does not collect in pools in the crevices. (Clean the brush with methylated alcohol.) Allow to dry for half an hour. Then paint on another coat. Allow to dry.

3 Water down some raw-umber latex paint until it is the consistency of heavy cream. Using a household paint-brush, cover the cherub completely in paint.

4 While the paint is still wet, rub it off with a paper towel. Make sure you use a clean piece of the towel each time you rub or you will put the paint back on. Leave the paint in the crevices. Thread the ribbon through the picture cord loop for hanging.

MATERIALS AND EQUIPMENT YOU WILL NEED

WOODEN CARVING OF CHERUB • MATERIALS LISTED FOR BASIC TECHNIQUE 1 • SHELLAC SANDING SEALER • ARTIST'S PAINTBRUSH •
METHYLATED ALCOHOL • RAW-UMBER LATEX PAINT • ½ IN HOUSEHOLD PAINTBRUSH • PAPER TOWELS • RIBBON

"ANTIQUE" GILDED FRAME

ANTIQUE FRAMES ARE BEAUTIFULLY ORNATE, BUT OFTEN VERY EXPENSIVE TO BUY. IT IS RARER STILL TO FIND A MATCHING PAIR OR SET. THIS PROJECT RECREATES, IN EXACT DETAIL, A FINELY CARVED AND GILDED FRAME MADE BY A NINETEENTH-CENTURY CRAFTSMAN. IN THIS INSTANCE, THE FRAME IS RELATIVELY SMALL, BUT THE SAME TECHNIQUE CAN BE APPLIED TO ANY SCALE ONCE THE PROCESSES INVOLVED HAVE BEEN MASTERED.

1 This mold was made from an original frame, following Basic Technique 1, Steps 1–4.

2 Since this mold is larger than those in previous projects, it may become distorted once plaster is poured in, so it will need a support. Fine casting plaster mixed with water is ideal for this. It dries quickly, so only mix a small amount at a time. Mix it in the same way as casting plaster (see Basic Technique 1, Step 5). Using a spoon, spread it on to the outside of the mold, leaving 2 in all around the side uncovered.

3 Mix enough casting plaster (see Basic Technique 1, Step 5) to fill the mold halfway up. Allow to dry for about one hour at room temperature.

4 Lay wax plasticine around the inside edge of the mold on top of the plaster. This will give the frame a rebated edge in which to insert the glass, picture, and backing. The plasticine should be approximately $^1/_2$ in wide. ▶

MATERIALS AND EQUIPMENT YOU WILL NEED

FRAME • MATERIALS LISTED FOR BASIC TECHNIQUE 1 • FINE CASTING PLASTER • WAX PLASTICINE • TWO PICTURE RINGS • SANDPAPER • LATEX PAINT: RED AND RAW UMBER • $^1/_2$ IN HOUSEHOLD PAINTBRUSH • WATER-BASED GOLD SIZE • GOLD DUTCH METAL LEAF ON TRANSFER PAPER • DUST MASK • GOLD BRONZE POWDER • GILDING BRUSH • PALE-SHELLAC VARNISH • METHYLATED ALCOHOL • PAPER TOWELS

5 Mix more casting plaster. Pour into the mold on top of the first layer of plaster. While the plaster is still wet, insert two picture rings on each side of the frame so that you will be able to hang it on the wall. Allow the plaster to dry for one hour.

6 Remove the plaster cast from the mold and take off the plasticine. If the edges are not completely smooth, rub them down with sandpaper. Paint the frame with two coats of red latex paint, allowing it to dry for two hours after each coat.

7 Paint a coat of water-based gold size on to the frame. Allow to dry for approximately half an hour. When it is ready, the size will become transparent.

8 Cut gold Dutch metal leaf into pieces approximately 2 in square, and place on top of the size. Rub your finger all over the transfer paper so that the gold is firmly stuck to the size. Remove the paper. Put on the next piece of metal leaf, which should slightly overlap the last piece. Again, rub with your finger. Then remove the transfer paper. Repeat until the whole frame is covered. Don't worry if there are some gaps. Brush the frame lightly with a dry brush to remove the excess metal leaf.

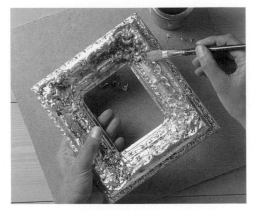

9 For this step, it is important to wear a dust mask. With something this intricate, it is impossible to cover it completely with metal leaf, but the use of gold bronze powder will remedy this. Dip the gilding brush into the gold bronze powder – the color should match the metal leaf as closely as possible. Lightly tap the brush on the jar to remove excess powder. Then work the powder into all the crevices.

10 Paint the frame all over with pale-shellac varnish to seal the gold. (Clean the brush with methylated alcohol.) Water down some raw-umber latex paint until it is the consistency of heavy cream. Stir well. Cover the frame with paint, making sure you work it into the crevices. Wipe the paint off immediately with a paper towel. Use a clean piece each time you wipe or you may put the paint back on.

PLASTER BOW

Not all plasterwork has to be cast from a mold. Dipping objects in plaster is another method with a long tradition. This decorative bow can be used to hide a picture hook, with the picture hanging below it on ribbon. It would also make a wonderful decoration for curtain valances. The bows can be made any size by cutting the cord and reattaching it where the knot of the bow falls.

1 Tie a belt from a bathrobe into a bow. Leave the ends hanging to slightly different lengths.

2 If the bow is to be hung, sew a slip ring on to the back of the knot.

3 Measure the bow and cut a piece of fiberboard 6 in longer top and bottom than the bow, and 6 in wider on each side. Cut a piece of aluminum foil slightly wider than the bow and long enough to fold over the top and bottom of the fiberboard. Cover the foil with petroleum jelly. Then fold the ends over the fiberboard. Lay the bow on the foil. Using a hammer, gently tap ³/₄ in panel pins into the fiberboard at each corner of the bow. Place the pins just inside the bow, not through it. These pins will be used later to hold the plaster bow in place while it dries.

4 Mix the plaster in a plastic container as described in Basic Technique 1, Step 5. Remove the belt bow from the fiberboard, and dip it in the plaster.

5 While the bow is still wet, attach it to the fiberboard around the panel pins. Stand the fiberboard vertically to allow the excess plaster to run off. ▶

MATERIALS AND EQUIPMENT YOU WILL NEED

BELT FROM BATHROBE • SLIP RING (OPTIONAL) • NEEDLE AND THREAD (OPTIONAL) • FIBERBOARD • ALUMINUM FOIL • PETROLEUM JELLY •
³/₄ IN PANEL PINS • HAMMER • WATER • PLASTER • SPOON • PLASTIC CONTAINER • CRAFT KNIFE • ¹/₂ IN HOUSEHOLD PAINTBRUSH •
ROYAL-BLUE LATEX PAINT • GILT CREAM

6 Allow to dry for two hours. Remove the plaster bow from the panel pins. Scrape off any plaster which does not follow the contours of the belt.

8 Lightly rub on gilt cream with your finger to highlight the contours.

7 Using a household paintbrush, paint the plaster belt with royal-blue latex paint.

Right: The plaster bow looks equally stunning gilded with gold Dutch metal leaf.

DECORATIVE BELL PEPPER

FRUITS AND VEGETABLES COME IN ALL SHAPES AND SIZES, AND ARE READILY AVAILABLE. ANY SHAPE, AS LONG AS IT IS NOT TOO INTRICATE, IS PERFECT FOR CASTING. A BELL PEPPER IS IDEAL BECAUSE IT WILL STAND UPRIGHT. THE COLOR CHOSEN HERE IS ONE OF THE PEPPER'S NATURAL COLORS, BUT BY ADDING A GILDED STALK, IT BECOMES A STYLISH ORNAMENT. SEVERAL OF THESE PEPPERS WOULD LOOK WONDERFUL CLUSTERED TOGETHER IN A WOODEN BOWL.

1 Cast the bell pepper as described in Basic Technique 2.

3 Paint the rest of the pepper with red latex paint. Allow to dry for at least two hours. Then paint on a second coat. Allow to dry for twenty-four hours.

5 Using a scouring pad dipped in water, gently rub off the burgundy paint in places to reveal the red paint underneath. Allow to dry for one hour.

2 Paint the stalk with two coats of red latex paint. Allow to dry for two hours after each coat. Using your finger, rub the stalk with gilt cream. Leave a little of the red showing to give a "distressed" look.

4 Add water to burgundy latex paint in a 50/50 ratio. Paint all over the pepper except the stalk. Allow to dry for one hour.

6 Varnish with two coats of satin-finish acrylic varnish.

MATERIALS AND EQUIPMENT YOU WILL NEED

BELL PEPPER • MATERIALS LISTED FOR BASIC TECHNIQUE 2 • LATEX PAINT: RED AND BURGUNDY • $^1/_2$ IN HOUSEHOLD PAINTBRUSH • GILT CREAM • SCOURING PAD • SATIN-FINISH ACRYLIC VARNISH

SHELL WALL PLAQUE

YOU DO NOT ALWAYS NEED TO USE SILICONE TO CREATE PLASTERWORK DESIGNS. SUBMERGING OBJECTS IN WET PLASTER ALSO WORKS VERY WELL. THIS PROJECT USES SHELLS, BUT OTHER OBJECTS, SUCH AS VEGETABLES OR FISH, WOULD BE EQUALLY SUITABLE. THE ARRANGEMENT OF THE SHELLS IS CRUCIAL FOR BALANCE AND COMPOSITION, SO SPEND SOME TIME PLANNING OUT THE EFFECT ON A PIECE OF PAPER THE SAME SIZE AS THE PLAQUE. IT IS ALSO IMPORTANT NOT TO USE TOO MANY OR THEY COULD LOOK CRAMMED, AND CHOOSE DIFFERENT SHAPES AND SIZES TO GIVE VARIETY AND STYLE.

1 Grease the shells well with petroleum jelly so that they do not stick in the wet plaster.

2 Mix some casting plaster in a jug as described in Basic Technique 1, Step 5. Pour into a large plaster container until half full. Allow to dry for one hour. Mix some more plaster, and pour it on top of the first coat to fill the plastic container. Press the shells into the wet plaster as far as they will go without being totally submerged.

3 Allow the plaster to dry for one hour. Then remove the shells.

MATERIALS AND EQUIPMENT YOU WILL NEED

SHELLS • PETROLEUM JELLY • CASTING PLASTER • WATER • SPOON • JUG • LARGE, SHALLOW PLASTIC CONTAINER •
LATEX PAINT: DARK GREEN AND PALE GREEN • TWO $1/2$ IN HOUSEHOLD PAINTBRUSHES • GILT CREAM • GIMLET • PICTURE CORD •
TWO-PART EPOXY RESIN GLUE • STICKY TAPE

4 Turn the plastic container upside down, and gently tap the base to remove the plaster.

5 Paint the cast all over with a coat of dark-green latex paint. Allow to dry for one hour.

6 Using two separate household paint-brushes, one for dark-green paint and the other for pale-green paint, stipple pale-green latex paint on to a small area of the plaque. While the pale-green paint is still wet, stipple some dark-green paint next to it. Blend in the two colors where they join by slightly stippling the dark-green paint on top of the wet pale-green paint. Repeat the process until the whole plaque is covered.

7 Allow the paint to dry for two hours. Using your finger, rub gilt cream into the shell impressions.

8 Using a gimlet, make a hole in the back of the plaque. Tie a piece of picture cord into a loop. Place glue in the hole. Then insert the knot of the loop. Put a piece of sticky tape over the hole to keep the cord in place. Allow to dry for twenty-four hours. ▶

Above: Vary the choice of colors and painting and decorating techniques for different effects. This plaque has been color-washed in pale blue for a fresh, contemporary look.

AUTUMN SEEDHEADS

AUTUMN OFFERS AN ABUNDANCE OF IDEAS FOR CASTING. SEEDHEADS AND BERRIES APPEAR IN STUNNING SHAPES AND COLORS WHICH, AS LONG AS THEY ARE REASONABLY FIRM, CAN EASILY BE CAST IN PLASTER. ONCE DECORATED, THEY MAKE SUPERB DECORATIONS FOR FRAMES, BOXES, AND FURNITURE. IN THIS CASE, THE SEEDHEAD CASTS, TAKEN FROM WATER IRISES, HAVE BEEN USED TO CREATE A DELIGHTFUL FRAMED PICTURE.

1 Cast several seedheads as described in Basic Technique 1, omitting Step 7.

3 Mix 2-parts pale-blue paint to 1-part water. Using a damp sponge, pat the color on the board to create a sponged effect. Allow to dry for one hour.

5 Paint the seeds within the seedheads with red acrylic paint.

2 Paint a piece of fiberboard with two coats of sky-blue latex paint. Allow each coat to dry for at least two hours at room temperature.

4 Using an artist's paintbrush, mix yellow-ocher and green acrylic paint together on a white tile or saucer. Paint the seedhead casings, and allow to dry for one hour.

6 Using a small spatula and two-part epoxy resin glue, attach the decorated seedheads to the painted board. Leave to dry for twenty-four hours then mount the board in the frame.

MATERIALS AND EQUIPMENT YOU WILL NEED

SEEDHEADS • MATERIALS LISTED FOR BASIC TECHNIQUE 1 • PIECE OF FIBERBOARD • LATEX PAINT: SKY BLUE AND PALE BLUE •
½ IN HOUSEHOLD PAINTBRUSH • WATER • BOWL • SMALL, NATURAL SPONGE • ARTIST'S PAINTBRUSH •
ACRYLIC PAINT: YELLOW OCHER, GREEN, AND RED • WHITE TILE OR SAUCER • TWO-PART EPOXY RESIN GLUE • FRAME

LETTERS OF THE ALPHABET

CASTING LETTERS IN PLASTER TO CREATE NAMES OR INITIALS IS A VERY USEFUL AND ATTRACTIVE IDEA, AND THE LETTERS CAN BE DECORATED IN A VARIETY OF WAYS. THEY CAN BE USED TO IDENTIFY ROOMS, TO MARK PERSONAL POSSESSIONS, OR TO CREATE DECORATIVE MOTTOS OR FRIEZES. THE INITIAL DESIGN IS TAKEN FROM A SHEET OF DRY TRANSFER LETTERING AND CAN BE ENLARGED BY PHOTOCOPYING TO WHATEVER SIZE YOU NEED.

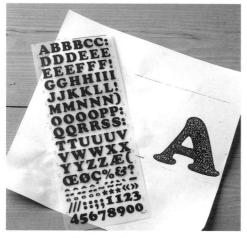

1 Using a sheet of dry transfer lettering, photocopy and enlarge a letter to the size you need.

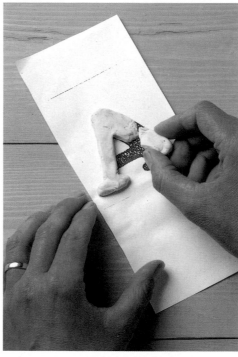

2 Place wax plasticine on top of the photocopied letter, following its shape exactly. Using your finger, smooth it flat. If necessary, cut off any excess with a craft knife. Cast the letter as described in Basic Technique 1, omitting Step 7.

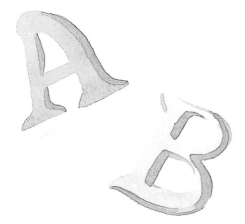

3 Using an artist's paintbrush, paint the plaster letter with two coats of dark-blue latex paint. Allow to dry for two hours after each coat.

4 Outline the letter in gold, using a gold felt-tipped pen.

MATERIALS AND EQUIPMENT YOU WILL NEED
SHEET OF DRY TRANSFER LETTERING • WAX PLASTICINE • CRAFT KNIFE • MATERIALS LISTED FOR BASIC TECHNIQUE 1 •
DARK-BLUE LATEX PAINT • ARTIST'S PAINTBRUSH • GOLD FELT-TIPPED PEN

WOODLAND COLLAGE

WOODS ARE FULL OF INTERESTING MATERIALS — LEAVES, BARK, BERRIES, AND FUNGI — ALL HIGHLY DECORATIVE AND EASY TO CAST. IF YOU KEEP YOUR EYES OPEN, EVERY WOODLAND WALK WILL SUGGEST WONDERFUL PROJECTS. BARK IS EXTREMELY DIVERSE, WITH BEAUTIFUL CONTOURS SPECIFIC TO EACH TREE.

THE BARK USED IN THIS PROJECT IS FROM AN OAK. THE ACORNS AND OAK LEAVES HAD BEEN CAST PREVIOUSLY FOR THE "BRONZED OAK DECORATION" PROJECT, WHERE THEY WERE USED TO DECORATE AN OLD BOX. COMBINED WITH THE CAST BARK, THEY MAKE A WONDERFUL NATURAL COLLAGE.

1 Cast the acorns and oak leaves as described in the "Bronzed Oak Decoration" project. Cut the fungi in half, and cast as described in Basic Technique 1, omitting Step 7.

2 Fill in any large splits in the bark, using a small spatula and some wax plasticine.

3 Because the bark is so intricate, it is best to spread a thick coat of silicone (see Basic Technique 1, Step 3) rather than a coat that is poured which may tear when removed. Cast as described in Basic Technique 1.

MATERIALS AND EQUIPMENT YOU WILL NEED
ACORNS • OAK LEAVES • THIN WHITE CARDBOARD • PENCIL OR BALLPOINT PEN • WAX PLASTICINE • ROLLING PIN •
CRAFT KNIFE • MATERIALS LISTED FOR BASIC TECHNIQUE 1 • FUNGI • BARK • LATEX PAINT: DARK GREEN, PALE GREEN, RED, AND RAW UMBER •
$^1/_2$ IN HOUSEHOLD PAINTBRUSH • PAPER TOWELS • ARTIST'S PAINTBRUSH • WATER-BASED GOLD SIZE •
GOLD DUTCH METAL LEAF ON TRANSFER PAPER • WATER • TWO-PART EPOXY RESIN GLUE

4 Paint the cast bark all over with dark-green latex paint. Allow to dry for two hours.

5 Water down some pale-green latex paint in a 50/50 ratio. Paint on top of the dark green paint, covering the bark completely.

6 While the paint is still wet, rub it off with paper towels, leaving some paint in the crevices.

7 Using an artist's paintbrush, paint the fungi and oak with red latex paint. Allow to dry for two hours.

8 Paint the acorns, oak leaves, and fungi with gold size. Leave for one hour, by which time the size will have become transparent, showing that it is ready for the next stage.

9 Cut gold Dutch metal leaf into small pieces, and place on top of the size. Smooth over with your finger until it sticks. Then remove the transfer paper. Each piece should slightly overlap the last piece. Remove the excess metal leaf with your finger.

▶

10 Water down some raw-umber latex paint until it is the consistency of light cream. Paint on top of the gold. Rub off at once with a paper towel. Leave some paint in the crevices.

12 Using an artist's paintbrush, stipple dark-green latex paint on to the acorns, oak leaves, and fungi, so that they blend with the bark.

11 Using a small spatula and two-part epoxy resin glue, stick the acorns, oak leaves, and fungi on to the bark. Allow to dry for twenty-four hours.

DECORATIVE TIN

CHINA TUREENS OFTEN HAVE BEAUTIFULLY SCULPTED HANDLES AND KNOBS, WHICH CAN BE CAST AND ADDED TO OTHER OBJECTS TO COMPLETELY CHANGE THEIR APPEARANCE. FOR THIS PROJECT, THE KNOB IS CAST FROM THE LID OF AN OLD BLUE-AND-WHITE VEGETABLE DISH, WHOSE BASE WAS LONG AGO EITHER BROKEN OR LOST. THE TIN, FROM A THRIFT SHOP, HAS BEEN GIVEN A SPLATTER GILDED FINISH TO MAKE AN EXOTIC YET PRACTICAL CONTAINER.

1 Cast the knob from the china lid as described in Basic Technique 1. Omit Step 1. Do not use a pouring coat as described in Step 2 since it is not possible to contain it. Instead, the first coat should be spread on as described in Step 3. Once dry, remove the mold from the knob, and hold it up to the light. If there are any holes or thin patches, mix more silicone as described in Step 3, and spread it on over the first coat.

2 Seal the tin with shellac sanding sealer. (Clean the brush with methylated alcohol.) Allow to dry. Then paint with two coats of black latex paint. Allow to dry for two hours after each coat.

4 Paint the knob with two coats of black latex paint, and allow to dry. With your finger, rub the high points of the knob with gilt cream.

3 Paint on a coat of water-based gold size and leave for approximately half an hour. Tear off small pieces of Dutch metal leaf, and tap them on to the tin with your finger.

5 Using a small spatula and two-part epoxy resin glue, attach the knob to the tin lid. Coat the tin with pale-shellac varnish to seal the metal leaf. (Clean the brush with methylated alcohol.)

MATERIALS AND EQUIPMENT YOU WILL NEED

CHINA LID WITH KNOB • TIN • MATERIALS LISTED FOR BASIC TECHNIQUE 1 • SHELLAC SANDING SEALER • METHYLATED ALCOHOL • BLACK LATEX PAINT • 1/2 IN HOUSEHOLD PAINTBRUSH • WATER-BASED GOLD SIZE • LOOSE GOLD DUTCH METAL LEAF • GILT CREAM • TWO-PART EPOXY RESIN GLUE • PALE-SHELLAC VARNISH

"CARVED" CANDLESTICK

ONE OF THE JOYS OF BEING ABLE TO CAST MOLDS IS THE ABILITY IT GIVES YOU TO TAKE A DECORATION FROM ONE OBJECT AND MAKE IT INTO SOMETHING COMPLETELY DIFFERENT. THERE ARE MANY BEAUTIFUL DECORATIVE FEATURES ON FURNITURE, FIREPLACES AND CEILINGS WHICH CAN BE CAST AND THEN TRANS-FORMED INTO SOMETHING QUITE NOVEL. THIS PROJECT USES THE DECORATION FROM AN OLD CHAIR AS THE BASIS FOR A CANDLESTICK.

1 Follow Basic Technique 1, omitting Steps 1, 2 and 7. The first coat of silicone has to be spread on with a small spatula, so mix it as in Step 3.

3 Cast in plaster as described in Basic Technique 1. Using a small modeling drill, gradually drill out the center until it is large enough to hold a candle.

5 Using an artist's paintbrush, paint the smaller petals and the center of the flower with gold acrylic paint. Allow to dry for one hour.

2 Remove the mold and hold it up to the light. If there are any holes or thin patches, mix another thick coat of silicone as described in Step 3. Spread it on over the first coat.

4 Paint two coats of olive-green latex over the candlestick. Allow to dry for two hours after each coat.

6 Water down some raw-umber latex paint until it is the consistency of cream. Paint it all over the candlestick. Wipe off immediately with a paper towel, leaving some paint in the crevices. Allow to dry for two hours. ▶

MATERIALS AND EQUIPMENT YOU WILL NEED

CHAIR BOSS OR OTHER SIMILAR DECORATION • MATERIALS LISTED FOR BASIC TECHNIQUE 1 • MODELING DRILL • CANDLE •
LATEX PAINT: OLIVE-GREEN AND RAW-UMBER • $1/2$ IN HOUSEHOLD PAINTBRUSH • GOLD ACRYLIC PAINT • ARTIST'S PAINTBRUSH • PAPER TOWELS •
SATIN-FINISH ACRYLIC VARNISH

7 Paint on two coats of satin-finish acrylic varnish.

8 Paint the bottom of the candlestick with olive-green paint.

Above: The candlestick can be painted and decorated to match a favorite table setting. The holder in the foreground has been gilded with gold Dutch metal leaf.

HOUSE PLAQUE

MAKING A PERSONALIZED NUMBER PLAQUE FOR YOUR HOUSE IS A VERY USEFUL PROJECT. PLASTER CAN BE USED OUTDOORS AS LONG AS IT DOES NOT GET FROZEN. THE PLAQUE CAN DEPICT THE SURROUNDINGS OF THE HOUSE OR THE NAME OF THE ROAD. A PLAQUE FOR A HOUSE NEAR THE SEA MIGHT BE DECORATED WITH AQUATIC MOTIFS, FOR EXAMPLE. IN THIS PROJECT, THE ACORNS REPRESENT "WOODLAND DRIVE," THE NAME OF THE ROAD.

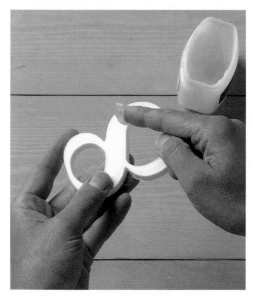

1 Grease a plastic number with petroleum jelly.

2 Grease some aluminum foil with petroleum jelly. Using plastic building bricks, build a box on top of the foil, at least three-bricks high. Leave a gap four-bricks wide at the top. Insert into this gap a brass attachment plate with two screws in the screwholes. Allow the top of the attachment plate to stick out above the box so that it can be used later for attaching the plaque to the wall. Surround the gap with wax plasticine to seal the gap. Mix casting plaster as described in Basic Technique 1, Step 5, and fill the box with plaster.

3 Press the greased number into the wet plaster and allow to dry for one hour. ▶

MATERIALS AND EQUIPMENT YOU WILL NEED

PLASTIC NUMBER • MATERIALS LISTED FOR BASIC TECHNIQUE 1 • PLASTIC BUILDING BRICKS •
BRASS ATTACHMENT PLATE WITH TWO SCREWS • WAX PLASTICINE • ACORNS • TWO-PART EPOXY RESIN GLUE • ARTIST'S PAINTBRUSH •
EXTERIOR PAINT: BLACK AND BLUE • ½ IN HOUSEHOLD PAINTBRUSH • OIL PAINT: PALE BLUE AND REDDISH BROWN • TURPENTINE •
PAPER TOWELS • EXTERIOR VARNISH

4 Remove the plastic number from the plaster.

5 Cast the acorns as described in Basic Technique 1, omitting Step 7. Attach to the plaque with glue. Allow to dry for twenty-four hours.

6 Using an artist's paintbrush, paint the indented number with black exterior paint. (Clean the brush as described on the paint can.)

7 Paint the rest of the plaque with blue exterior paint, using a household paintbrush.

8 Thin down some pale-blue artist's oil paint with turpentine. Wipe on to the plaque with a paper towel to give a mottled effect. Highlight the acorns in the same way, using reddish-brown oil paint. Seal the plaque with an exterior varnish.

KITCHEN BLACKBOARD

A BLACKBOARD IS VERY USEFUL IN THE KITCHEN FOR JOTTING DOWN SHOPPING LISTS AND MESSAGES. WHEN YOU ARE DESIGNING SOMETHING FOR A PARTICULAR ROOM, TRY TO USE DECORATIONS THAT RELATE TO THE SETTING. MANY VEGETABLES AND FRUITS ARE IDEAL FOR MOLDING. FOR THIS PROJECT, CHILIES AND MUSHROOMS HAVE BEEN CHOSEN TO DECORATE THE FRAME OF THE BLACKBOARD, BUT SEEDHEADS, BERRIES, AND WHEAT WOULD BE EQUALLY EFFECTIVE.

1 Cut the vegetables in half, and cast as described in Basic Technique 1, omitting Step 7. Repeat the process to give a total of eight chili halves and four mushroom halves.

2 Place the smaller piece of fiberboard in the center on top of the larger piece, and stick with wood glue. Drill a small hole in the center of the top of the larger piece. This will be used to hang the blackboard from a picture hook. Using a 2½ in household paintbrush, paint the smaller piece of fiberboard with two coats of blackboard paint. Allow to dry for two hours after each coat. (Wash the brush with turpentine.)

3 Paint the outside "frame" in royal-blue latex paint, using a smaller ½ in household paintbrush.

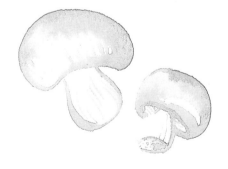

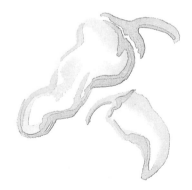

MATERIALS AND EQUIPMENT YOU WILL NEED
CHILIES AND BUTTON MUSHROOMS • MATERIALS LISTED FOR BASIC TECHNIQUE 1 •
PIECE OF ¼ IN THICK MEDIUM-DENSITY FIBERBOARD (MDF), 27½ x 20 IN •
PIECE OF ½ IN THICK MDF, 20 x 20 IN • WOOD GLUE • DRILL • 2½ IN HOUSEHOLD PAINTBRUSH • BLACKBOARD PAINT • TURPENTINE •
ROYAL-BLUE LATEX PAINT • ½ IN HOUSEHOLD PAINTBRUSH • ARTIST'S PAINTBRUSH • ACRYLIC PAINT: RED AND GREEN •
SHELLAC SANDING SEALER • METHYLATED ALCOHOL • TWO-PART EPOXY RESIN GLUE

4 Using an artist's paintbrush, paint the plaster chilies with red acrylic paint. Allow to dry for half an hour. Then paint the stalks with green acrylic paint.

5 Again using an artist's paintbrush, paint the plaster mushrooms with two coats of shellac sanding sealer. Allow to dry for half an hour between each coat. (Clean the brush with methylated alcohol.)

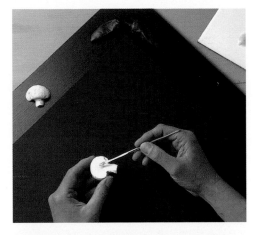

6 Arrange two chilies at each corner of the frame, with the stalks touching. Put two mushrooms halfway down each side. Using a small spatula and two-part epoxy resin glue, stick all the decorated vegetables in place.

SEASHELL MIRROR

A MIRROR WILL IMPROVE ANY ROOM, GIVING A FEELING OF LIGHT AND SPACE. OLD FRAMES CAN BE PICKED UP VERY CHEAPLY IN THRIFT SHOPS OR AT AUCTIONS. FRAMES WITH PLAIN, WIDE SURROUNDS LOOK INITIALLY UNATTRACTIVE, BUT THEY ARE THE IDEAL BASE FOR IMAGINATIVE DECORATION. THE FRAME IN THIS PROJECT, ORIGINALLY COVERED IN THICK, DARK VARNISH, BECOMES AN EXOTIC MIRROR SURROUND, IDEAL FOR A BEDROOM OR BATHROOM.

1 Cast the shell, a small scallop, as described in Basic Technique 1, omitting Step 7. You will need four plaster shells. If the frame has been varnished, apply one coat of shellac sanding sealer. Allow the shellac to dry for half an hour. (Clean the brush with methylated alcohol.)

2 Apply two coats of terracotta latex paint to the frame. Allow to dry for two hours after each coat.

3 Water down some brown latex paint in a 50/50 ratio. Paint all over the frame. Then wipe off while still wet with paper towels. Leave enough of the paint on to give a dragged effect.

MATERIALS AND EQUIPMENT YOU WILL NEED

SCALLOP SHELL • MATERIALS LISTED FOR BASIC TECHNIQUE 1 • FRAME • SHELLAC SANDING SEALER • $\frac{1}{2}$ IN HOUSEHOLD PAINTBRUSH •
METHYLATED ALCOHOL • LATEX PAINT: TERRACOTTA, BROWN, RED AND RAW UMBER • PAPER TOWELS • SATIN-FINISH ACRYLIC VARNISH •
ARTIST'S PAINTBRUSH • WATER-BASED GOLD SIZE • PALE-SHELLAC VARNISH • GOLD DUTCH METAL LEAF ON TRANSFER PAPER •
TWO-PART EPOXY RESIN GLUE

4 Varnish with two coats of satin-finish acrylic varnish. Allow to dry for one hour after each coat.

6 Cut a page of gold Dutch metal leaf into pieces large enough to cover each shell. Apply to the size. Rub the gold with your finger. Remove the transfer paper once the gold has stuck. If there are any gaps, add more pieces of metal leaf. Coat the shells with pale-shellac varnish to seal the metal leaf. (Clean the brush with methylated alcohol.) Leave to dry for half an hour.

7 Water down some raw-umber latex paint until it is the consistency of light cream. Stir well. Paint on over the gold with a household paintbrush. Wipe off, while wet, with paper towels, leaving some paint in the crevices.

5 Using an artist's paintbrush, paint the shells with red latex paint. Allow to dry for one hour. Paint on a coat of gold size. Leave for half an hour, by which time the size will have become transparent.

8 Using a spatula and two-part epoxy resin glue, stick the decorated shells to each corner of the frame. Allow to dry for twenty-four hours. ▶

Above: Seashells and land shells in all shapes and sizes can be cast, decorated with paint or Dutch metal leaf and applied to picture and mirror frames.

ADAPTING A WOOD CARVING

WOOD CARVINGS, WITH THEIR BEAUTIFUL AND, SOMETIMES, INTRICATE DESIGNS, CAN EASILY BE REPRODUCED IN PLASTER. IF THEY ARE OVER ONE-HUNDRED YEARS OLD, THEY ARE OUT OF COPYRIGHT, AND PERMISSIBLE TO COPY. THIS CARVING WASN'T LARGE ENOUGH FOR THE FIRESCREEN IT WAS INTENDED FOR, SO IT NEEDED TO BE ADAPTED. THIS PROJECT SHOWS HOW TO TAKE PARTS OF A CARVING AND RECAST THEM TO CREATE AN ADAPTED DESIGN.

1 The original wooden carving was cast twice in plaster as described in Basic Technique 1, omitting Step 7.

3 Allow to dry for half an hour before removing from the mold. Neaten the edges with a craft knife.

5 Allow twenty-four hours for the glue to dry. Then, using a spatula, fill in any gaps with wax plasticine.

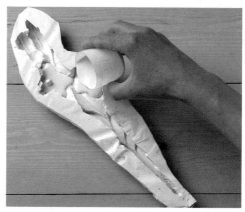

2 Mix a small pot of casting plaster as described in Basic Technique 1, Step 5. Pour the plaster into the parts of the mold which cast the two flowers.

4 Using a small spatula and two-part epoxy resin glue, stick the two main pieces together. Arrange the two flowers on the lower half and stick in place.

6 Cast as described in Basic Technique 1, omitting Step 7. Alow the plaster to dry for one hour before removing it from the mold.

MATERIALS AND EQUIPMENT YOU WILL NEED

WOOD CARVING • MATERIALS LISTED FOR BASIC TECHNIQUE 1 • SMALL PLASTIC POT • CRAFT KNIFE • TWO-PART EPOXY RESIN GLUE •
WAX PLASTICINE

RESTORING AN OLD FRAME

WHILE GILDED ANTIQUE FRAMES IN GOOD CONDITION ARE NOW EXPENSIVE TO BUY, YOU OFTEN FIND BEAUTIFUL OLD FRAMES IN THRIFT SHOPS AND ANTIQUE SHOPS WHICH ARE DAMAGED AND, THEREFORE, VERY REASONABLY PRICED. COLD-CURING SILICONE RUBBER IS IDEAL FOR RESTORING THEM. MISSING PIECES CAN BE COPIED EXACTLY, AND MATCHING THE GOLD IS MADE EASY USING THE DIFFERENT-COLORED GILT CREAMS AVAILABLE NOW.

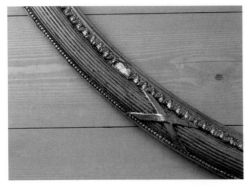

1 A small area on this frame is missing. Because it is intricately molded, it needs to be copied exactly in order to blend in with the rest of the frame.

3 Support the mold on a bag that is loosely filled with sand. Mix a small amount of plaster in a plastic pot (see Basic Technique 1, Step 5). Pour the plaster into the mold. When the mold is full, shake it to allow the air bubbles to rise. Allow to dry for two hours.

5 Using an artist's paintbrush, paint the repaired area with red latex paint. Give it a another coat if the plaster is not completely covered by the first coat. Allow to dry for three hours.

2 Mix a thick coat of silicone rubber as described in Basic Technique 1, Step 3. Spread it on to an area nearby which is undamaged. Remove when dry.

4 Using a craft knife, cut the cast to size to fit the missing area. Stick it to the frame with glue then allow to dry for twenty-four hours. Fill any gaps between the cast and the frame with two-part epoxy putty, using a small spatula. Allow to dry for two hours.

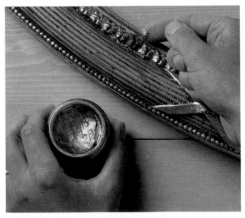

6 Dip your finger in gilt cream, and gently rub it on top of the red paint. Carefully blend in the edges to match the existing gold.

MATERIALS AND EQUIPMENT YOU WILL NEED

DAMAGED FRAME • COLD-CURING SILICONE BASE • CURING AGENT • PLASTIC CONTAINER • SPOON • SMALL SPATULA • BAG OF SAND • CASTING PLASTER • WATER • SMALL PLASTIC POT • CRAFT KNIFE • TWO-PART EPOXY RESIN GLUE • TWO-PART EPOXY PUTTY • ARTIST'S PAINTBRUSH • RED LATEX PAINT • GILT CREAM

BOOKENDS

WHAT BETTER DESIGN FOR BOOKENDS THAN BOOKS THEMSELVES? IN THIS PROJECT THREE BOOKS ARE USED, ONE THINNER, SO THAT IT CAN LIE FLAT AND SUPPORT THE OTHER TWO. OLD BOOKS WITH INTERESTING PATTERNS ON THE COVER AND ORNATE SPINES ARE BEST FOR THIS PURPOSE. ONCE CAST AND PAINTED IN IMAGINATIVE COLORS, THE DECORATIVE PATTERNS ARE RECREATED PERFECTLY. THE SPINES CAN THEN BE DECORATED USING A GOLD FELT-TIPPED PEN.

1 Work out the design of your bookends. Use the thinnest of the three books for the base, the shortest for the outside "prop" and the tallest as the actual support for the real books. Cut three pieces of aluminum foil 3 in larger all around than each book. Grease with petroleum jelly. Place each book on top of the foil, and make a nest around it, leaving a $^1/_2$ in gap around the edge. The parts of the books you will not see when the casts are joined together should be against the foil.

2 Cast as described in Basic Technique 1, Steps 1, 2, and 3. Because the largest book will show completely on one side and slightly on the other side (up to the point where the smaller "prop" joins it), it is important to coat a small piece of the second side of this book with silicone rubber. Once dry, turn the book over and repeat the process on the other side as far down as necessary.

3 Because the molds are larger than usual, they need support. Fine casting plaster is ideal for this. Mix as described in Basic Technique 1, Step 5. Allow the plaster to cover the rubber completely at the top, but leave about $^5/_8$ in uncovered round the edge. The plaster hardens quickly, so only mix enough plaster to do one book at a time.

MATERIALS AND EQUIPMENT YOU WILL NEED

THREE BOOKS • MATERIALS LISTED FOR BASIC TECHNIQUE 1 • FINE CASTING PLASTER • SANDPAPER • LATEX PAINT: DARK RED, DARK BLUE, DARK GREEN AND RAW UMBER • $^1/_2$ IN HOUSEHOLD PAINTBRUSH • PAPER TOWELS • GOLD FELT-TIPPED PEN • GILT CREAM • TWO-PART EPOXY RESIN GLUE

4 Allow the casting plaster to dry for four hours before removing from the silicone rubber. Remove the books from the rubber, and support the mold in the hardened casting plaster support. Fill with casting plaster as described in Steps 5–9, omitting Step 7. Remove when dry. Shown here is the largest of the three books being removed, with its slight overlap of silicone rubber.

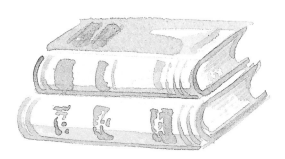

5 If the two sides of the books you are going to stick together are rough or uneven, rub them with sandpaper to smooth them down.

6 Using two coats of latex paint, cover each book in a different color. Allow two hours after each coat for the paint to dry.

7 Water down some raw-umber latex paint until it is the consistency of milk. Stir well. Dip a corner of a piece of paper towel into the paint, and rub on to the pages of each book.

8 Using a gold felt-tipped pen, mark in the lettering. ▶

9 If there are any larger pieces of decoration, use gilt cream as well.

11 Mix more glue, and stick the two upright books to the book which is to be the base. Allow twenty-four hours for the glue to dry.

10 Using a spatula and two-part epoxy resin glue, stick the two upright books together. Lay flat and allow twenty-four hours to dry.

POLYMER CLAYWORK
MARY MAGUIRE

POLYMER CLAY IS A VERSATILE, EASY TO HANDLE MODELING MEDIUM THAT CAN BE USED FOR MAKING OBJECTS AS DIVERSE AS ORNATE JEWELRY, DOLLS, TOY THEATERS, LAMPS, TABLEWARE AND MIRROR FRAMES. KNOWN TO DOLL AND MODEL MAKERS FOR SEVERAL DECADES, THIS REMARKABLE MATERIAL IS NOW WIDELY AVAILABLE FOR ANYONE TO USE, AND NEW TECHNIQUES ARE BEING DEVELOPED ALL THE TIME.

SIMILAR IN SOME WAYS TO ORDINARY CLAY, POLYMER CLAY HAS MANY ADVANTAGES. IT IS MADE IN A WIDE RANGE OF COLORS, INCLUDING FLUORES-CENT AND GLOW-IN-THE-DARK, AND COLORS CAN BE MIXED OR JUXTAPOSED TO CREATE SOME AMAZINGLY INTRICATE EFFECTS. IT DOES NOT SHRINK, MAKING IT SUITABLE FOR EMBEDDING OBJECTS, AND ONCE BAKED IT IS WATERPROOF AND DURABLE. IN ADDITION, POLYMER CLAY CAN BE TREATED WITH SHINY METALLIC FINISHES.

ALL YOU NEED TO WORK WITH POLYMER CLAY ARE YOUR HANDS, A CRAFT KNIFE, A KITCHEN TABLE AND AN ORDINARY DOMESTIC OVEN, ALTHOUGH MORE SPECIALIZED TOOLS WILL BE NECESSARY FOR MORE ADVANCED TECHNIQUES. THE TECHNIQUES REQUIRED ARE STRAIGHTFORWARD AND EASY TO LEARN, AND ONCE YOU HAVE ACQUIRED THE BASIC SKILLS AND MADE SOME OF THE MORE ADVANCED PROJECTS SHOWN IN THIS SECTION, YOU WILL BE ABLE TO CREATE YOUR OWN PROJECTS AND DESIGNS AND PERHAPS EVEN ACHIEVE THE LEVEL OF CRAFTSMANSHIP ILLUSTRATED IN THE GALLERY.

Left: Polymer clay can be used to create a dazzling array of colorful objects, from simple buttons to quirky cutlery and eye-catching decorations for the home.

HISTORY OF POLYMER CLAY

POLYMER CLAY ORIGINATED IN GERMANY IN THE LATE 1930S. IT WAS AN ACCIDENTAL CHEMICAL BY-PRODUCT THAT WAS DISCOVERED BY MRS REHBINDER, THE DAUGHTER OF THE FAMOUS DOLL-MAKER KÄTHE KRUSE. DURING THE SECOND WORLD WAR SHE DID NOT HAVE A SUITABLE RAW MATERIAL FROM WHICH TO MAKE DOLLS' HEADS. SHE EXPERIMENTED WITH THIS BY-PRODUCT AND FOUND THAT IT COULD BE MODELED AND HARDENED IN AN OVEN. SHE CONTINUED TO EXPERIMENT WITH THE MATERIAL FOR SOME YEARS, USING IT TO CREATE MOSAICS, AS WELL AS FOR HER INITIAL PURPOSE OF DOLLS' HEADS. SHE DEVELOPED A LIMITED COLOR RANGE, WHICH SHE STARTED TO SELL UNDER THE NAME OF FIFI MOSAIK — DERIVED FROM HER NICKNAME FIFI AND ITS MOSAIC APPLICATION.

Until 1964 she marketed her product alone, without advertising. Then she approached Eberhard Faber and acquired a license for industrial production. The product is now sold as Fimo.

Sculpy, the American equivalent, was developed in the late 1960s by a company called Polyform products in Illinois. Other brands of polymer clay are mostly produced in Germany, such as Formello, Modello and Cermit. The production and quality of polymer clay have improved enormously in its sixty-year existence. Each brand of polymer clay has its own color range and they all differ in consistency and cooking directions.

Because its history is so recent, it is really still establishing and defining itself - and polymer clay artists tend to draw heavily on well-established techniques from other disciplines. The most popular of these are

Above: Cane work was used in Ancient Egypt to produce faces made from mosaic glass slices. The two slices here show an exaggerated expression on a male face, suggestive of a Greek mask.
Left: An example of the late medieval art of millefiori: a glass bead embellished with canes and traces of gilding.

cane work and millefiori, which are now undergoing a renaissance.

These partner arts of glassworking are thought to have developed in Mesopotamia, and quality works of great craftsmanship were being produced in Alexandria and ancient Egypt. The art was rediscovered by the Italians in the late fifteenth century. It was they who called it millefiori, which literally means a thousand flowers.

Cane work is used to make a batch of multiple images. Long colored rods of glass are placed next to each other to form a picture or pattern and fused together so that the picture runs through the length of the cane. Slices are taken from the cane at this point, or the picture or pattern can be miniaturized by a process called reduction – by rolling the molten canes they can be elongated, then sliced. These perfect little miniatures can be applied to the surface of a glass bead, under a hot flame. This process is known as lampwerk. The slices are fused onto the surface of the bead, side by side, until the bead is completely covered – hence millefiori.

It is an enchanting technique with various applications. Beads and paperweights made by Murona craftsmen, or those from the French company Campagne des Cristallenes de Baccavat are much sought after by collectors.

Polymer clay is ideally suited to this technique, and brings new dimensions to this art form. What it lacks in transparency it makes up for in its versatility and its wide range of colors. Polymer clay objects and jewelry are now attracting collectors in their own right.

Cane work and millefiori, ancient techniques in the art of glasswork, have proved to be extremely well-suited to the modern material of polymer clay. Left: In cane work, long rods of pictures are made, from which slices are taken. For the next stage of millefiori, above, the slices of cane are then used to completely cover a plain bead, providing diverse, intricate decoration. (Beads and picture canes by Ingrid Proudfoot.)

GALLERY

Although polymer clay has yet to be taken seriously by the art world at large, there is no doubt about its huge potential as an art medium, and exciting and innovative developments are occurring all the time. A growing number of artists have already recognized the unique properties of polymer clay and used them to develop their own particular styles and techniques. To inspire you to explore and experiment with this fascinating medium, some of these artists are featured here with examples of their work, which help to show the material's versatility and attraction.

Left: CITY ZEN CANE
David Forlano and Steven Ford trained as painters at the Tyler School of Art in Rome where they drew inspiration for their mosaic picture frames and eggs. Each design consists of thousands of tiny colored squares of various tints to make them look like ancient stone. The eggs are made by placing cane slices of real shells from blown-out duck and goose eggs. Founding members of the National Polymer Guild in the USA, both artists teach intermediate and advanced polymer clay workshops.
DAVID FORLANO &
STEVEN FORD

Below: HEART BROOCH AND FLOWER JEWELRY
Lara Bohnic designs jewelry and also works as a product and fashion designer. Attracted by the lightness, color and easy workability of one of the softer of the polymer clays, she takes her inspiration from nature, pop art and kitsch culture.
LARA BOHNIC

Left: PEOPLE BEADS
These people beads are made by layering tiny pieces of polymer clay onto a basic bead then incorporating cane work into the costumes. Each bead is unique and takes anywhere from several hours to weeks to complete.
CYNTHIA TROOP

Below: PAPERWEIGHTS
Ingrid Proudfoot began experimenting with making polymer clay jewelry a decade ago and now makes various artifacts including buttons, door knobs, clocks and umbrella handles. She mainly uses cane work in which a strong African influence is detectable. Her beads and picture canes are also illustrated in the history section of this book.
INGRID PROUDFOOT

Below: IRIDESCENT EARRINGS
Mary Maguire has been making
polymer clay jewelry since 1986.
She prefers to use just one base
color with a metal leaf applied to
the surface and likes to incorporate
shells and other found objects into
her work.
MARY MAGUIRE

Right: MINIATURE THEATER
Theresa Pateman first started to
use polymer clay to make jewelry
but when she discovered its
versatility she began creating
figures around wire armature.
Inspired by a visit to the Musée
Grevin in Paris, a wax museum,
she devised the miniature theater.
THERESA PATEMAN

Right: BROOCHES
These two brooches (pins) were made
using a technique adapted from the
Japanese metalworking art of *Mokume
Gane,* which usually consists of laminating
thin sheets of silver, gold and copper
alloy, fusing the layers together, then
distorting the shape to create a watermark
or woodgrain pattern when sliced
through. This effect is much easier to
achieve with polymer clay by layering thin
slices of translucent clay, which have very
small amounts of color mixed in, with
silver leaf. The block is then deformed to
create an uneven surface and thin slices
are taken off it. These are then collaged
onto the surface of a base shape.
LINDLY HAUNANI

Left: HAT PIN & JEWELRY Sandra Duvall and Julia Hill designed the hat pin, the three-piece brooch and the brooch and earring set which are all made by the millefiori technique. They also specialize in buttons, barrettes, drop earrings, cufflinks and tie pins. They draw inspiration from Matisse and primitive decoration.
SANDRA DUVALL & JULIA HILL

Left: CENTRAL PARK The buildings in this dazzling picture of New York's Central Park are constructed from wood, and the figures, trees and windows are made from polymer clay. The choice of bright colors captures the energy of the city.
KAREN KRIGE

Above: CLOCK JEWELRY Although she had been making jewelry for a decade, Eileen Mahony first began using polymer clay in about 1990. Her soft watches, influenced by Dali's painting *The Persistence of Memory*, are built up from three-dimensional layers of clay, then gilded with bronze powders. The numerals are painted on. She also makes psychedelic millefiori jewelry as well as small boxes and mirrors.
EILEEN MAHONY

Left: GILDED BROOCHES
Drawing from their
backgrounds in illustration
and ceramics, Eric Pateman
and Fiona French taught
themselves the art of
jewelry making. They lay
gold and silver leaf onto
polymer clay, then paint
the cooked pieces. Their
work has strong Celtic and
Egyptian flavors.
KITCHEN TABLE STUDIO

Left: BLACK AND
GOLD CANDLESTICKS
Sarah Nelson Shriver
makes jewelry and
decorations out of
polymer clay. These
candlesticks are 10
inches high, with an
interior vertical support
of nylon-reinforced
plastic tubing. The
decorative elements
were applied using the
millefiori technique.
SARAH NELSON SHRIVER

Below: FACE PINS
Iridian Faces are vibrant
character face pins
created by Ellen Watt.
She has been making the
faces since 1989 and
each one is unique. Ellen
uses customized cookie
cutters to form the basic
shapes from polymer
clay slabs. They are
hand-manipulated
from there.
ELLEN WATT

Left: HEARTS OF GOLD
Deborah Banyas and T. P.
Speer are sculptors working
with polymer clay. *Hearts of
Gold* is constructed out of
wood and stuffed cotton. The
polymer clay was then applied
and the piece finished in
acrylic paint and gold leaf.
DEBORAH BANYAS &
T. P. SPEER

MATERIALS

POLYMER CLAY IS ACTUALLY A PLASTIC KNOWN AS POLYVINYL CHLORIDE. WITH ALL THE ADVANTAGES OF REAL CLAY, IT HAS NONE OF THE DISADVANTAGES. IT CAN BE MOLDED, MODELED, SCULPTED, STRETCHED AND EMBOSSED PRIOR TO BEING BAKED. IT IS CLEAN TO WORK WITH, IT DOES NOT SHRINK AND IT IS ALREADY COLORED, MAKING GLAZING OR PAINTING UNNECESSARY EXCEPT FOR CREATING DECORATIVE EFFECTS. IN ADDITION, IT DOES NOT REQUIRE FIRING AT HIGH TEMPERATURES, LIKE OTHER TYPES OF CLAY.

BAKING POLYMER CLAY IN AN ORDINARY DOMESTIC OVEN AT 215–275° F, ACCORDING TO THE MANUFACTURER'S INSTRUCTIONS, FUSES PARTICLES TOGETHER IN THE POLYMERIZATION PROCESS WHICH TRANSFORMS THE CLAY FROM A MALLEABLE SUBSTANCE INTO A SOLID ONE. ONCE BAKED, THE CLAY CAN BE SANDED, SAWN, DRILLED AND GLUED.

VARIOUS BRANDS OF POLYMER CLAY ARE SOLD. ALTHOUGH THEY ARE ALL BASICALLY THE SAME, SOME HAVE A SLIGHTLY DIFFERENT CONSISTENCIES AND SOME ARE MORE SPECIFICALLY DESIGNED AS ECONOMICAL MODELING CLAYS FOR MAKING DOLLS AND MODELS. EXPERIENCE WILL SOON TELL YOU WHICH TYPES OF POLYMER CLAY YOU PREFER FOR DIFFERENT TYPES OF PROJECTS.

THERE IS AN EVER-INCREASING RANGE OF COLORS AVAILABLE WHICH NOW INCLUDE STARTLING FLUORESCENT, PEARLESCENT, AND METALLIC COLORS AS WELL AS GLOW-IN-THE-DARK, TRANSPARENT AND MOTTLED STONE EFFECTS.

MOST MANUFACTURERS SELL THEIR CLAYS IN BLOCKS THAT WEIGH ABOUT 2 OUNCES BUT FOR ECONOMY, LARGER BLOCKS ARE AVAILABLE IN LIMITED COLOR RANGES AND OF THE SPECIALIZED MODELING CLAY.

Doll-making polymer clay is stiffer than most and is available in large blocks.

Modeling polymer clay is easier to work but stronger once baked and is available in large blocks.

Pearlescent polymer clay has a creamy sheen.

Translucent polymer clay can be used in a number of interesting ways.

Glow-in-the-dark polymer clay can be used to make items that show up in the dark.

Mix quick polymer clay is easy to work and suitable for use by children.

Mottled stone is an imitation stone effect that can be applied to polymer clay in a number of colors.

Glamour colors provide a metallic effect on polymer clay.

Softer polymer clay is available in a range of colors.

Fluorescent and ordinary colors are exciting and fun to use.

Epoxy resin glue is used in two parts and is very strong glue.

Aluminum wire can be used for building support structures.

Jewelry wire is used for connecting pieces for earrings and necklaces.

Metallic leaf in gold, silver, copper and aluminum is used for decorating the surface of clay.

Fridge magnets are produced by polymer clay manufacturers for use with their clays.

Button backs are useful for making clay buttons.

Barrettes can be decorated with clay beads or strips.

Beads and gemstones must be flat backed and, if they are to go into the oven, made of glass.

Clip-on earring backs and metal button backs are used to make jewelry pieces.

Bronze powders A limited range is produced by polymer clay manufacturers. A wide range of colors is available at art-suppy stores.

Varnish, gloss or matte, is supplied by polymer clay manufacturers.

Acrylic paint can be used for covering the surface of polymer clay.

Enamel paint is used for painting small areas or patterns.

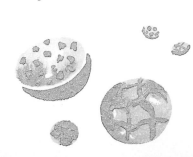

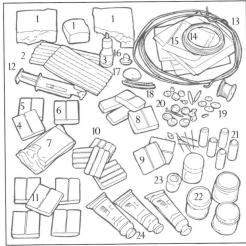

KEY

1 Doll-making polymer clay
2 Modeling polymer clay
3 Diluent
4 Pearlescent polymer clay
5 Translucent polymer clay
6 Glow-in-the-dark polymer clay
7 Mix quick polymer clay
8 Mottled stone effect
9 Glamour colors
10 Softer polymer clay
11 Fluorescent and ordinary colors
12 Epoxy resin glue
13 Aluminum wire
14 Jewelry wire
15 Metallic leaf
16 Fridge magnets
17 Button back
18 Barrette
19 Beads and gemstones
20 Clip-on earring backs and metal button backs
21 Bronze powders (branded)
22 Bronze powders
23 Acrylic paint
24 Enamel paint

EQUIPMENT

IN ADDITION TO AN ORDINARY HOUSEHOLD OVEN, THE MOST IMPOR-
TANT TOOLS REQUIRED FOR WORKING WITH POLYMER CLAY ARE YOUR
HANDS. WHEN YOU FIRST START, HOUSEHOLD ITEMS GLEANED FROM
KITCHEN DRAWERS AND SEWING, KNITTING AND TOOL BOXES WILL DO.
PINS, KNITTING NEEDLES, CHEESE SLICERS, SCREWS, PENS AND EVEN
MATCHES CAN ALL BE IMPROVISED AS TOOLS, AND YOU WILL FIND THAT A
VARIETY OF OBJECTS CAN PRODUCE PATTERNS. BUT FOR MORE ADVANCED
WORK, MORE SPECIALIZED EQUIPMENT WILL BE USEFUL. WHATEVER
EQUIPMENT YOU USE FOR POLYMER CLAY, KEEP IT EXCLUSIVELY FOR THAT
PURPOSE AND NEVER USE IT FOR PREPARING FOOD.

Oven An oven is necessary for baking the clay at specified temperatures. For those who prefer not to place plastic materials in their domestic ovens, at least one polymer clay manufacturer markets a special oven.

Mirror Placed behind the work, a mirror will enable you to see all around when slicing large canes or blocks, ensuring neat, even cuts.

Oven thermometer Using an oven thermometer ensures that your oven is working at the correct temperature for the clay. This is important because undercooked clay can be fragile, and overcooking burns the clay.

Pasta machine This can be used for rolling out clay to different thicknesses and is useful when precision and evenness are required, especially when producing several sheets of the same thickness. It can also be used for mixing colors. Buy one just for use with polymer clay and do not wash it between different colors, just wipe it clean with a cloth.

Dust mask Always wear a dust mask when sanding or drilling baked polymer or when using bronze powders.

Aluminum foil Layers of foil can be used to create bulk when making up shapes.

Waxed paper Tape a sheet of waxed paper to your work surface to ensure a smooth area. Also useful as a non-stick surface for baking clay.

Punches Metal- and leather-working punches are good for indenting and texturing clay surfaces.

Dentistry tools These precision tools are excellent for modeling. Ask your dentist for old ones or buy them from modeling shops.

Cookie cutter Good for patterns or cutting zigzag edges.

Dividers Useful for marking circular shapes to be cut out.

Toothpicks Good for reinforcing structure, especially joints.

Straws These can be used for making holes big enough for ribbon to pass through or for hanging over a nail.

Kebab sticks Use these to hold beads during baking.

Scissors are an essential piece of equipment useful for cutting out cardboard or paper templates.

Cheese slicer This can be used for taking even slices from an oblong cane.

Soft dough cutters For cutting out a wide variety of shapes, dough cutters are useful, but you may have to trim the edges of plastic ones to make them sharp enough for a clean cut.

Airtight box Polymer clay has a shelf life of approximately 2 years but goes crumbly if exposed to heat and ultraviolet light. Wrap the clay in waxed paper before storing it in a box.

Craft knife and scalpel A craft knife is good for cutting out heavy-duty cardboard, while a scalpel is perhaps the most useful tool for working with polymer clay.

Plastic cutting mat To protect your work surface, always cut clay on a cutting mat. Scrub the mat thoroughly to remove all traces of clay after use, as residues seem to react with the mat material.

Tissue blade Designed for taking human tissue samples, these razor-sharp blades enable thin slices to be cut from clay and are especially useful in canework and detailed modeling.

Round-nosed jewelry pliers Use these when making polymer jewelry pieces.

Pliers are essential for bending wire used structurally in projects.

Wire cutters are for cutting wire.

Vinyl gloves Many people prefer to wear gloves to protect their hands. Others wear them so as not to leave fingerprints on the clay. Gloves should be changed with each change of color to avoid transferring residual polymer particles from one color to another.

Fine palette knife This is useful for lifting thinly rolled out polymer clay.

Paintbrushes are essential for applying bronze powders and paints.

Plate A plate is useful for mixing paint colors.

Steel ruler A steel ruler guarantees straight lines.

Rolling pin A vinyl or straight-sided glass roller is best for rolling out clay by hand, although marble is excellent during hot weather, especially if the clay is overworked.

Brayer Sometimes referred to as a small roller, this is a good implement for smoothing over clay and wrinkled paper, or for applying metal leaf.

Plexiglass rollers A homemade device consisting of a small sheet of plexiglass with a wooden block as a handle is excellent for rolling out logs and canes. Make two sizes, about 3 inches x 3 inches and 8 inches x 7 inches for rolling out different sized items.

Petit four and aspic cutters are handy for cutting out interesting shapes.
Clay extruder Difficult to use, but useful if you do a lot of polymer clay work, this device should be secured with a small vice. Clay must be soft or thinned before use.

Smoothing tools These rubber-tipped implements for smoothing areas smaller than your fingertips resemble paintbrushes.

KEY

1 Oven	**19** Craft knife and scalpel
2 Mirror	**20** Plastic cutting mat
3 Oven thermometer	**21** Tissue blade
4 Pasta machine	**22** Round-nosed
5 Dust mask	jewelry pliers
6 Aluminum foil	**23** Pliers
7 Waxed paper	**24** Wire cutters
8 Punches	**25** Vinyl gloves
9 Dentistry tools	**26** Fine palette knife
10 Cookie cutter	**27** Paintbrushes
11 Dividers	**28** Plate
12 Toothpicks and	**29** Steel ruler
cocktail sticks	**30** Rolling pin
13 Straws	**31** Brayer
14 Kebab sticks	**32** Plexiglass rollers
15 Scissors	**33** Petit four and aspic
16 Cheese slicer	cutters
17 Soft dough cutters	**34** Clay extruder
18 Airtight sandwich box	**35** Smoothing tools

BASIC TECHNIQUES

POLYMER CLAY IS A WONDERFULLY VERSATILE MATERIAL, WHICH CAN BE SHAPED, MOLDED AND MODELED IN VARIOUS WAYS TO PRODUCE QUITE DIFFERENT EFFECTS. INSTRUCTIONS ARE GIVEN HERE FOR THE GENERAL TECHNIQUES WHICH HAVE BEEN APPLIED TO MANY OF THE PROJECTS IN THIS BOOK, SO DO READ THROUGH THIS SECTION CAREFULLY BEFORE EMBARKING ON A PROJECT. AS POLYMER CLAYS WILL PICK UP ANY DIRT AND DUST AROUND, IT IS IMPORTANT TO MAKE SURE YOUR HANDS ARE SCRUPULOUSLY CLEAN. YOU WILL ALSO NEED TO WASH YOUR HANDS WHEN CHANGING FROM ONE COLOR TO ANOTHER AS ANY RESIDUES WILL DISCOLOR THE NEXT PIECE OF CLAY YOU KNEAD.

PREPARING POLYMER CLAY

Polymer clays need to be manipulated or kneaded before they can be worked, the degree varying according to the brand. As clays are responsive to temperature, the warmth of your hands contributes to the conditioning process, and there is a world of difference between working with clay on a cold winter's day and on a hot summer's day. Some people go so far as to carry the clay in their pockets, or even bras, before working it.

To get your clay to its optimal working consistency, work small amounts, about an eighth of a block at a time, in your hands. Roll it between your palms to form a sausage, fold it over and roll again, then repeat the whole process until the clay is soft and pliable. Try to avoid trapping air bubbles in the clay. A pasta-making machine can be pressed into service to help the softening process.

MIXING COLORS

Although there are several commercially available colors, the choice becomes unlimited when you mix colors yourself. You can experiment by using small amounts to tailor colors to your needs. When mixing dark and light colors, add tiny bits of the darker clay to the lighter color as the darker one can easily overpower the lighter one.

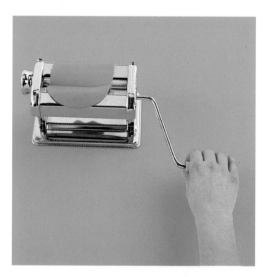

Mixing with a Pasta-making Machine
A pasta-making machine is excellent for mixing colors. Feed two differently colored sheets through the machine together, feeding them from opposite sides. As the sheets go through the machine they will become fused, and any air bubbles will be squeezed out.

Mixing by Hand

1 Twist together two or more differently colored sausages. This attractive effect is called candy cane.

2 Roll the cane into a smooth log, then twist, stretch and double over, excluding any air bubbles, to achieve a marbled pattern. This is another stage that can be used as it is. To blend the colors completely, continue to work the clay as described.

Rolling Out

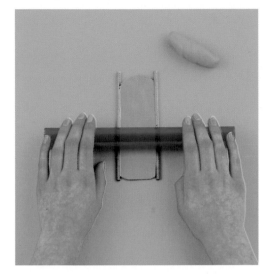

Roll the clay out on a smooth, clean surface, using a marble or acrylic rolling pin. A marble surface is excellent in a hot environment or if the clay is very soft, but not advisable in cold conditions. To ensure an even thickness, roll the clay between two pieces of metal, wood or plastic. Alternatively, pass it through a pasta-making machine, which is useful for producing several sheets of uniform thickness. If the clay is sticky, dust it with a thin film of flour or talcum powder.

PATTERNING

Patterned blocks can be used for various decorative effects. For instance, the slices of the striped block are used in the Eye-catching Cutlery project and to represent fabric in the Magnetic Theater project, while slices of the checkerboard design are used to make the hat of one of the players in the Magnetic Theater project. Slices can be cut off the block with a tissue blade or, if the block is long, with a cheese slicer.

Striped Block

1 Roll out several sheets of differently colored clay, trim them to the same dimensions, and stack them on top of each other, smoothing each layer to exclude air bubbles. Make the last layer a different color from the first. Trim the edges to neaten, if necessary.

2 When you have stacked a few layers, cut the block in half horizontally and stack. Roll with gentle pressure using a brayer.

Checkerboard Block

1 Make up a striped block. Using a tissue blade, cut off a slice the same thickness as the stripes. Stand the slice up alongside the block, staggering the colors, and cut another slice. Press this against the first slice and repeat the process to create a checkerboard block. Placing a mirror behind the block will help ensure that you slice the clay evenly.

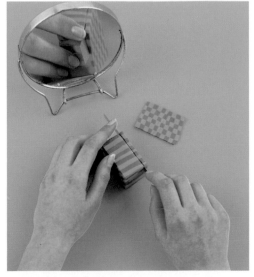

2 Press each side of the block evenly against a flat surface to consolidate it and trim if necessary.

Polka Dots

1 Press the head of a glass-headed pin into a rolled-out sheet of clay to make a regular pattern of indentations.

2 Roll out a thin sausage or cane in a contrasting color and slice off small disks using a scalpel. Roll these into balls and press each one into an indent.

3 Place a smooth piece of paper over the clay sheet and roll using a brayer or pass through a pasta-making machine to smooth the surface.

Jelly roll

1 To make a jelly roll, roll out two or three differently colored sheets and stack them. Trim to neaten the edges into a rectangle.

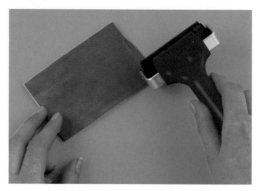

2 Roll over one of the shorter edges with a brayer to taper it.

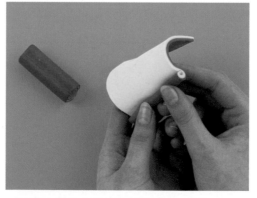

3 Starting at the flattened end, roll up the layers tightly and evenly. Gently roll the cane to smooth over the seams. Trim each end flat.

MAKING BEADS

Beads can be made in all sorts of shapes and sizes. A simple round bead is made by rolling a small ball of clay between the palms of your hands. Flat round ones are made by cutting thick disks from a log. More complicated beads can be made following the technique described in the Composite Beads project. Making the hole through the middle can be tricky, as the bead has to be held firmly enough to take pressure without distorting the shape. For this reason, many people prefer to drill the hole after the clay has been baked. Make the hole large enough to take whatever the bead is to be threaded on.

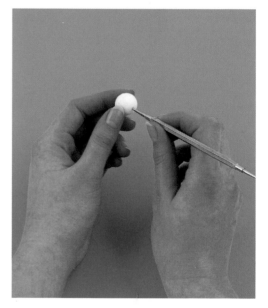

1 Make a hole through an unbaked bead using a tapered point such as a thin modeling tool or darning needle, with a drilling action. When the point emerges from the other side, remove the tool and push it through from the other side to neaten the hole. After the bead has been baked, you may need to sand down around the hole gently, using sandpaper, so that there are no jagged edges which could snag or catch on hair or clothing. ▶

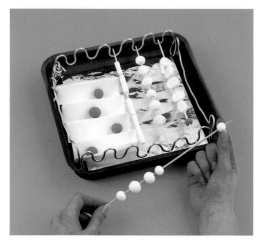

2 Beads need to be supported during baking to keep their shapes from distorting. String the beads on wooden skewers or wire, depending on the size of their holes, and suspend them across a baking tray; make a wire support if you make beads regularly. If you are drilling the holes after baking, place them in the folds of corrugated cardboard to bake them.

CANE WORK

Deriving from ancient glassworking techniques, a cane is a log with a design running along its length, like a stick of rock. The designs can be simple or complex patterns or images. Thick slices cut from these canes can be made into beads or pendants. Thin slices can be used like a veneer to decorate beads or sheets of clay. Slices are best cut using a tissue blade. If necessary, chill the cane before slicing to avoid distorting the shape of the soft clay.

Canes can be reduced in diameter to make delicately small designs which may also be joined together to make complex designs such as millefiori beads.

The simple flower cane shown here is used in the Night Light and the Magnetic Theater projects. There is sufficient cane for both projects, plus enough left over for making into beads.

Simple Flower Cane

1 Roll one cane for the flower center (yellow), two canes of another color (green) and five canes from a third color (pink) for the petals. Make all the canes with a diameter of about $\frac{3}{4}$ inch and a length of 3 inches.

2 Roll out two thin sheets in different colors (coral and red) to cover the flower center, and a large thin sheet in a color to contrast with the petals (purple). Wrap the canes in these sheets, rolling each slightly to smooth the joints.

3 Using a tissue blade, cut the green canes lengthwise into quarters.

4 Roll out a thin sheet of an entirely different color (blue). Arrange the canes to form a flower, filling in the spaces between the petals with five of the quarter canes.

5 Wrap the bundle in the prepared sheet, rolling lightly to smooth the joint.

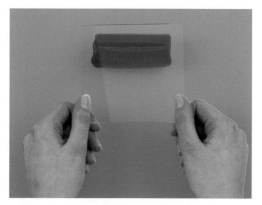

6 Using a small sheet of plexiglass, roll the cane to compact it. The ends will become concave. Trim these off.

Simple Picture Cane

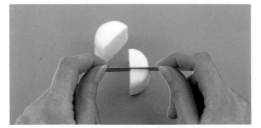

1 Roll a cane of white polymer clay about $1\frac{1}{2}$ inch in diameter and 3 inches long. Using a tissue blade, cut the cane in half lengthwise, then cut one of the halves into two to make two quarters.

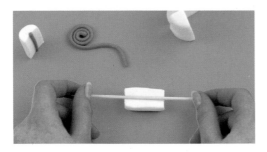

2 Roll one of the quarters into a round cane and cut it in half lengthwise. Press a groove down the middle of one flat side with a thin, round wooden or metal skewer and run a thin sausage of blue clay along it. Groove the other half and sandwich the two halves together to make the head and eye. Roll lightly to smooth the joints.

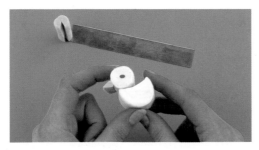

3 Curve the remaining half of the original white cane to form the duck's body. Place the head on the body. Cut a triangular wedge from a $\frac{1}{2}$ inch diameter yellow cane 3 inches long and press it firmly against the head for the bill.

4 Pack the gaps around the duck with wedges of pale blue cane, rolled to the same length, to make a circular shape. Wrap this with a thin sheet of pale blue to hold it together, and roll to consolidate it.

5 Surround the new cane with a sheet of dark blue, and roll again, smoothing the join. Trim off the concave ends.

Reducing Canes

Roll a cane under a small sheet of plexiglass to elongate it and reduce its diameter. Trim off the resultant concave ends as you work.

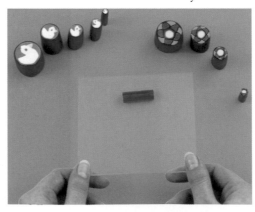

To make canes with different diameters with the same design running through them, stop rolling at each desired size and cut the cane in half. Continue rolling one half while reserving the other. Repeat until you have the sizes of cane you require.

Complex Canes

Gently squeeze several previously reduced picture or flower canes together and roll to produce a fascinatingly complex cane.

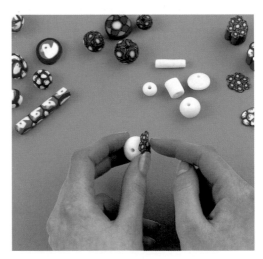

To make millefiori beads, cut thin slices from complex canes and press them onto the surface of clay beads. Previously baked beads give a better overall shape, but the millefiori slices may not adhere as well as on unbaked ones. Cover the bead completely and roll it between your palms.

METALLIC FINISHES

Polymer clays can be finished with metallic powders or metal leaf. Metal leaf may be gold, silver, copper or aluminum and is available in book form from art supply outlets. The sheets are very thin and easily marked by fingerprints so be careful when handling.

Metallic powders are brushed onto the surface of the clay. They go a long way, so use sparingly. For permanence, they should be varnished. As the particles of these powders are minute and spread everywhere, a fine dust mask should always be worn when using them.

Using Metal Leaf

1 Carefully lay a sheet of transfer leaf over a sheet of rolled-out polymer clay with the metal face down. As you lay it down, roll over it using a brayer to eliminate air bubbles. Rub all over the backing tissue paper before gently and slowly peeling it off. If any metal leaf clings to the tissue paper, replace it and rub over the area with your finger.

2 If you want a cracked finish, cover the surface of the applied metal leaf with a smooth piece of paper or tissue and roll over it using a brayer until the required amount of cracking is achieved. The cracking on silver and gold is finer than on copper or aluminum.

EMBOSSING AND TEXTURING

Being soft and pliable, polymer clay is easy to texture. It will take the impression of any pattern you press onto it, such as lace, a shell or a button. Alternatively, a pattern can be sculpted on using modeling tools or leather- and metal-workers' chasing and punching tools. Textured clay can be used to make molds for embossing other pieces of clay with a design.

1 Make a mold, such as the cup-shaped one shown here for making buttons, and transfer a relief design to it by pressing it into the clay. Bake the mold following the manufacturer's instructions, then use it to make positive images on other pieces of raw clay.

2 To highlight a textured piece before embossing, lightly brush the mold with metallic powder.

SPANGLY STARS

STARS ARE A PERENNIALLY POPULAR MOTIF, WELL SUITED TO LIGHTING. LOTS OF THEM CAN BE QUICKLY STAMPED OUT FROM A SHEET OF POLYMER CLAY TO WHICH GOLD LEAF HAS BEEN APPLIED. ALTERNATIVELY, PAINT THE STARS WITH GOLD PAINT AFTER THEY HAVE BEEN STAMPED OUT.

IF YOU MAKE A HOLE IN ONE POINT OF THE STARS, THEY CAN BE DANGLED FROM THE EDGE OF THE LAMP SHADE.

YOU COULD ALSO MAKE LOTS OF STARS FROM GLOW-IN-THE-DARK POLYMER CLAY AND HANG THEM FROM A CHILD'S BEDROOM CEILING.

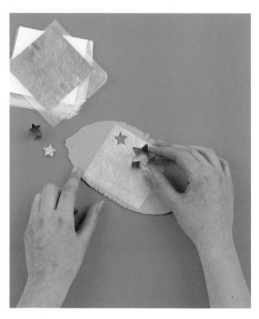

1 Apply gold leaf to rolled-out clay. Using small cookie or aspic cutters, stamp out the stars. Make some of the large ones hollow by stamping out their centers with a tiny cutter.

2 To make hanging holes, pierce through the center of the small stars and a point of the large ones using one of the jewelry head pins. If you wish, indent the centers of the small stars with a pen cap for decoration.

3 Lay the stars flat on a sheet of waxed paper and bake according to the manufacturer's instructions. When cool, apply varnish to protect the gold leaf.

4 Attach the stars to the lampshade using double-sided tape or jewelry head pins pushed through the holes and the shade. Twist the wires behind the shade to hold the stars in position.

MATERIALS AND EQUIPMENT YOU WILL NEED

SMALL BLOCK YELLOW POLYMER CLAY • DUTCH GOLD LEAF • STAR-SHAPED COOKIE OR ASPIC CUTTERS • JEWELRY HEAD PINS •
LAMPSHADE • STRONG DOUBLED-SIDED TAPE • ROUND-NOSED JEWELRY PLIERS • VARNISH • PAINTBRUSH

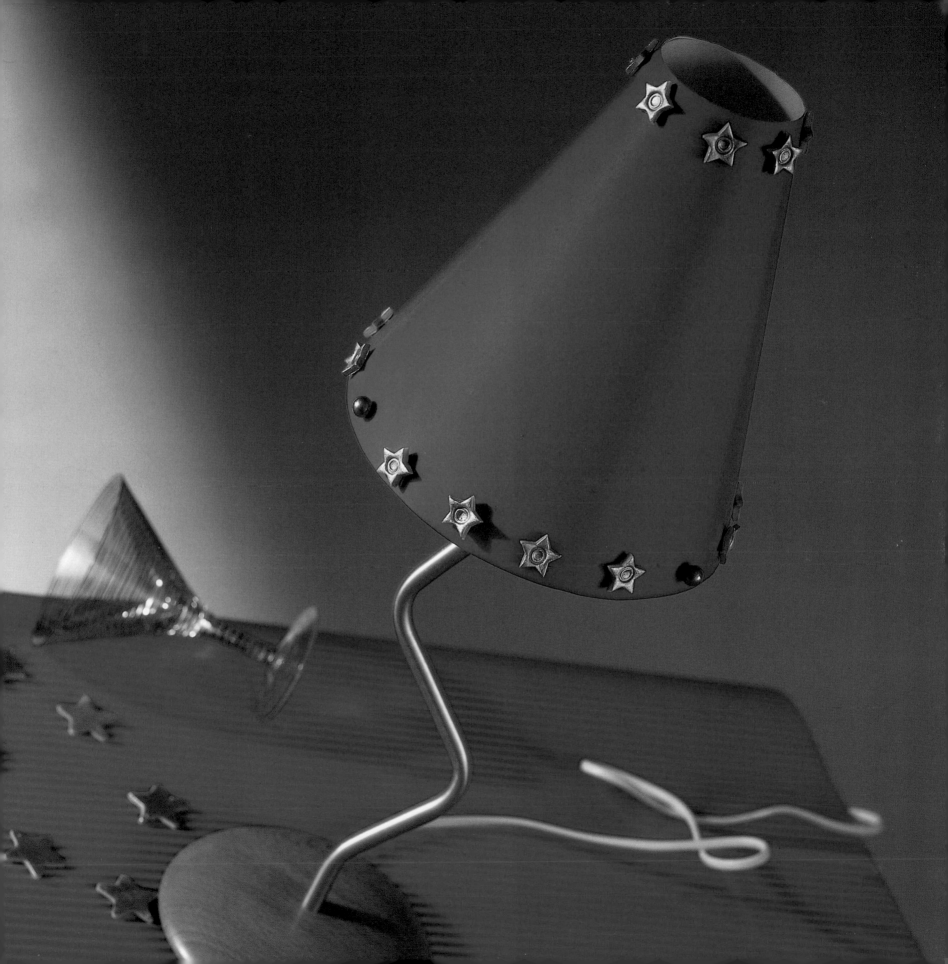

JAZZY TASSELS

TASSELS ARE EXPENSIVE TO BUY AND ARE USUALLY MADE IN AN OLD-FASHIONED STYLE, BUT THESE BLACK-STRIPED, FLUORESCENT VERSIONS, WHICH MAKE USE OF INEXPENSIVE SILKY TASSELS, ARE FRESH AND LIVELY (FOR SUPPLIERS SEE BACK OF THE BOOK). THE POLYMER CLAY BEADS ARE MODELED AROUND A CORK WRAPPED IN ALUMINUM FOIL WHICH IS REMOVED AFTER BAKING TO CREATE A HOLLOW HEAD THROUGH WHICH THE TASSEL END IS THREADED. MAKE PAIRS OF TASSELS FOR TIE-BACKS ON CURTAINS OR SINGLE ONES AS LIGHT PULLS.

1 Attach a marble on top of a cork or similarly shaped object using plasticine. Wrap a doubled strip of aluminum foil around the cork and secure with masking tape. Pinch the foil together at the top of the shape.

3 Snip off the excess clay at the top and smooth over to round the tassel top's shape. Push a sharp implement through the foil from the top to ensure the hole will be big enough for the tassel string. Bake for 5 minutes.

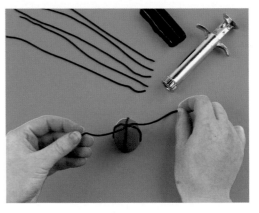

5 Roll or extrude thin threads of black clay. Drape over the top, tucking the ends inside at the bottom. Cut off the excess.

2 Roll out some modeling clay and cut a strip to wrap around the cork with enough to be pinched in at the top.

4 Pass a sharp implement through the hole at the top to push the cork out through the bottom of the tassel top. Roll out a thin sheet of fluorescent pink clay and wrap it around the tassel top. Cut off the excess and smooth over the joint.

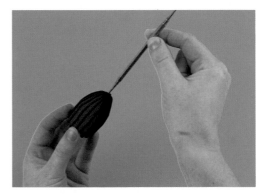

6 Press down where the threads cross over the top. Pierce through the hole once again. Return to the oven and bake for another 10 minutes. Thread the tassel through the top.

MATERIALS AND EQUIPMENT YOU WILL NEED

MARBLE • CORK OR SIMILAR SHAPE • PLASTICINE • ALUMINUM FOIL • SCISSORS • MASKING TAPE • $\frac{1}{8}$ BLOCK MODELING POLYMER CLAY • SHARP IMPLEMENT SUCH AS CROCHET HOOK • CRAFT KNIFE • $\frac{1}{2}$ BLOCK FLUORESCENT PINK POLYMER CLAY • SMALL AMOUNT BLACK POLYMER CLAY • EXTRUDER • TASSEL

SPOTTED EGG CUPS

COVERING METAL OBJECTS WITH POLYMER CLAY IS A SHORTCUT TO CREATING A SHAPE, LEAVING ONLY THE DECORATION TO BE APPLIED. THE METAL MUST NOT BE PREVIOUSLY PAINTED OR VARNISHED. HERE, STAINLESS STEEL EGG CUPS HAVE BEEN USED, BUT SALT AND PEPPER SHAKERS COULD ALSO BE TREATED (AFTER REMOVING THE PLASTIC STOPPERS), AS COULD TIN BOXES, WHISTLES OR CUTLERY. A THIN LAYER OF POLYMER CLAY APPLIED OVER A METAL BASE REQUIRES JUST 10 MINUTES BAKING TIME; LEAVE IT IN THE OVEN FOR A WHILE AFTER TURNING IT OFF, TO COOL DOWN.

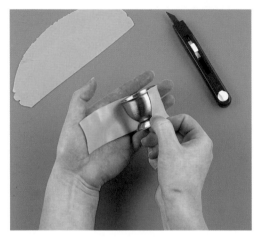

1 Roll out a thin sheet of yellow clay and cut out a strip to wrap around an egg cup.

3 Using the beaded head of a pin make small indentations in the clay in a regular pattern.

5 Use the beaded head of the pin to push the balls firmly in position, flattening them.

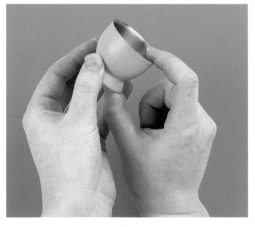

2 Smooth the clay to fit the contours of the egg cup and to join the ends together. Trim off any excess.

4 Roll a thin sausage of red clay. Cut into slices and roll each into a tiny ball. Pick each one up with the sharp end of the pin and place on an indentation.

6 Roll a slightly thicker red sausage to wrap around the rim, waist and bottom. Overlap the ends, trimming diagonally to fit, and smooth joints with fingertips or a smoothing tool. Bake the egg cups at a lower temperature and for a shorter time than recommended by the manufacturer.

MATERIALS AND EQUIPMENT YOU WILL NEED

1 BLOCK YELLOW POLYMER CLAY • 4 METAL EGG CUPS • GLASS-HEADED DRESSMAKER'S PIN • 1 BLOCK RED POLYMER CLAY • CRAFT KNIFE • SMOOTHING TOOL

CHEERY CANDLE HOLDER

THE STAINED GLASS EFFECT OF THIS CANDLE HOLDER GIVES OUT A WARM GLOW WHILE PROTECTING THE FLAME. A VARIATION ON TRADITIONAL MILLEFIORI WORK, THIN SLICES OF FLOWER CANE ARE ROLLED OUT AND USED TO LAMINATE A GLASS TUMBLER. THE SAME TECHNIQUE CAN BE USED TO DECORATE GLASS JARS, PANES OF GLASS OR EVEN GOLDFISH BOWLS. WHEN POLYMER CLAY IS USED THIS THINLY, THE BAKING TIME SHOULD BE REDUCED BY HALF; IT IS POSSIBLE TO BAKE IT WITH A HAIRDRYER IF YOU CAN ASCERTAIN THE TEMPERATURE.

1 Cut five slices from the flower cane, all the same thickness (see Basic Techniques).

3 Run the brayer up and down the extra center cane to shape it into a triangular log. Cut off ten slices and roll them out thinly as described in step 2.

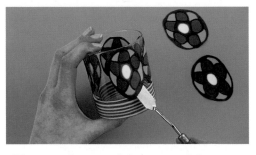

5 Wrap the striped slices around the bottom of the tumblers. Cut off any extra and smooth the joints. Using the palette knife, carefully transfer the flowers to the sides of the tumbler.

2 Place a piece of paper over one of the slices and roll the brayer over it in different directions to thin out the flower design with minimal distortion. Check regularly that the edges are not splitting. Roll the other slices.

4 Make a striped block and shave off two strips using the cheese slicer. Roll these between paper until they stretch about 1 inch in length.

6 Fill the gaps between the flowers with the triangular slices. Edge the top with a thin strip of blue clay. Place the tumbler on its side and roll firmly over a hard surface. Place in the oven before it heats up and bake, reducing the recommended cooking time by 5 minutes. Allow to cool completely before removing.

MATERIALS AND EQUIPMENT YOU WILL NEED

2½-INCH FLOWER CANE PLUS CENTER CANE (SEE BASIC TECHNIQUES) • CRAFT KNIFE • SMOOTH PAPER • BRAYER •
1 INCH x 4 INCHES STRIPED BLOCK OF POLYMER CLAY: FLUORESCENT YELLOW AND ORANGE (SEE BASIC TECHNIQUES) •
CHEESE SLICER • GLASS TUMBLER • PALETTE KNIFE • SMALL STRIP BLUE POLYMER CLAY

MINIATURE THEATER

THIS ENCHANTING THREE-DIMENSIONAL PICTURE SCONCE ENSHRINES THE MYTHICAL UNICORN IN A THEATRICAL SETTING. IT CAN BE HUNG ON A WALL BY A RIBBON OR PLACED ON A SHELF. THE FRAMEWORK IS MADE FROM COLLAGED AND PAINTED CARDBOARD, WHILE THE UNICORN ITSELF IS VERY SIMPLY MODELED OUT OF POLYMER CLAY. TO ENLARGE THE TEMPLATE FOR THIS AND OTHER PROJECTS, DRAW A GRID OF 1-INCH SQUARES AROUND THE TEMPLATE. DRAW A SEPARATE GRID OF LARGER SQUARES AND COPY THE TEMPLATE ONTO IT.

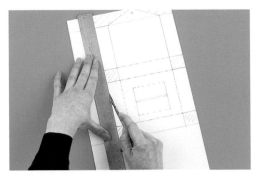

1 Draw the theater plan on thick cardboard and cut out, scoring along the dotted lines (see template at the back of the book). Make a small hole where shown for hanging.

2 Using gouache paint, paint the theater frame outside purple, the stage yellow, and the ceiling blue with yellow stars. When the paint is dry, paint the backdrop blue with yellow stars. Embellish further if you wish. Stick a photograph of a pair of velvet curtains to the front. When dry, varnish the front for protection.

3 Glue the wings to the front at all points of contact. Fold along all the score lines. Glue the top backdrop to the edges of the wings.

4 Fold the sides in and glue along the edges and adhere to the back.

5 Shape the unicorn form. Pinch out the head, legs and tail shape, using a modeling tool for detail if you wish. Bake the unicorn following the manufacturer's instructions. When cool, smooth with wet-and-dry sandpaper if necessary.

6 Paint the unicorn white. When this is dry, add detail in pale purple. Varnish and allow to dry. Apply glue to the feet and stand in position center stage, propping up if necessary with plasticine.

MATERIALS AND EQUIPMENT YOU WILL NEED

PENCIL • ⅛ INCH THICK CARDBOARD • STEEL RULER • SCALPEL • GOUACHE PAINT: PURPLE, YELLOW AND BLUE • PAINTBRUSHES • SCISSORS • FURNISHING CATALOG • SPRAY ADHESIVE • ACRYLIC VARNISH • STRONG GLUE • MODELING POLYMER CLAY • MODELING TOOL (OPTIONAL) • WET-AND-DRY SANDPAPER • ACRYLIC PAINT: WHITE AND PALE PURPLE • PLASTICINE (OPTIONAL)

TIGER DOOR PLAQUE

IMPISH TIGERS ARE USED HERE FOR A CHILD'S DOOR PLAQUE BUT YOU CAN MAKE ANY DESIGN YOU WANT WITH ANY MESSAGE. ATTACH THE PLAQUE USING HEAVY-DUTY SELF-ADHESIVE TABS. FOR OUTDOOR USE, COAT THE PLAQUE WITH AT LEAST TWO THICK COATS OF VARNISH AFTER MAKING A HANGING HOLE AT EACH CORNER. BE CAREFUL NOT TO TURN THE SCREWS TOO TIGHTLY WHEN ATTACHING IT.

THE INDIVIDUAL TIGER'S HEAD CAN BE USED TO MAKE BUTTONS. MAKE TWO HOLES WHERE THE NOSTRILS ARE FOR THE THREAD BEFORE BAKING.

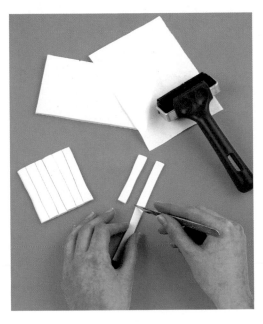

1 Roll out a rectangle of white clay, about 5 inches x 3 inches x $\frac{1}{4}$ inch, to form the base plate. Make 12 strips 3 inches long and $\frac{1}{8}$ inch thick and lay them on the base.

2 For the border, roll out two sausages from black clay, $\frac{1}{2}$ inch in diameter and a little longer than the base. Cut them in half lengthwise.

3 Cut the black strips to fit the base, mitering the ends. Arrange them around the edge of the base, smoothing the joints.

4 From a 10 inches x $\frac{1}{4}$ inch x $\frac{1}{16}$ inch strip of white clay, cut approximately 32 triangles. Arrange these at staggered intervals along the border.

5 To make the tigers' faces, roll three balls of white clay and flatten them to form disks about 1 inch in diameter and $\frac{3}{4}$ inch thick. Pinch out two ear shapes on each. Place a piece of paper over the shape, then smooth using the brayer. ▶

MATERIALS AND EQUIPMENT YOU WILL NEED

2 BLOCKS WHITE POLYMER CLAY • BRAYER • SCALPEL • $\frac{1}{2}$ BLOCK BLACK POLYMER CLAY • SMALL AMOUNT PINK POLYMER CLAY • SMOOTHING TOOL • SMOOTH PAPER

6 Roll a short $\frac{1}{8}$-inch-diameter cane from the pink clay and cut into nine slices $\frac{1}{16}$ inch thick. Roll each into a ball and flatten into $\frac{1}{4}$-inch-diameter disks. Place two disks on each face for the cheeks and smooth over. Cut the remaining three disks in half for the ear inserts and press in position.

7 Roll a thin thread of black clay and cut into six thin slices. Roll into balls and flatten for the eyes. Cut short lengths of black thread for the smiling mouths. Press into position.

8 Cut three triangles and three thin strips from the black clay to make the arrow-shaped noses. Press into position.

9 Cut 18 black triangles, long sides $\frac{1}{4}$ inch and short side $\frac{1}{8}$ inch. Place three triangles on each side of the faces. Cut nine thinner triangles and arrange them between the ears to make fringes.

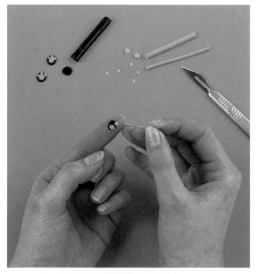

10 Roll a $\frac{1}{4}$-inch-diameter black cane. Roll two pink canes, one $\frac{1}{16}$ inch, the other $\frac{1}{8}$ inch in diameter. Cut four black disks, four from the thicker pink cane and 12 from the thinner pink cane. Roll the disks into balls and squash flat. Place one large and three small pink disks on each of the black disks to make the paws.

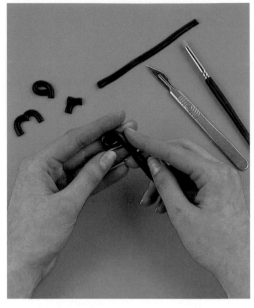

11 Roll a $\frac{1}{4}$-inch-diameter black cane, slice in half lengthwise and shape into letters. If more letters are required, make the cane narrower.

12 Arrange the tiger heads, paws and letters on the plaque and gently press them in place. Line a baking tray with waxed paper and bake following the manufacturer's instructions. Remove the paper immediately after baking.

MOBILE JUGGLERS

Mobiles can be structured in an infinite number of ways, and polymer clay is light enough to be made up into interesting shapes to suspend from them. They are fun to make and well suited to a circus theme. Here, four jugglers are mod-eled in the same basic shape to hang in formation from a frame made out of a bent coat hanger. These jugglers have been hand painted, but you could make them using bright polymer clay colors instead.

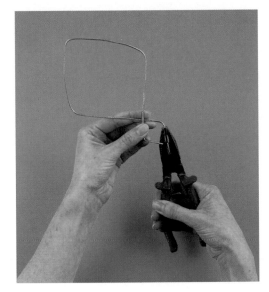

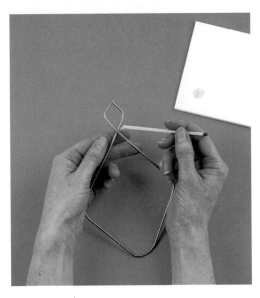

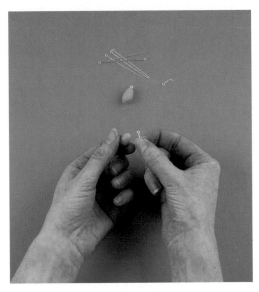

1 Using strong pliers or wire cutters, cut the hook and twisted section off a wire coat hanger and discard. Fashion half of the remaining wire into a double diamond shape as illustrated.

2 Spray the shaped wire with gold paint and glue the wires together to secure the point where they cross.

3 Mold four thumbnail-sized pieces of clay into egg shapes for the jugglers' heads. Trim an earring wire, form a hook in the end and embed this in one of heads. Repeat for the other heads. ▶

MATERIALS AND EQUIPMENT YOU WILL NEED

WIRE COAT HANGER • PLIERS OR WIRE CUTTERS • GOLD SPRAY PAINT • EPOXY RESIN GLUE • ¼ BLOCK MODELING POLYMER CLAY •
EARRING WIRES WITH LOOPS • MODELING TOOLS • SCALPEL OR COOKIE CUTTERS • NEEDLE • WET-AND-DRY SANDPAPER (OPTIONAL) •
ACRYLIC PAINT: PURPLE, RED AND YELLOW • PAINTBRUSH • VARNISH • NYLON FISHING LINE • SHELL-SHAPED JEWELRY CLASPS (OPTIONAL) •
GOLD CORD OR RIBBON FOR HANGING

4 Roll a small sausage of clay for the arms
and legs, and mold a rounded oblong for
the torso. Assemble the parts, shaping the
doubled legs into a curve. Using a modeling
tool, smooth over the joints.

5 Roll out some clay and cut out four
stars, two a little larger than the others,
thick enough to be pierced by a needle.
Either cut around a template using a scalpel
or use cookie cutters. Roll five marble-sized
beads. Pierce through all the pieces then bake
them with the 4 jugglers' figures, following
the manufacturer's instructions.

6 If necessary, smooth any rough edges
using wet-and-dry sandpaper.

7 Paint a purple, red and yellow harlequin
pattern onto the figures. Paint the beads
red with a yellow pattern. Spray the stars
gold. Varnish all these when the paint is dry.

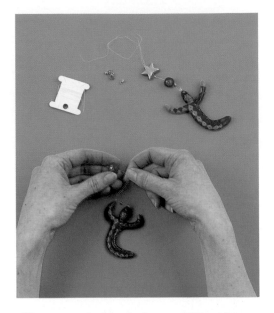

8 Loop a double thickness of fishing line
through the ring on a juggler's head, and
thread on a bead and a star. Use jewelry
clasps to keep these in position, or knot the
line, and glue them in place. Repeat for the
other jugglers but do not thread a star for the
fourth juggler.

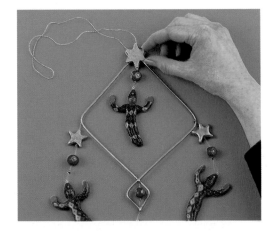

9 Tie the jugglers to the wire shape, with
the starless juggler tied to the top
corner. Hang the remaining bead inside the
small diamond. Dab glue on the knots to
prevent the fishing line from slipping. Tie a
length of gold cord or ribbon to the top for
hanging. Glue the large stars on either side,
sandwiching the wire in between.

POLY MERMAID

THIS DELIGHTFUL MERMAID WOULD ENJOY BASKING AMONG A COLLECTION OF SHELLS ON A SANDY SHELF IN A STEAMY BATHROOM. HER TAIL IS MADE OF STUFFED FABRIC AND IS DECORATED WITH ROWS OF BEADS AND SEQUINS. THE MODELING INVOLVED FOR HER TORSO, HEAD AND ARMS IS VERY SIMPLE, AND TRANSLUCENT CLAY IS USED TO GIVE HER A LOVELY WATERY HUE. THE MERMAID'S GOLDEN TRESSES ARE INGENIOUSLY MADE FROM AN UNRAVELLED PIECE OF CORD, WHICH IS GLUED ONTO HER HEAD.

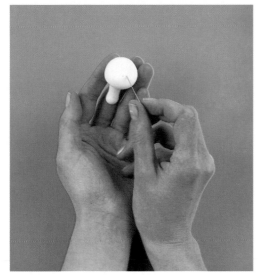

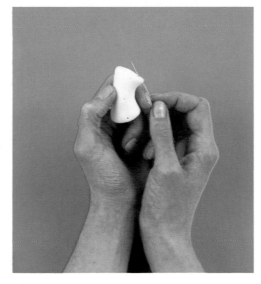

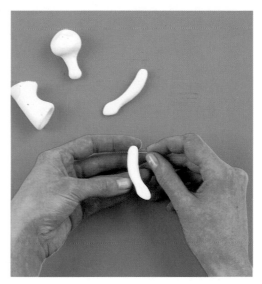

1 Roll about a quarter of the clay into a ball and form into the mermaid's head. Draw out the neck to one side, rounding it off into a wider knob. Pinch out the nose and use a needle to make nostrils. Pierce a hole through the side of the neck, halfway down.

2 For the mermaid's midriff, roll a thick, stumpy log. Roll the middle between your index fingers to shape the waist. Make concave recesses in each end with your thumbs. Pierce holes at the front and back of the top and bottom.

3 Fashion two stylized arms and hands and pierce the top of each with a needle. Bake all the body parts following the manufacturer's instructions. ▶

MATERIALS AND EQUIPMENT YOU WILL NEED

1 BLOCK TRANSLUCENT POLYMER CLAY • NEEDLE AND THREAD • ACRYLIC PAINT: BLUE, RED AND YELLOW • FINE PAINTBRUSH • VARNISH • CARDBOARD • PENCIL • SCISSORS • 2 DIFFERENT FABRICS • WADDING • PIPE CLEANER • BEADS • SEQUINS • GOLD CORD • GLUE

4 Wash the mermaid's face with soap and water to remove any surface grease. Using a fine paintbrush, paint on the features. Allow to dry.

5 Suspend each body part from a thread and dip it into varnish. Hang the pieces up until they are dry.

6 Make a template for the tail shape and cut out the fabric. Cut a bodice from different fabric. With wrong sides together, sew the seams then turn right side out. Gather in the top of the tail fin and sew to the tail. Pad the bodice with wadding and stitch across the top, leaving a gap for the neck.

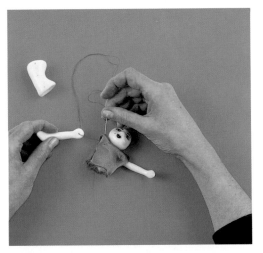

7 Insert the mermaid's neck and stitch the bodice to the neck. Attach the arms by sewing through the previously made holes to the bodice. Stitch the bodice to the top of the midriff, sewing through the previously made holes.

8 Push a pipe cleaner down inside the tail and stuff with wadding. Decorate the tail by sewing on rows of beads and sequins. Stitch the tail to the mermaid's midriff, sewing through the previously made holes.

9 Untangle a piece of cord and brush it out to make it look like hair. Glue the hair to the mermaid's head.

MIRROR WITH LIZARDS

ECORATED MIRROR FRAMES ARE VERY FASHIONABLE, AND THIS ONE IS EASY AND FUN TO MAKE. THE COLORFUL, BRIGHT-EYED LIZARDS WOULD BE IDEAL DECORATION FOR A CHILD'S BEDROOM, OR THEY WOULD ADD A WITTY NOTE TO YOUR BATHROOM WALL.

A CHEAP MIRROR WITH A PLASTIC FRAME WAS USED HERE. THE FRAME WAS BROKEN OFF WITH PLIERS AND REPLACED WITH POLYMER CLAY. THE REPEATING MOTIF IS A GOOD, RHYTHMIC WAY OF FILLING THE SHAPE, BUT A SINGLE LIZARD WOULD ALSO BE VERY EFFECTIVE.

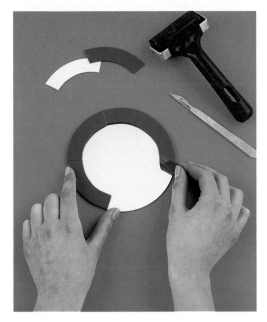

1 Roll out the light turquoise clay to about $^3/_{16}$ inch thick. Cut five curved strips (see the template at the back of the book) and place carefully around the edge of the mirror.

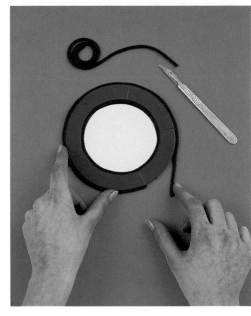

2 From the fluorescent mixed pink and magenta clay, roll out two long sausages, one slightly thicker than the other. Use the thinner sausage to edge the inner ring of the border, and the thicker sausage to edge the outer ring.

3 From the dark turquoise clay, fashion 20 lizard legs. Roll short sausages, flatten one end and bend for the knee and foot joints.

4 For each body, roll a tapered sausage from a medium-sized piece of dark turquoise clay. Create a neck in the thicker end by rolling between your two index fingers, and flatten out the head shape. Make four more lizard bodies. ▶

MATERIALS AND EQUIPMENT YOU WILL NEED

1 BLOCK LIGHT TURQUOISE POLYMER CLAY • BRAYER • SCALPEL • ROUND MIRROR, $5^1/_4$ INCH DIAMETER • $^1/_2$ BLOCK FLUORESCENT MIXED PINK AND MAGENTA POLYMER CLAY (2:1)• 3 BLOCKS DARK TURQUOISE POLYMER CLAY • SMALL AMOUNT POLYMER CLAY: GRAY, BLACK AND WHITE • SMOOTHING TOOL • D-RING • EPOXY RESIN GLUE

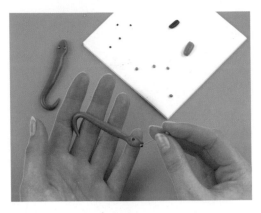

5 Roll tiny beads from gray, black and white clay for the eyes. Position the gray first and flatten, then add the black and finally the white on top.

6 Roll thin strands of light turquoise clay to make a stripe for each lizard's back and its legs.

7 Make a thin tapering sausage from the pink clay and slice thinly to make subtly graded disks. Make approximately 18 per lizard. Roll the disks into balls, flatten and apply to either side of the back stripe.

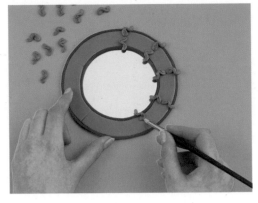

8 Position the legs at equal intervals on the mirror frame so that all the front legs cover up the joints. Press them into position using a smoothing tool.

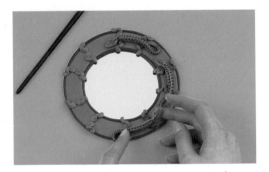

9 Place the lizards' bodies on top of the legs, carefully but firmly enough to ensure that they join properly. Bake for three-quarters of the manufacturer's recommended baking time.

10 Form another, thicker pink sausage and flatten it into a flat circle using the brayer. Press it in position around the back of the mirror edge, making sure that it adheres well.

11 Roll out a thin sheet of pink clay and trim a semi-circular shape to fit within the back frame. Bake for the remainder of the recommended cooking time.

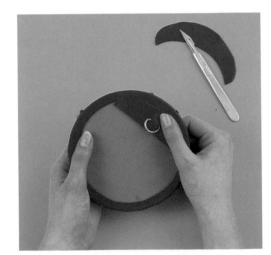

12 To position the D-ring for hanging, loop a thin strip of clay through the ring and make an indentation on the semi-circular shape but do not attach it yet. Remove the strip and the semi-circle and bake separately on a flat surface. When cool, glue the shape to the back of the mirror then glue the tab, making sure the D-ring can still move freely.

CHRISTMAS DECORATIONS

Christmas cookie cutters are ideal for making your own decorations — nothing could be easier! Decorate the shapes with a modeling tool and brush on your own pattern with bronze powder. Glue on small rhinestones for extra sparkle.

Instructions are given here for making one decoration, but you will probably want to make several, using different christmas shapes. As well as hanging them on the christmas tree, you can suspend them from a door knocker or christmas wreath.

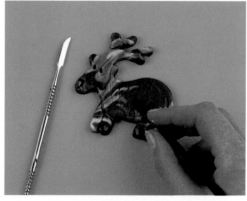

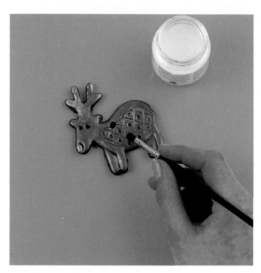

1 Roll out the clay and press out a shape using a cookie cutter.

2 Draw on markings with a modeling tool and make small indentations for the rhinestones with the blunt end of a paintbrush.

3 Using a plastic straw, make a hole in the center top for hanging.

4 Brush on differently colored bronze powders and blend together. Bake following the manufacturer's instructions.

5 Apply a protective coat of varnish.

6 Glue rhinestones in the indentations, using a toothpick. Thread a hanging ribbon through the hole.

MATERIALS AND EQUIPMENT YOU WILL NEED

POLYMER CLAY • ROLLER • CHRISTMAS COOKIE CUTTERS • MODELING TOOL • PAINTBRUSH • PLASTIC STRAW • BRONZE POWDER: VARIOUS COLORS • VARNISH • RHINESTONES • GLUE • TOOTHPICK • RIBBON

STARBURST HAND MIRROR

"MIRROR, MIRROR ON THE WALL, WHO'S THE FAIREST OF THEM ALL?" ALTHOUGH THIS MIRROR IS NOT ATACHED TO THE WALL, IT IS CERTAINLY REMINISCENT OF FAIRY TALES AND MYTHOLOGY. THE MAGICAL EFFECT IS ACHIEVED BY ENCASING THE MIRROR BETWEEN TWO LAYERS OF POLYMER CLAY WHICH HAVE BEEN COVERED WITH STRETCHED COPPER LEAF; COPPER LEAF CHANGES COLOR WHEN HEATED, ENHANCING ITS APPEARANCE. THE FRAME IS EMBELLISHED WITH GLASS GEMSTONES AND PAINTED. THE HANDLE IS REINFORCED WITH WIRE.

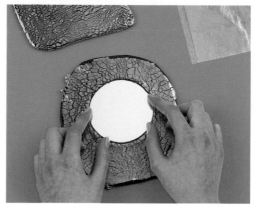

1 Roll out a ¼-inch-thick sheet of polymer clay, about 1½ inches larger all around than the mirror. Apply copper leaf and crackle the surface (see Basic Techniques). Press the mirror into the center of the clay to embed it firmly.

3 Prepare a thin strip of clay with copper leaf, rolled a little more thinly to give a finer crackle. Press it onto the clay base to frame the mirror.

5 Using a modeling tool, press all around the inner and outer edges of the mirror frame to neaten them and to secure the mirror. Do the same around the cross points.

2 Cut two pieces of rectangular clay to form the handle. Press one into the edge of the mirror base. Prepare the second piece with crackled copper leaf as in step 1 and set it aside for use in step 8.

4 Cut out three trapezoidal pieces of clay to form the three points of the cross. Apply copper leaf and crackle as in step 3, then press in place.

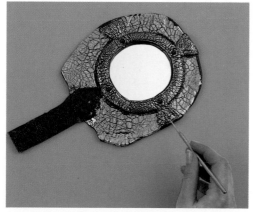

6 Place a small cabochon stone on the mirror frame opposite each cross point and the handle. Score the cross points outward to create a ray-like pattern. ▶

MATERIALS AND EQUIPMENT YOU WILL NEED
LARGE BLOCK BLACK POLYMER CLAY • COPPER LEAF • MIRROR • SCALPEL • MODELING TOOL • 4 SMALL BLUE GLASS CABOCHON STONES •
WIRE • 3 LARGE GEMSTONES • ACRYLIC PAINT: MAUVE, CORAL, BLUE AND WHITE • PAINTBRUSH

7 Etch a double-tiered zigzag pattern radiating out from the mirror frame to produce a sunburst effect.

9 Carefully mold the zigzag sunburst pattern around the mirror frame to create a staggered ray effect, then cut off the excess clay using a scalpel.

11 Roll out a thin piece of clay and apply copper leaf to it. Cut it into three narrow strips and frame each gemstone with one. Press a pattern into the strips to secure the stones in position. Bake following the manufacturer's instructions.

8 Bend a piece of wire to form a hook at one end. Embed it along the length of the handle with the hook towards the mirror. Cover with the second part of the handle prepared in step 2, pressing the edges together.

10 Press the large gemstones along the handle and delineate around them using the modeling tool.

12 Highlight the details with differently colored paints: variegated mauve on the outer spikes; variegated coral on the inner spikes; variegated blue on the cross points and down the handle (see Ornamental Book Cover project, steps 10 and 11).

CACTUS CANDELABRA

THE CACTUS SHAPE MAKES A DRAMATIC, SCULPTURAL CANDELABRA, AND THE FLUORESCENT COLOR ENSURES IT WILL BE A FOCAL POINT IN ANY ROOM. A BASIC STRUCTURE MADE FROM WIRE AND ALUMINUM FOIL IS COVERED WITH A SKIN OF CLAY TO MAKE THE CANDELABRA AN ECO-NOMIC PROPOSITION. CHECK THAT THE DIMENSIONS OF THE CANDELABRA WILL FIT IN YOUR OVEN BEFORE STARTING WORK. IT WILL BAKE MORE QUICKLY AT THE TOP OF THE OVEN THAN AT THE BOTTOM, SO YOU MAY NEED TO ROTATE THE CANDELABRA DURING BAKING.

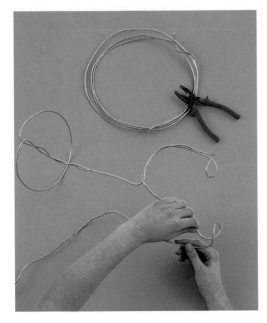

1 Work a long piece of wire into the basic structure of the candelabra. Make a circular base, bend the wire back to the center, then up to make the central stem. Form the three branches, looping the end of each in to make candle-holders. Twist the remaining end in.

2 Spread out five large sheets of foil, one on top of the other. Cut a piece of cardboard the size of a small plate and place it in the center of the foil. Stand the candelabra frame on the cardboard.

3 Fold up the foil, shaping it into a funnel around the wire frame.

4 Pour a pitcher of sand into the funnel to fill it out and also to weight the base of the candelabra.

5 Squeeze the foil together around the frame. Fold sheets of foil into thick strips and wrap these around the stem to make a bulbous shape. ▶

MATERIALS AND EQUIPMENT YOU WILL NEED

MALLEABLE WIRE, ABOUT 5 FEET • PLIERS • ALUMINUM FOIL • CARDBOARD • PLATE • SCISSORS • JUG • SAND • WIDE MASKING TAPE •
2 BLOCKS MODELING POLYMER CLAY • ROLLING PIN • SCALPEL • 2 BLOCKS FLUORESCENT GREEN POLYMER CLAY •
POLYMER CLAY: FLUORESCENT PINK, ORANGE AND DARK GREEN • DRESSMAKER'S PIN • STRONG GLUE

6 Roll the foil strips into cups and tuck them over the wire loops. Bind the cups in place to the required thickness using more folded foil.

7 Wrap masking tape around the structure to completely cover it.

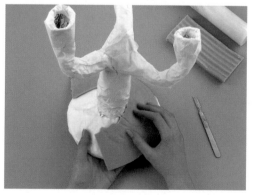

8 Roll the clay into broad strips, about ⅛ inch thick, and cover the candelabra with them. Do not press too hard as this will spoil its smooth form. Smooth over the joints.

9 Tuck the ends of the clay over the candle-holder edges. Bake for 10 minutes.

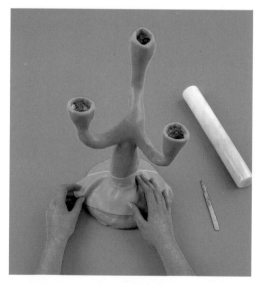

10 Roll out the fluorescent green clay into thin sheets and use it to completely cover the baked modeling clay, smoothing over the joints. Bake for another 10 minutes.

11 Roll one thick and one thin fluorescent green sausage, one thick fluorescent pink sausage and one thinner fluorescent orange sausage. Cut thin disks from all of these, make into balls, then flatten. Place pink dots on the larger green disks and orange dots on the smaller green disks. Pierce through both layers with a pin to help them hold together. Place the dots on a flat tray and bake following the manufacturer's instructions.

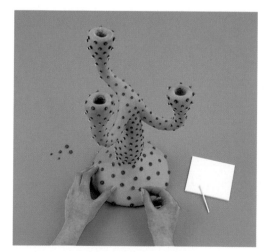

12 Glue the cooked dots to the candelabra to transform it into a cactus.

GLOW-IN-THE-DARK CLOCK

BECAUSE IT IS MADE WITH GLOW-IN-THE-DARK POLYMER CLAY, YOU WILL BE ABLE TO READ THE TIME FROM THIS AMUSING CLOCK IN THE DARK. THE FLOWER AND EGG MOTIFS ARE DETACHABLE, ALLOWING FOR OTHER ORNAMENTS, SUCH AS A CANDLE FOR A BIRTHDAY CELEBRATION (AS LONG AS THE CANDLE DOES NOT BURN RIGHT DOWN TO THE CLAY), TO BE ATTACHED TO THE CLOCK IN THEIR PLACE.

THE CLOCK MECHANISM IS INEXPENSIVE TO BUY (SEE PAGE 95 FOR SUPPLIERS) AND IS EASILY ASSEMBLED.

1 Roll out the glow-in-the-dark clay and trim to a 4-inch x 5-inch rectangle $^3/_{16}$ inch thick. Cut a circular template, place at one end and cut around it to shape the top. Squeezing an empty plastic film canister, stamp out an oval near the bottom.

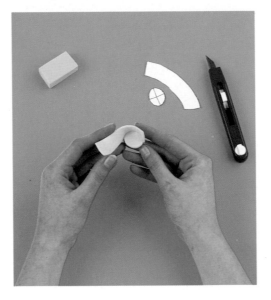

2 Make templates for a slightly curved strip and for the oval cut out in step 1. Roll out a small quantity of yellow clay and cut out these shapes. Wrap the strip around the oval to form a tapered cup.

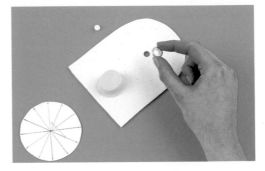

3 Fix the cup over the hole in the clock face and smooth over the joint. Mark the hour positions on the circular template and position it on the back plate. Prick through the center to mark the clock face. Using a narrow tube, stamp out a hole large enough to take the clock spindle.

4 Roll and cut out two strips of glow-in-the-dark clay $1^1/_4$ inches wide by $^3/_{16}$ inch thick. Make one $12^1/_4$ inches and the other 4 inches in length. Using a very narrow tube, stamp out a small hole at the mid-point of the longer strip. ▶

MATERIALS AND EQUIPMENT YOU WILL NEED
$2^3/_4$ BLOCKS GLOW-IN-THE-DARK POLYMER CLAY • CRAFT KNIFE OR SCALPEL • METAL RULER • THIN CARDBOARD • PENCIL • FILM CANISTER • $^1/_4$ BLOCKS POLYMER CLAY: YELLOW, LIGHT BLUE, DARK BLUE, LIGHT AND DARK GREEN • SMOOTHING TOOL • DRESSMAKER'S PIN • NARROW TUBES • JEWELRY WIRE • ALUMINUM FOIL • CROSSHEAD SCREW • BALLPOINT PEN • JEWELRY HEAD PINS • EPOXY RESIN GLUE • WIRE CUTTERS • CLOCK MECHANISM

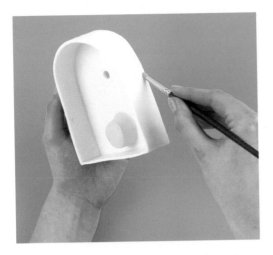

5 Assemble the strips to make the sides of the clock face, smoothing over the joints. Fix the sides to the back of the clock face and smooth over the joints.

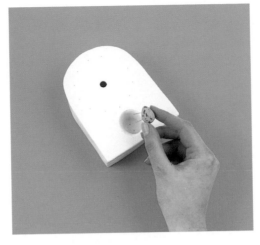

7 Push two short wires, about $\frac{5}{8}$ inch, into the egg. They should project sufficiently to push into the recess to hold the egg in place. Remove the egg and bake it following the manufacturer's instructions.

9 Twist together thin strips of yellow and light and dark green clay to create a marbled sausage.

6 Roll a marble-sized piece of light blue clay into an egg shape. Crumble some dark blue clay and roll the egg in it to speckle the surface.

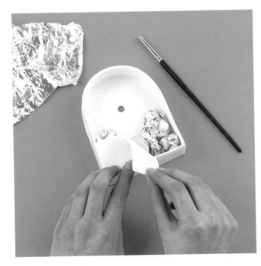

8 Cut a glow-in-the-dark clay rectangle to cover the bottom section of the back of the clock face. Fill up the cavity with scrunched-up aluminum foil. Bake the clock face following the clay manufacturer's instructions.

10 Cut the sausage into one long and four short pieces. Assemble the pieces to make a central stem with four branches. Taper one end of the stem.

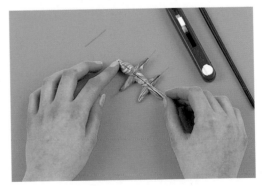

11 Make incisions along the branches and stem, and insert wires long enough to protrude from the ends of the branches and the non-tapered end of the stem. Close up the slits and smooth over. ▶

12 Roll out a small piece of yellow clay and form a three-petaled flower. Roll out a small piece of green clay and shape four leaves. Press patterns on the flower and leaves using the tip of a screw and a pen.

14 Twist together thin strips of light and dark blue clay and slice off 12 disks. Roll these into balls and flatten. Stamp each with the end of a screw and make a hole in the middle. Bake the disks following the manufacturer's instructions.

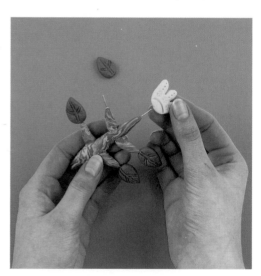

13 Push the flower and leaves onto the wires of the stem and branches and bake following the manufacturer's instructions. When assembled, the tapered stem slots into the hole at the top of the clock.

15 Push a jewelry head pin through each disk, dab a spot of glue on the back and push the pin into the clock face at an hour marking. When the glue has dried, snip off the excess wire at the back. Hold the clock movement at the back of the clock face. Push the spindle through the hole from the front and screw together.

WIREWORK TEMPLATES

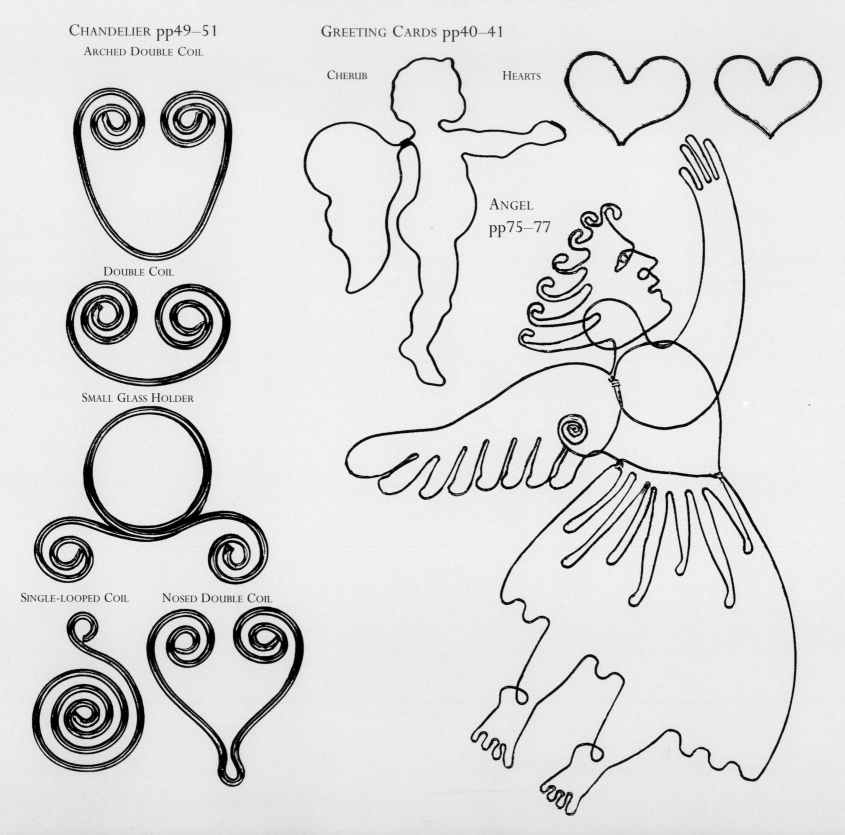

CHANDELIER pp49–51

ARCHED DOUBLE COIL

DOUBLE COIL

SMALL GLASS HOLDER

SINGLE-LOOPED COIL

NOSED DOUBLE COIL

GREETING CARDS pp40–41

CHERUB

HEARTS

ANGEL pp75–77

SEASHORE MOBILE pp54–57

LARGE FISH

SHELL

CRAB

SMALL FISH

SEAHORSE

LARGE STARFISH

SEAWEED

DOLPHIN

SMALL STARFISH

MOSAIC TEMPLATES

PRINCESS WALL MOSAIC pp163–65

BATHROOM CABINET pp132–33

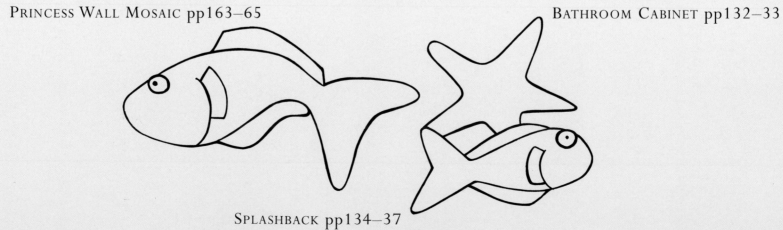

SPLASHBACK pp134–37

TINWORK TEMPLATES

EMBOSSED GREETINGS CARDS pp196–97

CANDLE COLLARS pp198–99

ROCKET CANDLESTICK pp250–51

CHRISTMAS DECORATIONS pp214–15

REINDEER pp224–26

BATHROOM SHELF pp227–29

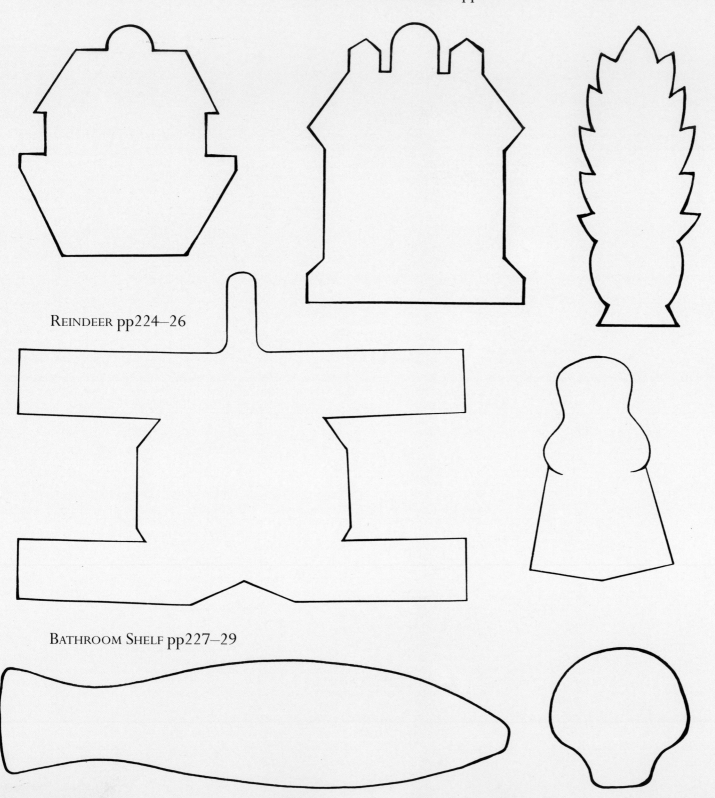

REGAL COAT RACK pp238–40

LUNCH BOX pp246–49

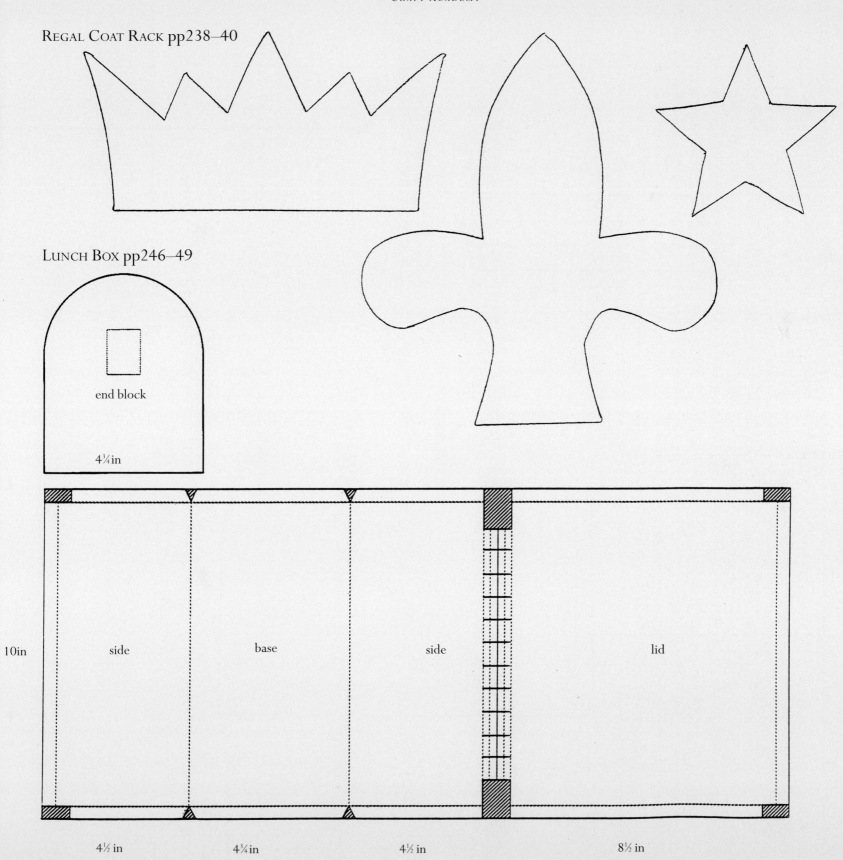

end block

4¾ in

10in

side

base

side

lid

4½ in

4¾ in

4½ in

8½ in

Plant Markers pp252–53

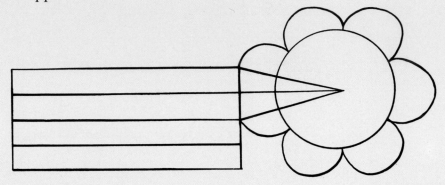

Pewter-look Shelf pp254–55

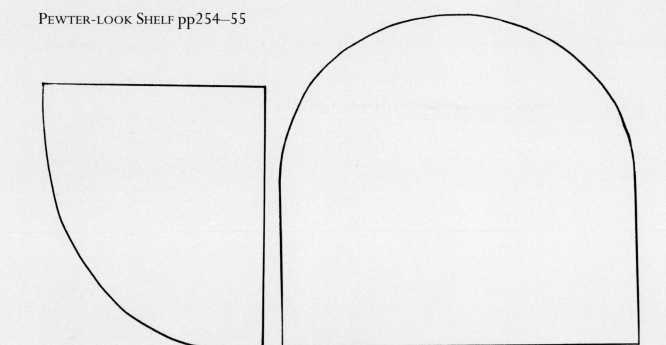

POLYMER CLAYWORK TEMPLATES

POLY MERMAID pp380–82

MIRROR WITH LIZARDS pp383–85

MINIATURE THEATER pp372–73

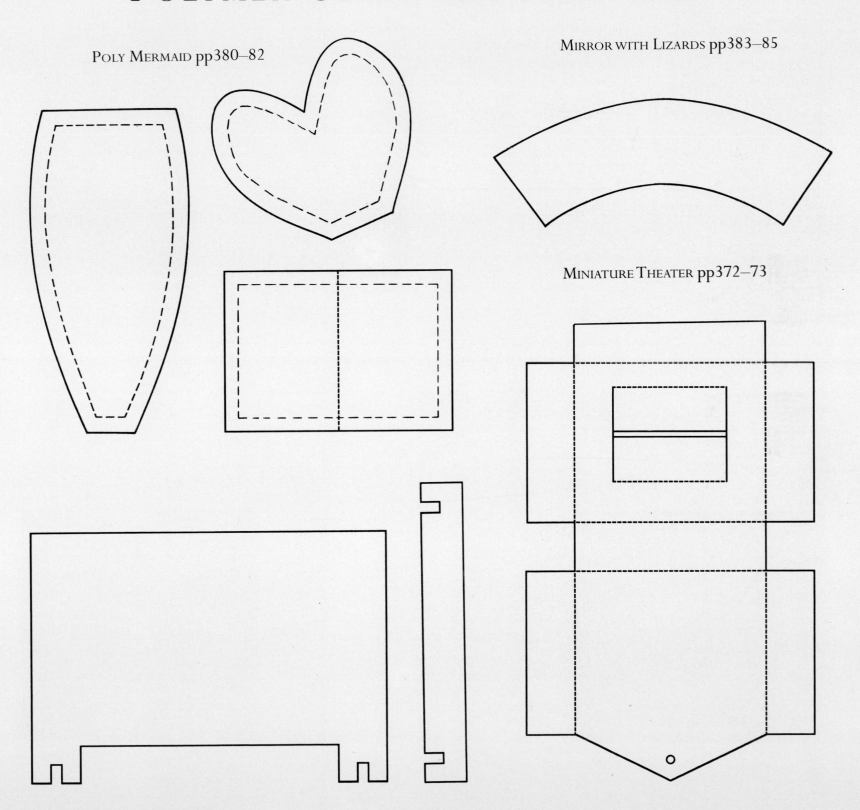

WIREWORK SUPPLIERS

United States
Are Inc.
P.O. Box 8
Greensboro
UT 05842
Tel: (802) 533 7007

Bourget Bros
1636 11th Street
Santa Monica
CA 90404
Tel: (310) 450 6556

Grieger's Inc.
P.O. Box 73070
Pasadena
CA 91109
Tel: (818) 795 9775

Universal Wirecraft Company
P.O. Box 20206
Bradenton
FL 34203
Tel: (813) 745 1219

United Kingdom
Southern Handicrafts
20 Kensington Gardens
Brighton BN1 4AL
Tel: (01273) 681901

Romany's Tools and Ironmongers
52–57 Camden High Street
London NW1 0LT
Tel: (0171) 9379570

Buck and Ryan Ltd
101 Tottenham Court Road
London W1 0DY
Tel: (0171) 6367475

Scientific Wire Company
18 Raven Road
London E18 1HW
Tel: (0181) 5050002

Alec Tiranti Ltd
70 High Street
Theale

Reading RG7 5AR
Tel: (01734) 302775

Stuart Stephenson Ltd
68 Clerkenwell Road
London EC1M 5QA
Tel: (0171) 2531693

Renaissance Creative Courses
Merlin House, High Street
Hindon, Salisbury
Wiltshire SP3 6DR
Tel: (01747) 820661

Canada
Michaels Arts & Crafts Superstore
200 North Service Road
Oakville Town Centre 2
Oakville
Ontario L6M 2V1
Tel: (905) 842 1555

Abbey Arts & Crafts
4118 East Hastings Street

Vancouver, BC
Tel: (604) 299 5201

Lewiscraft
2300 Yonge Street
Toronto, Ontario
Tel: (416) 483 2783

Australia
Mandrills
1 Transvaal Avenue
Double Bay NSW 2018
Tel: (02) 327 7477

Twin Plaza Metals
7th Floor
227 Collins Street
Melbourne Vic 3000
Tel: (03) 654 1477

Twin Plaza Metals
250 Pitt Street
Sydney NSW 2000
Tel: (02) 264 1667

ACKNOWLEDGMENTS

Mary Maguire and the publishers would like to thank the following for contributing projects to the wirework section of this book: Andrew Gilmore, Dawn Giullas and Adele Tipler.

They would also like to thank the following companies for loaning items for photography: African Fine Art and Craft, Bazar, Brats Ltd, Robert Young Antiques, Joss Graham Oriental Textiles, V.V. Rouleaux and Paperchase.

MOSAIC SUPPLIERS

United States
Are Inc.
P.O. Box 8
Greensboro
UT 05842
Tel: (802) 533 7007

Creative Craft House
P.O. Box 2567
Bullhead City
AZ 86430
Tel: (520) 754 3300

Sax Arts & Crafts
P.O. Box 51710
New Berlin
WI 53151
Tel: (414) 784 6880

Pearl Paint Co.
308 Canal Street
New York
NY 10013
Tel: (212) 431 7932

United Kingdom
South West Industrial Plasterers
The Old Dairy
Hawk Street
Bromham
Chippenham
Wiltshire SN15 2HU
Tel: (01380) 850616

Alec Tiranti Ltd
70 High Street
Theale
Reading RG7 5AR
Tel: (01734) 302775

E. Ploton Ltd
273 Archway Road
London N6 5AA
Tel: (0181) 3482838

Stuart Stephenson Ltd
68 Clerkenwell Road
London EC1M 5QA
Tel: (0171) 2531693

John Mylans Ltd
80 Norwood High Street
London SE27 9NW
Tel: (0181) 6709161

Renaissance Creative Courses
Merlin House
High Street
Hindon
Salisbury
Wiltshire SP3 6DR
Tel: (01747) 820661

Canada
Lewiscraft
2300 Yonge Street
Toronto
Ontario M4P 1E4
Tel: (416) 483 2783

Abbey Arts & Crafts
4118 East Hastings Street
Vancouver, BC
Tel: (604) 299 5201

Pottery Supply House
1120 Speers Road
Oakville
Ontario L6L 2X4
Tel: (416) 827 1129

Australia
Hobby Co.
402 Gallery Level
Mid City Centre
197 Pitt Street
Sydney NSW 2000
Tel: (02) 221 0666

Spotlight
(60 stores throughout)
Tel: freecall 1800 500021

Lincraft
(stores in every capital)
Tel: (03) 9875 7575

ACKNOWLEDGMENTS

Helen Baird and the publishers would like to thank the following for contributing projects to the mosaic section of this book: Tessa Brown, Sandra Hadfield, Cleo Mussi, Sarah Round and Norma Vondee.

Thanks to e.t. archive for the photographs on pages 94, 95, 96 and 97. Special thanks also to Gideon at Upstart Gallery and to all the mosaicists who kindly lent their pieces for photography.

TINWORK SUPPLIERS

United States

Creative Craft House
P.O. Box 2567
Bullhead City
AZ 86430
Tel: (520) 754 3300

Pearl Discount Art & Craft
3756 Roswell Road
Atlanta
GA 30342
Tel: (404) 233 9400

Pearl Paint Co.
308 Canal Street
New York
NY 10013
Tel: (212) 431 7932

Wood-met Services
3314 Shoff Circle, Dept CSS
Peoria
IL 61604

Sax Arts & Crafts
P.O. Box 51710
New Berlin
W1 53151
Tel: (414) 784 6880

Universal Wirecraft Company
P.O. Box 20206
Bradenton
FL 34203
Tel: (813) 745 1219

United Kingdom

Clay Brothers Metal Suppliers
The Green, High Street
London W5 5DA
Tel: (0181) 5672215

Alec Tiranti Ltd
70 High Street
Theale
Reading RG7 5AR
Tel: (01734) 302775

J. Smith & Sons
Tottenham Road
Islington
London N1 4BZ
Tel: (0171) 2531277

Europacrafts
Hawthorn Avenue
Hull HU3 5JZ
Tel: (01482) 223399

Canada

Fun Craft City Ltd
13890–104 Avenue
Surrey, BC
Tel: (604) 583 3262

Abbey Arts & Crafts
4118 East Hastings Street
Burnaby
Vancouver, BC
Tel: (604) 299 5201

Lee Valley
Steeles Avenue W. Westin
Toronto
Ontario
Tel: (416) 746 0850

Australia

Tinplate Distribution P/L
Angas Street
Meadowbank
NSW 2114
Tel: (02) 808 1522

NCI Diversified Products P/L
Separation Street
Northcote
Vic 3070
Tel: (03) 9489 0666

Spotlight
(60 stores throughout)
Tel: freecall 1800 500021

ACKNOWLEDGMENTS

Marion Elliot and the publishers would like to thank the following for contributing projects to the tinwork section of this book: Penny Boylan, Deborah Schneebeli Morrell, Evelyn Bennett, Mary Maguire and Andrew Gilmore.

They would also like to thank the following shops and collections for lending items for photography: Young & D Ltd, the Tony Hayward collection, Applachia Folk Art Shop and the Kasbah.

CREATIVE PLASTERWORK SUPPLIERS

United States
Dick Blick
P.O. Box 1267
Galesburg
IL 61402
Tel: (309) 343 6181

Windsor & Newton Inc.
US Office
11 Constitution Avenue
P.O. Box 1396
Piscataway
NJ 0885–1396

Design Consulting Service
41355 Covello Road
Willits
CA 05490
Tel: (707) 984 8394

Gold Leaf
381 Park Avenue South

New York, NY 10016
Tel: (212) 683 2840

Art Supply Warehouse
360 Main Street
Norwalk
CT 06851

United Kingdom
South West Industrial Plasterers
The Old Dairy
Hawk Street
Bromham
Chippenham
Wiltshire SN15 2HU
Tel: (01380) 850616

Alec Tiranti Ltd
70 High Street
Theale
Reading RG7 5AR
Tel: (01734) 302775

Stuart Stephenson Ltd
68 Clerkenwell Road
London EC1M 5QA
Tel: (0171) 2531693

Liberon Waxes Ltd
Mountfield Industrial Estate
Learoyd Road, New Romney
Kent TN28 8XU
Tel: (01797) 367555

John Mylans Ltd
80 Norwood High Street
London SE27 9NW
Tel: (0181) 6709161

Canada
Lewiscraft
2300 Yonge Street
Toronto
Ontario M4P 1E4
Tel: (416) 483 2783

Abbey Arts & Crafts
4118 East Hastings Street
Vancouver, BC
Tel: (604) 299 5201

Pottery Supply House
1120 Speers Road
Oakville
Ontario L6L 2X4
Tel: (416) 827 1129

Australia
Hobby Co.
402 Gallery Level
Mid City Centre
197 Pitt Street
Sydney NSW 2000
Tel: (02) 221 0666

Spotlight
(60 stores throughout)
Tel: freecall 1800 500021

ACKNOWLEDGMENTS

Stephanie Harvey and the publishers would like to thank all the artists who contributed to the plasterwork section of this book.

They would also like to thank the Bridgeman Art Library/John Rethell for the photographs on pages 263, 264 and 265t and The Hutchinson Library for the photographs on page 262 (Isabella Tree) and 265b (J.G. Fuller). Special thanks are also due to the following companies for lending items for photography: Robert Young Antiques, Joss Graham Oriental Textiles, V.V. Rouleaux and Paperchase.

POLYMER CLAYWORK SUPPLIERS

United States
American Art Clay Company Inc.
4717 West 16th Street
Indianapolis
IN 46222
Tel: (317) 244 6871

National Artcraft Company
23456 Mercantile Road
Beachwood
OH 44122
Tel: (216) 963 6011

Gold's Artworks Inc.
2100 North Pine Street
Lumberton
NC 28358
Tel: (910) 739 28358

The Art Store
935 Erie Boulevard East
Syracuse, NY 13210
Tel: (315) 474 1000

Brian's Crafts Unlimited
1421 South Dixie Freeway
New Smyrna Beach
FL 32168
Tel: (904) 672 2726

United Kingdom
Alec Tiranti Ltd
70 High Street
Theale
Reading RG7 5AR
Tel: (01734) 302775

Forsline & Starr International Ltd
P.O. Box 67
Ware
Herts SG12 OYL
Tel: (01920) 485859

Swann Morton Ltd
Owlerton Green
Sheffield S6 2BJ
Tel: (01742) 344231

Dryad
White Fire Avenue
Harrow
Middlesex HA3 5RH
Tel: (0181) 4274343

Canada
Opus
1360 Johnson Street
Granville Island
Vancouver, BC
Tel: (604) 736 7028

Abbey Arts & Crafts
4118 East Hastings Street
Vancouver, BC
Tel: (604) 299 5201

Pottery Supply House
1120 Speers Road
Oakville
Ontario L6L 2X4
Tel: (416) 827 1129

Salma Gundi
321 W. Georgia
Vancouver, BC
Tel: (604) 681 4648

Bead Works
2326 Bloor Street
Toronto
Ontario
Tel: (416) 736 5446

Australia
Spotlight
(60 stores throughout)
Tel: freecall 1800 500021

Boyle Industries P/L
4/14 Apollo Court
Blackburn Vic 3130
Tel: (03) 9894 2233

Rossdale Pty Ltd
Tel: (03) 9482 3988

ACKNOWLEDGMENTS

Mary Maguire and the publishers would like to thank the following for contributing projects to the polymer claywork section of this book: Sandra Duvall, Anne Dyson, Dawn Emms, Julia Hill, Kitchen Table Studios, Theresa Pateman, Rebecca Patterson and Helen Mahoney.

The photographs on page 346 are used by permission of the Trustees of the British Museum, and the photograph on page 353l is used with thanks to George Post. Special thanks also to Alec Tiranti, Green & Stone, Cornelisson & Son and V.V. Rouleaux for supplying materials for photography.

INDEX

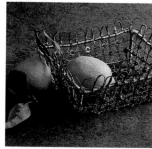